WITHDRAWN

D1223209

SECULARISM AND THE ARAB WORLD

Nazik Saba Yared

Secularism and the Arab World
(1850–1939)

Saqi Books

British Library Cataloguing-in-Publication Data
A catalogue record for this book is available from
the British Library

ISBN 0 86356 393 7 (hb)

Saqi Books
26 Westbourne Grove
London W2 5RH
www.saqibooks.com

Contents

Acknowledgements   7

Introduction   9

1. Historical and Social Background   13

2. Separation of the Spiritual and Temporal Powers   24

3. Religion and its Role. Anticlericalism   42

4. The Individual   66

5. The Status of Women   81

6. The Role of Education and Knowledge   95

7. Change, Progress and Civilization   107

8. Government and Law   128

9. Nationalism   149

10. Language, Literature, Art   181

Conclusion   194

Notes   201
Bibliography   234
Index   243

Acknowledgements

I would like to thank all those without whom this book would not have been possible. First and foremost my publishers: André Gaspard for his confidence in me, May Ghoussoub for having drawn my attention to the fact that my proposal did not include women. Thanks to her I looked for and discovered women whose writing was admirable for its days.

My infinite thanks also to Professor Roger Owen of the Center for Middle Eastern Studies at Harvard University who was gracious enough to accept my application as an Affiliate in Research. As a result, I was given borrowing privileges at the Widener Library where I was able to undertake most of my research. Those privileges his successor Professor Cemal Kafadar renewed. I am very grateful to both of them, as well as to the staff of the Widener Library for their kindness and help in assisting me. I would also like to thank the staff of both the Jafet Library at the American University in Beirut and the Stolzfus Library at the Lebanese American University in Beirut. My special thanks goes to Ms Aida Naaman who did all she could to help me and never hesitated to order whatever material I needed.

Last, but not least, I would like to thank my husband, Ibrahim Yared, for his infinite patience in bearing with me during the time it took to accomplish this book.

Introduction

Despite the strong religious and even fundamentalist trends in Arabic thought today, secularism is evident in the writings of many contemporary Arab authors, as well as in the social context and the political and legal systems of several Arab countries. Naturally, this could not have been the case had there been no earlier writings propagating secularism among the Arabs. These writings began to appear in the mid-nineteenth century, once the Arabs had come into contact with, and were influenced by, Western, mainly European, secular thought.

Rationalism was not foreign to Arabic philosophy, even as far back as the Middle Ages. Some philosophers applied a rationalistic interpretation of Islam itself but this rationalism was not identical to secularism. Secularism can be defined as a refusal to believe that nature and history are governed by external, supernatural forces, and a refusal to be guided by religion in political, social, educational, moral, economic and other matters, whether temporal, moral, spiritual or intellectual. Secular thought considers politics, society, law and ethics to be completely independent of religion, though it does not deny the influence of religion on moral principles. Secularism asserts that political and legal norms can be derived from ethical codes, though not necessarily from religious ones. 'Although secularism does not aim at eliminating religion, it believes in the epistemological independence of human reason in all fields of knowledge and research, including religion.' It thus believes not only in the independence of human reason, but in the independence of human actions as well and, as a result, in man's responsibility for his actions. In secular thought, political power and authority are no longer sacred, therefore political and social change are a necessity. As a result, secular thought looks towards modernization, progress and utilitarianism, and believes all values to be relative, even truth and religious and moral values. It considers that man is free to change these values. Nor is Nature a divine entity, but merely subject to man's needs and plans.

As to the beginnings of secular Arabic thought in the mid-nineteenth and the first third of the twentieth century, the focus will be on writers from Egypt, Lebanon and Syria since they formed the bulk of secular thinkers and influenced those in other Arab countries.

In Morocco, for example, the Egyptian 'Ali 'Abd al-Raziq's book *Al-Islam wa Usul al-Hukm* (Islam and the Bases of Government), published in 1925, 'was the founding discourse on secularism... Nothing similar existed in the Maghreb in the nineteenth and early twentieth centuries, when secularism was hardly mentioned as an ideology.'[2] One of the main Moroccan thinkers of this period was al-Wazzani (b.1910). He wrote mainly in French, and his political concepts are principally those of the Enlightenment and the French Revolution,[3] but his argument for separating religion and state was similar to that of 'Ali 'Abd al-Raziq whom he greatly admired.[4] And he, too, opposed the intervention of religious clerics in politics and allowing Islam to shape the Moroccan political system. A Moroccan newspaper called *Lisan al-Maghreb,* started by Syrians, called for constitutional government, equality before the law, freedom of thought, action and worship, and permitting all creeds to be treated equally. But it is not certain that 'young Moroccan scholars played any significant role either as columnists ... or as co-authors of the constitution project that appeared in the same periodical.'[5] Later than the period we are concerned with, liberal and to a certain extent secular writers like 'Alla al-Fasi (1906–1973) appeared.

In Tunisia, some rare seeds of secular thought are found in Khair al-Din al-Tunisi's (d.1890) writings, but his mindset is definitely Islamic, although he reinterpreted Islam in a manner that enabled it to accommodate Western principles.[6] Al-Tahar Haddad (d.1935), who wrote in *Imra'atuna fil-Shari'a wal-Mujtama'* (1930) (Our Woman in the Shari'a and Society) about 'The Essential and the Transient' wrote in a much more secular manner:

'One must take into consideration the important and obvious difference between the founding principles of Islam – its dogma and essence – immutable principles such as belief in the oneness of God, ethics, justice, and equality among human beings, and the contextual givens such as local human situations and mindsets rooted in the pre-Islamic era ... [In these latter cases], positions taken concerning their preservation or their modification are valid as long as these situations persist, but they become invalid as soon as the context changes. I cite the examples of slaves, of concubines, of polygamy, which do not come from Islam... To know if a question comes from the essence of Islam or not, one must ask oneself: is it part of the founding principle of Islam?'[7]

But Haddad wrote at a much later date than the Egyptian Qasim Amin, dealing with the same topic as will be seen later in this book, and he still refers to Islam as containing the principles of justice and equality among human beings, for example, but went a step farther than Amin when he saw that changing times called for a change in some Qur'anic laws, like those punishing adultery, allowing polygamy or treating women and men differently as regards the rights of inheritance.

Algierian resistance to the French occupation and its efforts to eliminate the Algerian Arab-Muslim identity caused this identity to be heavily stressed as opposed to the French-Christian identity, and the Algerian authorities 'aimed at re-Islamizing society through the state.'[8] One of the main political leaders between 1919 and 1924, for example, Prince Khaled al-Jaza'iri, (d.1936) called for reinstating the caliphate, and waved the banner of Islam in his speeches and articles until his death.[9] Another prominent political leader and writer who was active between 1925 and 1937 was Massali al-Haj (d.1974) who, in spite of collaborating with the French Communist party in his struggle for the independence of his country, also stressed the solid link between nationalism and Islam.[10] Farhat 'Abbas (d.1985) was one of the few Algerian intellectuals and political leaders to have been strongly influenced by French culture. Yet his articles and books, written between 1919 and 1941, did not differentiate between Arabism and Islam, and it was in Islam that he sought inspiration for building the ideal future state. It was only after 1943 that Farhat 'Abbas changed and asserted his secularism when he called for the separation between religion and politics and wanted freedom of faith for all citizens.[11] But this is a period beyond that with which we are concerned.

As for Iraq which was also under Ottoman rule until 1917, the books that appeared prior to this period were traditional, both in content and style.[12] By the Treaty of San Remo in 1920 Iraq was assigned to the British who appointed Feisal I (d.1933) as ruler. The number of schools increased, but only about 10% of the population was literate, and even as late as 1933 King Feisal complained that Iraqis were 'imbued with religious traditions and absurdities.'[13] It is true that, like other countries in the Middle East, Iraq had been exposed to Western influence since the nineteenth century through missionary activity, education and business interests, but the impact of the West became directly felt during and after the British Mandate, the strongest impact naturally being among the educated middle- and upper-classes in the cities. Westernization was opposed by large sections of traditionalists who criticized and even rejected Western civilization. Even less traditional thinkers like 'Abd al-Hamid al-Zahrawi (1871–1916) and 'Abd al-Rahman al-Bazzaz (1913–1971) were firmly grounded in Islam. The poet Jamil Sidqi al-Zahawi (1863–1936) was definitely more secular, especially regarding women's rights, but his poetry and writing are full of contradictions which make it difficult to deduce a cohesive, consistent train of thought.[14] Britain's control over Iraq's affairs and its broken promise to King Feisal about Syria led to the awakening of a very strong nationalist, anti-British feeling. In the 1930s, the Iraqis used the schools to inculcate Arab nationalism and Iraq's important role in a pan-Arab union.[15] But 'the lack of publishers, the limited size of the literate public and the tendency of intellectuals to be drawn into politics,[16] restricted secularism mainly to the political thought of this period. Its most enthusiastic spokesman was Sati' al-Husri (1882–1968) who was of Syrian origin. His significant writings are of a later period than the one with which we are concerned, so at the relevant time, Egypt, Lebanon and Syria still maintained the cultural leadership of the Middle East.

Constraints of space in this book have caused the author to be selective in choosing the writers covered, and some important figures whose thought was also more or less secular have had to be left out. These include the Egyptian nationalists 'Abd Allah al-Nadim (1844–1896) and Mustafa Kamil (1874–1908), the feminists Zeiza Nabarawi (1897–1985) and May Ziady (1895–1941), the socialist Salama Musa(1888–1952), the Darwinist Isma'il Mazhar (1891–1962), the liberal Husein Haykal (1888–1956), the atheist Isma'il Adham (1911–1940), and Mahmud 'Azmi (1889–1954) who campaigned to replace the shari'a laws by secular ones, to mention only a few. Musa, Mazhar and Haykal later recanted their secular thought, as did others who submitted to the conservative pressure of the society in which they lived. The author's choice has been based on writers from three different generations whose secular writings had an impact on their contemporaries, or raised a certain amount of controversy and who introduced new secular perspectives into Arab thought. These include the women writers of the period who have been sadly neglected in other books. Those aspects of their thought that are not relevant to secularism, the subject of this book, are not referred to.

The first chapter of this book will briefly summarize the main political and socio-economic conditions of the period. The second chapter will show what secularism meant to the writers chosen by the author and why they felt it was important and necessary. The following four chapters will try to indicate how their secularism influenced their outlook on religion, the individual, women, education and knowledge. Since the aim of these writers was to achieve progress and civilization, better government and law and a true spirit of nationalism in which language played an important role, these will be the subjects the last chapters of the book. Throughout these chapters a comparison will be made between the secularism of the various writers from the same or different generations.

CHAPTER ONE

Historical and Social Background[1]

In the early sixteenth century, Egypt became part of the Ottoman Empire, but thanks to his powerful military force Muhammad 'Ali Pasha (1769–1848) managed to weaken the tie between his country and Turkey. In 1841, he obtained an edict (*ferman*) from the Ottoman Sultan granting him the hereditary viceroyalty of Egypt, and the country enjoyed relative autonomy until its occupation by the British in 1882. During Muhammed 'Ali's rule, he reformed the taxation and agrarian systems, started the great cotton industry, encouraged Western cultural and technical assistance, developed the first system of secular state education in a Muslim country, founding primary, secondary and technical schools, and granted many students scholarships to study in Europe.

When Muhammad 'Ali's grandson, 'Abbas Hilmi I (ruled from 1848–1854) inherited the viceroyalty of Egypt he rejected the Western, mainly French, technical advice and resented European influence in Egypt. But when the Ottoman government tried to weaken him and regain more direct control over Egypt, he turned to the British, in return for allowing them to build a railway between Alexandria and Cairo to facilitate communications with India. During Sa'id's reign (ruled 1854–1863) the building of the Suez Canal was started, but the Ottomans never again tried to restrict his autonomous powers or those of Isma'il (ruled 1863–1879) who entertained friendly relations with the Sultan 'Abdülaziz (1861–1876). All the subsequent rulers of Egypt, until the monarchy was abolished in 1952, were descended from Isma'il.

Thanks to his friendly relations with the Sublime Porte, to whom he offered lavish gifts and the troops he supplied to help the Sultan suppress an uprising in Crete, in 1867 Isma'il obtained an edict formally conferring upon him the title of Khedive (*khidiwi*) and in 1873 he was recognized as the virtually independent sovereign of Egypt. In the early years of his reign, he greatly improved the administrative system, public works and communications, culminating in the opening of the Suez Canal in 1869. The huge funds required for this expansion were extorted, however, from the poverty-stricken population and from loans on the European market. Unable to raise more money, Isma'il had to sell his Suez canal shares to the British government in 1875. In May 1876, the *Caisse de la Dette Publique* was instituted and led to international control over a large portion of the Egyptian revenue. In the same year, British and French control of Egyptian revenue and expenditure was established, and the vast lands owned by the Khedive fell under international control. In June 1879, the Khedive was deposed and his son Tawfiq (ruled 1879–1892) appointed as his successor. But the continued foreign control of the Turkish and European powers over Egypt antagonized the Egyptians and led to a military revolt in 1882 under the leadership of Ahmad 'Urabi Pasha (1839–1911). Britain crushed the revolt and occupied Egypt.

Under Isma'il, Western influence on education and culture in Egypt increased. Learned institutions and societies, the Khedival Library and the Egyptian Museum were established, a number of periodicals were started, and towards the end of his reign Lebanese journalists who had fled from Ottoman tyranny in their country contributed significantly to the development of the Egyptian press. In 1873, the first girls' school was founded but it was not until 1914 that government secondary schools for girls were opened. '... yet from 1907 to 1929 only a few women took the secondary school certificate examination and none passed it'.[2] Nineteenth-century Egypt also faced the problem of the Capitulations. These were commercial treaties that granted foreign merchants enormous privileges, which were claimed not only by Europeans but also by local people who enjoyed the protection of foreign consulates. Under the British concessions, vast amounts of land were also granted to European companies. In addition, there were seventeen consular jurisdictions, each applying a different law. Foreigners could not be tried in the local criminal courts, the police could not enter their homes and they were able to avoid much of the local taxation. Thus, foreigners and their hangers-on had too many privileges the ordinary Egyptian could never enjoy.

When the British occupied Egypt, Sir Evelyn Baring (later to become Lord Cromer) (1841–1917) was sent as consul-general. During his term of office (1883–1907), he proved to be an autocratic decision-maker. Tawfiq, however, remained Khedive until his death, when he was succeeded by his son 'Abbas Hilmi II (r. 1892–1914). Nothing changed in the administration and legal systems, except for the introduction of mixed courts. But the British abolished the Dual Control and an Englishman alone supervised the Egyptian finances. Under Cromer, the Egyptian press enjoyed relative freedom, but his autocratic rule strengthened Egyptian nationalism which had already been opposed to the foreign occupation of the country. Between 1869 and 1887, Jamal al-Din al-

Afghani (1838/9–1897) attracted followers and fomented conspiracies in the Ottoman Empire with the aim of creating a pan-Islamic state uniting all the Muslim countries in opposition to Christian European influence, but his movement was religious, not national. The first spokesman for Egyptian nationalism was Mustafa Kamil (1874–1908), a young lawyer and journalist with whom 'Abbas Hilmi allied himself through exasperation with Cromer's autocracy. The measures Cromer and Horatio H. Kitchener (1850–1916) took in 1899 to deprive the Khedive of any influence over the Sudan and bring it completely under British control further fuelled Egyptian resentment, as did the barbaric incident of Dinshaway in 1906.[3]

Cromer retired in 1907, but he had restored financial stability to Egypt and improved the systems of transport, irrigation and agriculture. Industry, however, remained limited because the investors, mostly Europeans, did not want Egypt to become a competitor for European manufactured goods.[4] The education system stagnated, for the British did not encourage a Western-educated elite that might threaten their domination. The Egyptian university founded in 1908 was financed solely by Egyptian contributions. Cromer was replaced by Sir Eldon Gorst (1907–1911) who adopted a more flexible and less autocratic policy, but this did not stop the nationalist movement from expanding. One of its prominent spokesmen was Ahmad Lutfi al-Sayyid, theorist, publicist and editor of al-Jarida. Gorst died in 1911 and was succeeded by Lord Kitchener who restored strong, autocratic British rule, but when a new Legislative Assembly was created in 1913, Sa'd Zaghlul (1857–1927) was elected to it, and succeeded Mustafa Kamil as national leader.

When the Ottoman Empire sided with Germany in World War I, the British proclaimed a protectorate over Egypt, deposed 'Abbas II and appointed Hussein Kamil (1852–1917), a son of Isma'il, as sultan and head of state. A new high commissioner, Sir Henry McMahon, took over the control of Egyptian foreign affairs until he was replaced in 1916 by Gen. Sir Reginald Wingate (1861–1953). During the war, the British used conscription to help their campaigns in Palestine and the Middle East, requisitioned the peasants' animals, and ordered compulsory subscriptions to the Red Cross. To add to the social problems, the cost of living soared and there was a shortage of grain. All of this added to the unpopularity of the occupying forces.

When Sultan Hussein died in 1917, he was replaced by Prince Fuad (1868–1936), the sixth son of Isma'il. The principles formulated by the American president, Woodrow Wilson (1856–1924) at the end of World War I stating the right of all nations to self-determination were not applied by the British and French, but greatly encouraged the nationalists, led by Sa'd Zaghlul, to demand independence. After the British government refused to receive their delegation (*wafd*), arrested and deported Zaghlul and three others, a serious revolt broke out in 1919 and Zaghlul and his companions were liberated. Negotiations ensued between the British and the Egyptians, who wanted their independence, but they broke down and the disturbances continued until 1923. In that year, a constitution was promulgated and a parliamentary government was established after Fuad had been proclaimed king and Egypt became an independent state. British forces remained along the Suez Canal, however, to guarantee its security. In 1928, after a number of disagreements between the British and Egyptian governments and a crisis between the Wafdist government, now headed by Mustafa Nahhas, and the king, Fuad suspended the constitution and dissolved parliament. There followed a period of authoritarian government until Fuad's death in 1936. He was succeeded by his son Farook, and as the result of a treaty signed with the British, the high commissioner was withdrawn. Under the agreement drawn up in Montreux in the following year, the system of Capitulations was abolished, Egypt obtained full right of jurisdiction and taxation over all residents, and the mixed courts for non-Egyptians were thenceforth to apply only Egyptian law. However the tension and rivalry between the king and the Wafd continued, and some of the Wafd party broke away to form the Sa'dist party. 'Ali Maher Pasha was able to form a strong government in August 1939 which had the support of the Sa'dists.

After World War I, there was a rapid increase in the budget of the Ministry of Public Education. Apart from the government schools, there were many private schools, both Egyptian and foreign, besides the technical schools and the traditional *kuttabs*, or Qur'anic schools in the rural districts. The Egyptian university expanded, the Muslim university of al-Azhar underwent some reform, and graduates from both universities were sent to Europe for further specialist education.

Syria and Lebanon were provinces of the Ottoman Empire until the end of World War I, and most of the population, with the exception of Mount Lebanon, was mainly Sunni Muslim. Through four centuries of Ottoman occupation, these two provinces had witnessed very little material development. The people were governed by unscrupulous rulers who subjected them to heavy and unequal taxation, making them victims of injustice and poverty. Mount Lebanon, however, with its Maronite and Druze population, had never been under direct Ottoman control and had always enjoyed autonomous rule, especially during the reign of the Ma'n (1516–1697) and Shehab (1706–1840) princes. The mid-nineteenth century was a period of political instability in Mount Lebanon, due to the sectarian conflict between the Maronite and Druze communities, in which European interference played a major role. The

Europeans sought to further their interests in the region, France protecting the Catholic communities, Britain the Druze, and Russia the Greek Orthodox Christians of the Ottoman Empire. When the last Shehabi, Bashir III (d.1860), was deposed in 1842 as a result of the strong Druze opposition to him, the Ottoman sultan tried to place Lebanon under direct Ottoman administration by appointing a governor, 'Umar Pasha (1806–1871), who was of Croatian origin. But both Christians and Druze opposed having a foreign ruler, 'Umar Pasha was removed and a dual *qaimmaqamate* was installed in 1843, backed by the European powers. The plan was to divide Mount Lebanon administratively between two governors, a Druze and a Christian, each ruling over his own co-religionists. This did not solve the problem, however, in the mixed districts and hostilities broke out again in 1845. So the Ottoman government sent its minister of foreign affairs to Lebanon and a council was created in each *qaimmaqam,* consisting of representatives of the Muslims, Maronites, Druze, Greek Orthodox and Greek Catholics. Subsequent years witnessed conflicts inside the Maronite community. In 1858, under the leadership of a muleteer, Tanius Shahin, the peasants in the entirely Maronite Kisrawan revolted against the many injustices of the wealthy Khazin family and others, drove them out and seized their property, interpreting the equality between the various religious sects decreed by the Tanzimat to mean social equality. The Maronite Pariarch tried to end the rebellion by meeting at least some of the peasants' demands.[5] But their revolt spread to other parts of Mount Lebanon, and in 1860 a bloody war broke out between Maronites and Druze, for which several explanations were given.[6] The latter were supported by the Muslims of Damascus who were against emancipation of the Christians which the Sultan had made official in 1856 in the *Hatti-i-Hümayun.* Many Muslim manual labourers and artisans were unemployed due to competition from European goods, and they vented their anger on the prosperous Christians, popularly identified with European interests.[7] In 1860, the Christians in the mixed districts of Lebanon and in Damascus were massacred, and these massacres left a lasting effect on the people, as will be shown in the following chapters. In Lebanon, the Ottoman authorities were unable to contain the violence of the attackers, while in Damascus they made no effort to stop the murder and plunder. The only Muslim protector of the Christians in Damascus was the exiled Algerian hero Prince 'Abd el-Qadir al-Jaza'iri (1807–1883). These events were followed by a reign of terror during which the Ottoman authorities severely punished the Muslims and Druzes,[8] but they also led to renewed European intervention. In 1861, the Organic Regulation was signed by the powers. Under this regulation, the double *qaimmaqamate* was replaced by a unified regime that had authority only over Mount Lebanon proper. Its administration was headed by a non-Lebanese Christian *mutasarrif* (governor), directly responsible to the Sultan, and the different Lebanese communities were represented by delegates designated by their chiefs and notables. The Organic Regulation abolished feudal privileges and declared the equality of all citizens before the law. But the tension between the Druzes and Maronites was not eliminated, nor could the wealth and hereditary influence of the great families be removed by the decrees of the Organic Regulation.

The troubles in Lebanon and Syria also lead to an administrative reorganization by the Ottomans. In 1864, Syria was divided into two *wilayas* (provinces) with Aleppo and Damascus as their capitals, and in 1888 the *wilaya* of Beirut was created, stretching from Tripoli in the north to northern Palestine in the south and inland to the Jordan Valley. An autonomous Jerusalem *sanjaq* was created in southern Palestine.

After 1870, Syria enjoyed relative peace and prosperity, and under the *Mutasarrifiya* Lebanon had over fifty years of tranquility and development. It was supplied with good roads, bridges, public buildings and valuable public services, agriculture and the production of silk flourished, but the limited natural resources of Lebanon drove a large number of Lebanese to emigrate to Africa or the Americas, mainly during the last quarter of the nineteenth century. During the tyrannical reign of the Ottoman Sultan Abdulhamid II (1876–1909) numerous Lebanese intellectuals left for more liberal countries such as France and the Americas. Many settled in Egypt, where they started influential newspapers and magazines, such as *al-Ahram* founded in 1875 by Saleem Taqla (1849–1892) assisted by his brother Bishara (1852–1911), *al-Muqattam* founded in 1889 by Ya'qub Sarruf and Faris Nimr (c.1860–1952) who had also founded *al-Muqtataf* in Beirut in 1876 and which then moved with its founders to Cairo when they emigrated in 1883. *Al-Hilal*, a monthly magazine and a major publishing house, was founded by Jurji Zaydan in 1892. The Protestant missionary activity during this century had increased in Lebanon and Palestine, besides that of the Catholic church. In 1834, the American mission brought an Arabic press[9] to Beirut and established many schools, one of which, the Syrian Protestant College, founded in 1866, later became the American University of Beirut. The Roman Catholics, on the other hand, established the Imprimerie Catholique in 1853 and the Université St. Joseph in 1875, besides numerous schools in Syria and all over Lebanon. Thanks to these schools and printing presses, literacy spread in Lebanon, and 'no fewer than forty periodicals were published between 1870 and 1900'.[10] This was partly the reason for the intellectual ascendancy of the Christians during the second half of the nineteenth and the first quarter of the twentieth centuries, although Lebanese non-Christians, mainly Druze, also attended these schools, before the

Lebanese Muslims and Christians of various sects founded their own local community or national schools. While Egyptian and other Muslim intellectuals were trying to prove that modernism and Western concepts are not contrary to Islam, Christian intellectuals were not faced with such problems and easily accepted Western civilization, the more so because it was based on Christian beliefs like theirs. These schools produced many Christian scholars, writers and journalists, and the Christian graduates of and teachers in these schools played a significant part in reviving the Arabic language and literature, among them Nasif al-Yaziji(1800–1871), Faris al-Shidyaq, Ibrahim al-Yaziji (1847–1906), Butrus al-Bustani, Jurji Zaydan and the other journalists mentioned above." Through these men and others Arab nationalism spread among Lebanese Christians who felt alienated in the Muslim Ottoman Empire. This feeling was not shared by the majority of Muslims before the beginning of the twentieth century, since most were Sunnis like the Ottomans, and they held almost all the posts in the administration. A few Muslim exceptions to the rule were writers like 'Abd al-Rahman al-Kawakibi of Aleppo, but almost all the others were in favor of pan-Islamism upheld by Sultan 'Abdülhamid II who maintained that he was the Caliph of Islam.

When the Young Turks overthrew Sultan 'Abdülhamid in 1909 and tried to force the different peoples of the Ottoman Empire into a political unity by centralization and imposing Ottoman Turkish culture, the Arabs, both Christian and Muslim this time, who had had hopes of decentralization or home rule, reacted by forming nationalist societies in Syria, Lebanon, Cairo, Istanbul and Paris, where several Arab nationalists had sought exile. In 1913, they held the Arab Congress in Paris; most of the participants were Syrian and Lebanese, and their aim was to publicize their desire for the autonomy of the Arab provinces *within* the Ottoman Empire, Arab participation in the central administration and the recognition of Arabic along with Turkish as an official language. The Congress failed to force the Ottoman government to concede to its wishes. Alongside this Arab nationalist movement there existed a purely Christian Lebanese nationalism, encouraged by France, whose aim was to restore complete independence to Lebanon within its nineteenth-century borders.[12]

Agriculture and commerce were the main commercial activities in Syria and Lebanon before the World War I. There were some exports of agricultural and processed products, mainly silk, olive oil, tobacco, wine and local fabrics. Foreign trade was controlled by Europeans.

The nineteenth century also witnessed the beginning of Zionist immigration to Palestine, a movement which was to have a profound effect on Arab thought in the following century. Since Biblical times, a small, mostly poor Jewish community had always existed in Syria, Lebanon and Palestine, but the pogrom of 1881 perpetuated against the Jews in Russia started a wave of immigration. These Ashkenazi Jews were very different from the Sephardi and Oriental Jews already in the Middle East. With time, the problem was aggravated by the Balfour Declaration (1917) which did not take into account the Arabs who constituted 90% of the population, and by the massive Jewish immigration to Palestine which followed the Nazi persecution of the Jews in Europe. There ensued constant clashes between Arabs and Jews, of which the most violent were those that occurred in 1929, 1933 and the Arab Rebellion of 1936–1939, before the events of 1948 drove the Arab population out of most of Palestine.

When the Ottoman Empire entered World War I in 1914, Syria, Lebanon and Palestine were faced by more important changes than Egypt, since they were Ottoman provinces. In October, 1915, the autonomous status of Lebanon was abolished. In his negotiations (1915–1916) with McMahon, Sharif Hussein of Hijaz (1852?-1931) was promised an independent Arab kingdom which included the Hijaz, Lebanon, Palestine and parts of Syria. The negotiations between the British and French, culminated in the Sykes-Picot agreement that same year, giving France power over Syria and Lebanon, and Britain over Palestine. In 1917, the Balfour Declaration promised the Jews the establishment of a national home in Palestine, without caring about the disastrous effects it would have on the Arabs.[13] In 1916, Sharif Hussein proclaimed his revolt in the Hijaz and under the military rule of Jamal Pasha (1872–1922) twenty-two Arab Christian and Muslim nationalists in Syria and Lebanon were executed in May, eleven having been executed in Beirut in the previous year. In the year 1915 a plague of locusts struck the Near East, and the devastating famine of the following year, exacerbated by Jamal Pasha's blockade of Mount Lebanon, in reprisal against Christians accused of disloyalty, caused the death of more than one third of the population. The famine in Beirut and the coastal towns was caused by the Allied blockade of the coast.

In 1917, Hussein's son Feisal (1883–1933) occupied Aqaba and was able to operate on the flank of the forces of the British General Allenby (1861–1936) as they advanced into Palestine. In 1918, Feisal was operating in Transjordan and in October, he and Allenby reached Damascus. At the end of that month, the Armistice was signed and the Ottoman Empire withdrew from the war.

Feisal established his administration in Damascus on 1 October, 1918 and declared an independent Arab kingdom that included Syria, Lebanon and Palestine. The Sharifian flag was hoisted in Beirut, much to the consternation of the Christian nationalists in Lebanon who still wanted an independent country, to avoid being swallowed up in a greater Muslim state. Feisal's kingdom lasted no longer than a week in Lebanon, which was soon occupied by British and French forces. Most of the Christian population welcomed the French occupation that they perceived as rescueing them from pan-Arab, i.e. Muslim, unity and fulfilled their hopes for a separate country. But Feisal's kingdom persisted for almost two years in Syria, in spite of its economic weakness, chaotic government and the French claims on Syria that were stated in the secret Sykes-Picot agreement. Negotiations and several meetings were held between the British, the French and the Arabs, but to no avail. Feisal and the Arabs were betrayed by the British and French, their participation in the war against the Ottomans as well as the promises made by the British to Sharif Hussein forgotten. Under the terms of the Treaty of San Remo (April 1920)[14] the whole of Syria and Lebanon became a French mandate while Palestine and Iraq were allocated to Britain. The Arabs in Syria took to arms but were crushed by the French in the battle of Maysalun on 24 July, 1920, and the French were able to enter Damascus and affirm their mandate over the whole of Syria. However, continued resentment against the French occupation forces, both in Syria and to a lesser degree in Lebanon, obliged the French to keep a large number of troops in the area to ensure peace and order. Although armed action against the French did not wholly cease, it came to a head in 1925 when the Jabal Druze revolted against General Sarrail (1856–1929) who rejected their petitions and exiled their representatives. This revolt quickly spread to most of Syria and parts of southern Lebanon, leading, mainly in Damascus, to looting, the destruction of roads, railways and buildings and the attacking and murdering of Christians. To put an end to the troubles, the French bombarded Damascus, but General Sarrail had to be removed. It was not until 1927 that the French were finally able to control the unrest, looting and banditry that had taken hold throughout Syria.

Even before the Druze revolt broke out, the French felt the hostility mainly of the Muslim population in Syria and Lebanon, and applied a policy of 'divide and rule' in these two countries, with their different religions and sects. The French perpetuated the system begun by the Turks of having representatives of every sect on all government councils proportionate to their numbers. Their main support lay among the Maronites of Lebanon. In 1920, they enlarged the old *sanjaq* of Lebanon to three times its size, to include the South, the Beqa' valley and the coastal towns of Beirut, Tripoli and Sidon, a step which was opposed by the majority of the Muslim population, who wanted to remain part of Syria. Since the population of these newly annexed areas was predominantly Muslim (Sunni and/or Shi'a) the Maronites no longer had an absolute majority as they had in the old *sanjaq*, though the various Christian sects together formed a precarious majority. 'This weakening of the

Christian position may have been designed to make them more dependent on French protection"[15] and, indeed, most of the Christians were less inclined to follow the nationalist movement. In 1926, the constitutional Lebanese Republic was proclaimed and an eminent Greek Orthodox lawyer, Charles Dabbas, elected as its first president (1926–1934), but the French retained control as before.

Due to Syrian resistance to the French, elections in Syria were not held before 1928. The Constituent Assembly met in Damascus. However, the Syrians and, to a lesser degree, the Muslim and some Christian Lebanese, continued opposing French rule in its control of the administration, the judiciary, the army and the financially important Common Interests.[16] Strikes and demonstrations were organized, political figures dismissed from their jobs by the French or arrested, and in 1936, Lebanese Muslims again demanded that predominantly Muslim districts of the country be annexed to Syria. Finally. in 1936. a treaty was signed between the French and the Syrians, and later between the French and the Lebanese, modelled on the Anglo-Iraqi treaty of 1930,[17] under the terms of which France would support the admittance of Lebanon and Syria as independent states to the League of Nations (within a period of no longer than three years). Jebel Druze and Latakia would be annexed to Syria, but would retain special military and diplomatic privileges, as well as their existing monetary affinity. The National Bloc party was elected in Syria and the exiled nationalists returned. During the following three years Lebanon enjoyed a constitutional government and witnessed some progress in governmental organization and administration, but in Syria there were political unrest and riots. France's yielding the *sanjaq* of Alexandretta to Turkey in 1939, in contradiction to what had been stated in the text of the Syrian Mandate, only made matters worse. In 1939, the French High Commissioner, under pressure from the French Foreign Affairs Commission, suspended the Syrian constitution and appointed a council of directors to rule under his orders; separate administrations were again established in the Jabal Druze, Latakia and the Jazira. The Franco-Lebanese Treaty remained untouched, however.

During the Mandate period, the French had absolute control over everything, and were determined to impose French culture and language in the schools and governmental departments and to further the interests of French companies; they favored the Christians and Alawites and restricted the freedom of the people and the press. Deportation without trial was not uncommon. The economic and social conditions of the people improved as compared with Ottoman rule, however. Criminal, civil, commercial and administrative laws were improved, as were, to a certain extent, the administration of justice and the standard of the judiciary. State and private schools became more numerous and were controlled by the French, but there were more private schools than state schools, and their standard of education was higher, whether they were foreign, community or national schools. Relief was organized for the poor and sick in the first years after the war. State and private hospitals and clinics increased in number and were often staffed by graduates of the medical schools of the Damascus University and the St. Joseph and American Universities in Beirut. The police force was modernized, communications, ports and telecommunications improved, all of which was of great benefit to trade, agriculture, industry, tourism and society in general. Although agriculture remained the main source of income, there was also livestock-breeding, fishing, light industry, trade and commercial services, as well as the money sent home by the emigrants. Assistance was given to encourage agriculture and light industry, and some effort was made to protect and replant forests.

The standard of living improved slightly, mainly in the towns where modernization and change were noticeable. A growing number of women were educated and became teachers, writers and journalist. They also became involved in charitable societies and clubs. At the same time, polygamy among the Muslims became rare. In the villages, however, the feudal system persisted and the peasants were poor and backward.

This was the political and social situation in Syria and Lebanon at the outbreak of World War II.

CHAPTER TWO

Separation of the Spiritual and Temporal Powers

Not all the writers chosen for discussion here openly stated their desire to separate the temporal power from the spiritual. Although it can be inferred from their opinions about nation and government, for example, that this would have been their view, this chapter will deal solely with those who explicitly advocated this separation of powers, leaving the writers' secular stand on other subjects to later chapters.

Since, unlike Islam, the Christian religion does not deal directly with worldly affairs, it is not surprising that it was much easier for Christians to take a secular stand. Thus, not only did Christian writers insist on separating the temporal from the spiritual before Muslims, but Christian secularism had different causes and took on a different form from that of the Muslims whose religion, as such, deals with many worldly matters besides the spiritual.[1]

As early as 1855, Faris al-Shidyaq[2] a Lebanese Christian Maronite, severely criticized the Maronite Church for having tortured his brother As'ad to death (in 1830) because he had become a Protestant. In his attack on the Church, Shidyaq writes that Christ himself asked us to give unto Caesar that which is Caesar's, and if his brother had committed a crime, it was for the ruler, not the Church, to judge and punish him; for when the Church judges and punishes people for what it believes to be a crime, it is breaking the law and infringing the ruler's prerogatives.[3] Thus it is obvious that, by rejecting the idea that the Church had the power of a state within the state, Shidyaq clearly endorses the separation of the temporal from the spiritual.

It is not only his personal tragedy, however, that made him take this secular stand. Shidyaq, who knew both English and French, was a great admirer of Voltaire (d.1778)[4] and French culture[5] which gave the world some of its earliest and most prominent secular thinkers. He may well have been influenced by other Western secular thinkers.

As'ad al-Shidyaq's tragedy moved another Lebanese Christian Maronite to comment on the evil of mixing religion with secularism. In his book *Qissat*

As'ad al-Shidyaq (The Story of As'ad al-Shidyaq) Butrus al-Bustani[6] writes that 'the evil the Patriarch did to As'ad is an evil done to the Sultan, since As'ad is under his rule.'[7]

Yet it was not only As'ad's personal tragedy that moved Bustani, but that of the whole of Lebanon when the intense religious strife broke out in 1860, the year in which he published his book. Bustani tried to combat it by writing articles in the periodicals he had started. These were *Nafir Suriyya* (1860) with the help of his son Saleem, *al-Jinan* and *al-Janna* (both in 1870) and *al-Junayna* (1871). In *Nafir Suriyya*, for example, he writes that evil and damage are the only results of mixing religion with politics and failing to separate the spiritual from the temporal.[8]

Yet it is important to note that both he and Shidyaq sought the separation of the spiritual from the temporal power of the Church, and not from that of the Ottoman Sultan. One of the reasons might have been their refusal to add fuel to an already inflamed atmosphere by antagonizing both the Muslims and the Turkish administration, besides the fact that As'ad had been a victim of the Church rather than of the Sultan. Another reason might be the Ottoman *Tanzimat* that had decreed equality between the various religions and creeds and made the Christians feel that the Sultan had separated his temporal from his religious power.[9]

Bustani also explains that he has non-personal and non-political reasons for his secular stance when he writes that religion deals with internal, personal matters that do not change, whereas politics deals with external matters that change and can improve with time and circumstance. Vesting both powers in one person, therefore, can only lead to disaster in both religion and politics, and 'I do not exaggerate if I say that civilization and progress would then become impossible.'[10]

Thus al-Shidyaq's and Bustani's clearly secular stance was not due only to personal or national tragedies, but also to their intellectual approach. As can be deduced from al-Shidyaq's admiration for Voltaire and Bustani's statement quoted above, they believed that secularism should be the basis for all the material and intellectual aspects of society if there was to be any hope of progress, since civilization encompasses both the intellectual and the material. However, neither of them went into detail on the subject; this was left to writers of the next generation.

It is among the writers of this next generation that we find the first Muslim requiring separation of the spiritual from the temporal. In his book *Um al-Qura* (Mother of Cities), published in 1898, the Aleppan 'Abd al-Rahman al-Kawakibi(1854–1902)[11] clearly states that:

... religion is one thing and royalty another... It is neither the aim nor the business of the [Ottoman] sultans to give precedence to religion over the interest of the state... Even had they wanted to, they have been unable to do so because their empire comprises peoples of different religions and races.[12]

He then cites both Arab and Ottoman history in support of his argument:

If we examine history carefully we find that religion and the state were never one, except under the rule of the Rashidun (Orthodox) Caliphs and that of the [Umayyad] 'Umar ibn 'Abd al-'Aziz. Sometimes the spiritual and the temporal were partially united during the Umayyad and the 'Abbasid periods, but after that religion was separated from matters of state.[13]

As proof, al-Kawakibi cites several examples, among them the secret agreement between the Ottoman Sultan Muhammad II the Conqueror (d.1481) and the Spanish Catholic monarchs, Ferdinand and Isabella, to help them eliminate the last Arab Muslim kingdom in Spain, allowing the murder and burning of Muslims. This was in return for the favour Rome had done him by abandoning the Eastern Empire when he attacked Macedonia and then Constantinople.[14]

In al-Kawakibi's second book, *Taba'i' al-Istibdad* (The Characteristics of Tyranny)[15] he reiterates that politics, religion and education should be separated.[16] If there should be a caliph in modern times, al-Kawakibi insists that his role and that of his assistants should be a purely spiritual one, leaving all the political, administrative and military matters to the sultans and princes.[17] This contradicts the traditional Muslim view whereby the title of 'caliph' has both a spiritual and a temporal connotation, and which, as will be shown later in this chapter, was discussed in detail and strongly disputed by 'Ali 'Abd al-Raziq.

As a result of his belief in the separation of the spiritual from the political, al-Kawakibi enjoins Muslims to obey any government that is just, even if it is non-Muslim or even atheist, for a just ruler who is an atheist is better that an unjust Muslim ruler.[18] This, too, contradicts Muslim political thought which insists on Muslims being ruled by none but a Muslim, let alone an atheist, since the ruler's role is to protect religion as well as the country, as al-Mawardi had stated.

Like al-Shidyaq and Bustani, a personal factor might also have been the reason for Kawakibi's secularism. Because he had criticized the Sultan 'Abdülhamid's tyranny in his newspaper articles and freely expressed his desire for reform, his newspapers were banned, he was imprisoned and his property confiscated before he managed to escape to Egypt. His personal plight was that of many in an Empire which was starting to crumble militarily, politically, socially and economically. This might have been another reason for his hoping that separating the religious from the political could be a means of improvement, for he clearly states that 'many thinkers in developed countries assure that they only started progressing after separating matters of religion from those of the state.'[19]

However, besides merely stating that separating the two powers was a reason for progress, al-Kawakibi does not go into the various aspects of this progress, or show the political and social results of this separation. Could this be for fear of reaching a conclusion that might be incompatible with Islam?

It is here that the difference emerges between himself and his two Christian precursors. First of all, note that he calls for separating the spiritual only from the political and not from all aspects of temporal life. Even when he attacks tyranny and injustice in his book *Taba'i' al-Istibdad,* he supports his attacks by citing the Qur'anic verses that call for justice and equanimity. This proves that, for al-Kawakibi, religion was still the foundation of society, as opposed to the secular political principles of the West. When he lays down the rules for an imaginative ideal society in the future, he calls for Islamic unity, headed by a caliph who would rule from Mecca,[20] and a society made up solely of Muslims.[21] This is not surprising since he was in close contact with the Muslim reformers al-Afghani, Muhammad 'Abdu (1849–1905) and Rashid Rida (1865–1935) with whom he collaborated in editing his periodical *al-Manar.*

Even when al-Kawakibi sought to separate the spiritual from the political he did not dwell on intellectual reasoning, but merely reinterpreted Arab Muslim history, choosing from it that which suited his purpose and not criticizing, but trying to defend it by showing that it contained the principles that produced progress in the West. Yet it did not occur to him to ask why separating the spiritual from the political had led to progress in the West, even though it had not yielded the same results in what he claimed to be the history of Islam.

The Egyptian Qasim Amin (1865–1908)[22] was a Muslim contemporary of al-Kawakibi but unlike al-Kawakibi he did not confine himself to the separation of the spiritual from the temporal in politics. Amin's main concern was liberating Muslim women from all that kept them ignorant and backward. Since the personal status laws were in the hands of the *'ulama* (doctors of religion), he claimed that those ignorant Islamic 'scholars' who neither understood science nor religion should not be allowed to express an opinion in any of the nation's affairs, least of all in one of the utmost importance such as that of women's liberation.[23] From this and his saying that science, and as a result the whole of Europe, only developed after eliminating the power of the clergy,[24] one can easily deduce his desire to separate the temporal from the spiritual and not merely in the political sphere. Although what he seeks to eliminate here is the power of the *'ulama*, the chapter on 'Women' will show that Amin went much further in wanting to separate the spiritual from the social aspects of life.

The contradictions in Kawakibi's thought are not found in the writings of six Lebanese Christians in the next generation who dealt with separation of the spiritual from the temporal. Four of them emigrated to Egypt, like al-Kawakibi, and the other two to France.

Jurji Zaydan,[25] unlike his three compatriots Adib Ishaq (1856–1885)[26], Shibli al-Shummayyil (1850–1917)[27] and Farah Antun (1874–1922)[28] never openly insisted on a secular state. Yet this can be inferred from his strong support of the Union and Progress Party whose members claimed that they intended to institute a democracy and advocated equality between all citizens of the Empire, which would mean separating the spiritual from the temporal. Besides, they were against 'Abdülhamid who had proclaimed himself Caliph of the Muslims, thus restoring the traditional Islamic concept of the state. Zaydan expressed his bitterness in a letter to his son on October 12, 1910, when he was forced to resign from the Egyptian University, even before having started to teach the course on Islamic history, just because he was a Christian and 'the university felt it to be improper for a Christian to be a professor of Islamic history.'[29] This cannot but show his desire for separation between religious and temporal matters.

Without going into details, Ishaq, who was a great admirer of the French Revolution and its slogans, attacked the religious clerics who interfered in politics and the government, clearly believing in the separation of religion and the state, and if he defended the nihilists it was because they also wanted this separation.[30]

Shibli al-Shummayyil was more open and direct in dealing with the subject. He stated in 1908 that 'the temporal power must be completely separated from the spiritual.' Unlike his predecessors, al-Shidyaq and Bustani, who avoided the subject completely, Shummayyil says that so long as the ruler was not the 'Ottoman Sultan' but *'Amir al-Mu'minin'*, i.e. Commander of the Faithful and Caliph of the Muslims, as 'Abdülhamid had declared himself to be, an Ottoman Christian, Jewish or atheist subject could not have any real patriotic feeling, or a Muslim's rights and duties. Therefore Shummayyil clearly called for the divesting of all of the Sultan's spiritual powers and transferring them to someone else.[31] This, in his eyes, was the only hope for progress, because 'society can only advance by separating the temporal from the spiritual,'[32] and Christian Europe had progressed only after wresting power from the hands of the Church, putting religion aside and advancing in the world independently of religion and its clergy.[33] This demand to dispense with religion in all worldly matters was a very far cry from al-Kawakibi's limited secularism.

Farah Antun went a step further by directly comparing Christianity and Islam in this respect, pointing out the differences between them. A long polemic between him and Muhammad 'Abdu followed Antun's articles in his periodical *al-Jami'a* concerning Ibn Rushd's (Averroes, d. 1198) philosophy[34] and published in 1903 in his best-known book, *Ibn Rushd wa Falsafatuhu* (Averroes and his Philosophy). He dedicated it to:

> ... those men of sense in every community and every religion in the East who have seen the danger of mingling the world with religion in an age such as ours, and who have come to demand that their religion should be placed on one side in a sacred and honoured place, so that they will be able really to unite, and to flow with the tide of the new European civilization, in order to be able to compete with those who belong to it, for otherwise it will sweep them all away and make them the subjects of others.[35]

He thus not only clearly advocates the necessity of separating the spiritual from the temporal aspects of life, but in an answer to 'Abdu shows why this happened in Christendom which does not deal with the temporal, unlike Islam,[36] and that, even in Europe, this separation came about after many wars against the pope. He then points out to 'Abdu the reasons why he advocates this separation, stating that the role of religion is to prepare for the hereafter and not for this world, which is no longer what it used to be when religions were revealed, and therefore cannot be administered in the way it was in the past.[37]

Antun then explains all the disadvantages of mingling the spiritual with the temporal. He sees them as both intellectual and socio-political. In an article about persecution under Christianity and Islam, he writes that it is easier for Christian countries to be tolerant than it is for Muslim ones because the Christians, who comply with Christ's exhortation to 'render unto Caesar that which is Caesar's, and unto God that which is God's' separated the temporal from the spiritual power and deprived the latter of the right to interfere in people's beliefs by persecuting and even killing them. Thus science and philosophy were no longer persecuted by the Church and managed to develop and create modern civilization, whereas they could not avoid being persecuted in Muslim countries where the temporal and spiritual powers were and still are united.[38]

Antun thus feels that 'the most important reason for separating the temporal power from the spiritual is the release of the human intellect from any bonds, and this is a service performed for the future of humanity.'[39] It was thanks to great kings like Frederick II of Germany (d.1797) and great men like Voltaire that the power of the Church was weakened and man's intellect in Europe freed. He writes, 'but it is impossible to have such kings and men in the East so long as the religious power is capable at all times of putting the temporal power to the sword.'[40] And as long as intelligence and reason are persecuted by the clergy, the nation will remain weak, because the spiritual power, being weak by nature, strives to win favour among the people by pandering to their feelings of spirituality, even if this leads to fanaticism and religious strife within the nation.[41]

Antun then indicates the socio-political advantages of separating the temporal from the political. This is where feelings of unease and fear lurk in a person who is a member of the Christian minority in a Muslim world and state. Thus he insists that all citizens should be absolutely equal, no matter what their religion, and the government should no longer defend one religion against the other.[42] Then the individual will have his/her rights as an individual, and the head of the temporal power can belong to any faith without this affecting the government's decisions.[43] In fact, by separating them, it is 'the temporal that should have the right to power and to rule over the spiritual,'[44] otherwise it would be normal for the government to favour those who profess its own faith. Speaking from his experience as a Lebanese who saw what happened after the 1860 incidents, he says that the underprivileged, weaker section of the population will then resort to a foreign power for protection, and this power will interfere, considering its own interests first and foremost and leading to great disaster for all.[45] From his purely secular stance, Antun believed that even the Christian missionaries had been sent to the Middle East primarily for political reasons, although he did not deny the good they had done.[46] In fact, the missionaries were not extraneous to political Europe and had played a role in accentuating sectarianism between the Christians, Druzes and Muslims in Lebanon.[47] But in the wake of 'Abdu's severe attack on him, and the feeling of unease and alienation he shared with the whole Christian minority, Antun might also have criticized the sincerity of the missionaries because he wanted to distance himself and other Arab Christians from the West with which the Muslims associated them, and bring them closer to their Muslim compatriots.

This attitude, as well as his secular stance, led Antun to directly attack al-Afghani's call for Pan-Islamism as a means of fighting the West.[48] Pan-Islamism, Antun believed, could only annoy the West without thwarting any of its aims; depending on a deep faith in religion alone, he claimed, makes people loose all ambition and incentive to work and improve, since for them this world is ephemeral and vain, and their reward awaits them in paradise. In answer to those who claim that in the past Muslims had built a great empire and civilization based on their religion combined with strength, Antun retorts that it was their love of conquest and their desire for wealth that made them succeed, besides their longing to spread Islam through *jihad* (holy war). Thus:

> Their love of conquest and *jihad* were their strongest drive and what most whetted their ardour and will. In those days Nietsche's philosophy of power and energy took on a religious connotation which is no longer possible today, for the only result of mixing religion with politics is to make the Easterners even weaker. [49]

Pan-Islamism, he says, might be a temporary hope because the Muslim countries share the same misfortunes and suffering, but unlike its supporters and al-Kawakibi, he believes religious unity to be impossible because the Muslim countries differ in language, ethnicity and creed, and conflict between them is unavoidable just as it was when they were independent states since the days of the Caliph Mu'awiya.[50]

Thus, for Antun, unless the temporal and the spiritual are separated there can be no real civilization, tolerance, justice, equality or security, harmony, freedom, science, philosophy and progress; nor can the nation enjoy peace and be powerful vis-à-vis other nations.[51] For him, civilization today is based on two things, science and secularism, without which no progress is possible.

Yet Philipp rightly believes that those Christian writers were not seeking the separation of the temporal from the spiritual merely as a reaction to the danger of Muslim domination, but also in order 'to emancipate themselves from the social and intellectual narrowness of the life in their own Christian minorities,' and from 'the power that the Church wielded over the members of the Christian minorities.'[52] Both al-Shidyaq and Bustani were severely criticized by the Maronite Church for having embraced Protestantism, the former's brother murdered, as has been shown, and all three: Zaydan, Shummayyil and Antun were as strongly attacked by the Islamic revivalist Rashid Rida's *al-Manar* as by the Jesuit Louis Shikho (d.1927) in his book on the history of Arabic literature in the nineteenth and early twentieth centuries.

Two Lebanese Christian contemporaries, Nejib Azoury (d.1916)[53] and Georges Samné (1877– ?)[54] wrote from Paris. Azoury's book *Le Réveil de la Nation Arabe* (The Awakening of the Arab Nation), published in 1905, clearly states that separating the temporal from the spiritual is in the interest of both the Arabs and Islam, one of the main reasons for the fall of the great Arab empire having been that both powers were in the hands of one person. This is also why the caliphate has become ridiculous and despicable in the hands of the Turks since, according to Azoury, the successor of Allah's prophet must have impeccable morality and spotless honour,[55] if he is to be considered a religious leader. Although he was a Christian, Azoury, unlike al-Kawakibi, saw the problem Islam would face if the two powers were separated. He tried to solve this problem in an original manner. The population of the then-Ottoman province of Hijaz was, as it still is, entirely Muslim. He therefore suggests that, together with the terrritory of Madina, it should form 'an independent state whose ruler would also be the religious Caliph of all the Muslims. Thus the great difficulty of separating the civil power from the religious in Islam would have been solved for the good of all.'[56] Since this Caliph would have real moral authority over all the Muslims in the world, Azoury believes he should be a descendant of the Prophet.[57] By keeping both powers in the hand of a descendant of the Prophet in the Hijaz and Madina, Azoury felt he would be satisfying the Muslims, and by separating the temporal from the spritual in the rest of the Arab world he would be satisfying his belief in secularism.

In his book, *La Syrie*, Samné directly addresses the history of Islam. Years before 'Abd al-Raziq wrote his famous book *al-Islam wa Usul al-Hukm* Samné believed, as did 'Abd al-Raziq later on, that Islam only formed a moral, religious unity between Muslims. Such a belief was no problem for a Christian living in France and writing in French. He insisted that although the caliphs were undoubtedly the spiritual heads of Islam, their temporal authority did not extend beyond their own army, tribe and the country they had conquered. For example, three of the four Orthodox Caliphs were murdered, as numerous others had been during the history of Islam. This lead to the break-up of the Empire into numerous autonomous and virtually independent states, the caliph having been a mere figurehead since the mid-eighth century.[58] He then provides a detailed draft of the constitution he proposes for Syria, insisting on two provisions to be inserted, namely, that the state should be purely secular and that it should be absolutely neutral vis-à-vis the different religions, beliefs and faiths.[59] His theory about this state will be developed later in the chapter concerning his belief in secular nationalism.

However, it was not only Christian writers who attacked Pan-Islamism. One of the most prominent Muslim thinkers in Egypt, Ahmad Lutfi al-Sayyid (1872–1963)[60,] considered that mixing politics with religion was dangerous, for politics is based only on the common interest (*manafi' 'amma*) shared by certain people.[61] He admits that a shared religion is a solidarity factor between people, but considers it unfit to be the basis of politics in the twentieth century, an age in which politics is based on the common interest, as opposed to faith. Otherwise the British and the Germans, for example, would have been one nation instead of fighting each other because of conflicting interests and patriotism.[62] Al-Sayyid also mentions religion as being merely a factor of 'solidarity', undoubtedly realizing that solidarity does not mean unity, not even moral or social unity between all Muslims, to say nothing of political unity.

Consequently, al-Sayyid considers Pan-Islamism a mere ideal that can never be implemented, adding that what really exists is 'Pan-Islamic disunity, not Pan-Islamic unity'. This discord between Muslims dates as far back as the rule of 'Ali Ibn Abi Taleb (d. 660), the fourth and last Orthodox caliph.[63] Using a contemporary example, he claims that the [Muslim] Ottoman Sultan did nothing to help the Muslim Egyptians in their struggle for independence from [Christian] British rule.[64]

Although al-Sayyid, like al-Kawakibi, advocates the separation of religion only from politics and not from the other temporal aspects of life, later chapters will show that he did not want to restrict this separation to the political sphere.

The writings of the Syrian Muslim Muhammad Kurd 'Ali (1876–1953)[65] indicate an ambivalence regarding the separation of the spiritual from the temporal. In an article written in 1906, he divides knowledge ('ilm) into temporal and religious, the former dealing with what is good for people's livelihood and the preservation of order in society, the latter dealing with the hereafter and moral guidance so that people may gain everlasting bliss in paradise.[66] The Qur'an regulated most of the private, social and economic lives of the Muslims, i.e. 'what is good for people's livelihood and preserves order in society.' In this, Kurd 'Ali is closer to his Christian contemporaries, Shummayyil and Farah Antun, and takes a step towards secularism further than that of al-Kawakibi, since he separates the spiritual from the whole of temporality, not merely from politics. However, he avoids going into details that might conflict with Islam.

Then, contrary to what al-Kawakibi claimed, Kurd 'Ali states that the temporal and religious were only separated for a short time in the history of Islam, but as early as the first century after the coming of Islam (the seventh century C.E.). Especially in the second and third centuries of Islam, he claims that the temporal became mingled with religion because the political rulers saw that this was to their advantage, bribing the 'ulama to lend support to whatever deeds they performed. In an article written in the following year, Kurd 'Ali calls Saladin (d.1193) wise and intelligent because he was the first to realise that mixing politics with religion was one of the main causes of a nation's weakness.[67]

Consequently, when he took his first trip to Europe in 1909 he wrote that the power of the Church in politics had been eliminated thanks to the 1789 French Revolution,[68] and he extolls the virtues of Paris which taught the world:

> ... the meaning of liberty, equality and fraternity... thus putting an end to any differentiation between people as regards their rights and obligations, and any discrimination against class and religion.[69]

This clearly shows that Kurd 'Ali realized the secular connotation of the French Revolution's slogans, yet he expresses no desire to transpose them to his own country, nor does he criticize their absence there. One reason for this might be his fear of Ottoman rule of which he, like others, had been a victim. Another reason might be the realization that complete secularism would contradict many of Islam's principles and the injunctions that discriminate against women, slaves and non-Muslims, for example, besides the fact that he felt comfortable belonging to Sunni Islam which ruled the country and represented the majority of Syrians. Even after Syria had become a French mandate, when visiting Spain in 1922 and criticizing the Church which opposed all reform and kept the country backward compared to other European countries[70] that had made progress thanks to the separation of church and state,[71] he still does not allude to the interference of religion in secular matters as being a cause of the backwardness in Muslim countries. He also severely criticizes Mustafa Kamal Atatürk's (d.1938) secularism in Turkey,[72] and as late as 1934 still refers to the Christians and Jews by the Qur'anic term of '*ahl dhimma*'.[73]

However, at the same time, he reverts to the stance he had taken in 1906 and 1907. He writes that when the ignorant '*ulama* got the upper hand in the Muslim countries after the 12th century AD, free thought no longer existed, philosophers and thinkers were terrorized, the people became ignorant and fanatical, and 'these ignoramuses harmed both the spiritual and the temporal because they saw everything through the eyes of religion and did not let the temporal follow the path that was best for it.'[74] Later in his *Memoirs* he becomes more explicit when he criticizes the interference in politics of all the theologians (*fuqaha'*) because this causes the nation to degenerate, unlike the Christian nations that had started to deal soundly with temporal matters when they separated them from the spiritual.[75] Therefore he urges the Muslims to:

> ... put the hereafter aside and let us examine the temporal. Could matters be sound if they are not based on order and justice, and can they be achieved without applying laws like the Westerners... who only pay attention to this life. That is why they are more successful than us in

everything: they are richer, more honest and just, whereas all that which our religion forbids, such as cheating, lying and slander, is amply found in our country... and accepted by our *'ulama* and rulers.[76]

Here, a Muslim not only seeks to separate the temporal from the spiritual, but even believes that Western secular laws are more effective than Islam in redressing society and morals. This shows to what extent some Muslim thinkers had started to adopt Western secularism in the 1930s, although Kurd 'Ali did not go into detail to show how these secular temporal laws might contradict the Islamic *shari'a* laws.

It is not surprising to find a Lebanese Christian woman and journalist, Julia Tohmi Dimashqiyya (1880–1954)[77] strongly criticizing all sectarianism and asking not to teach religion in schools. Religion can be taught at home, in churches and mosques; schools, however, should be free from any sectarian or religious spirit, and instead instil in the children a spirit of true patriotism and nationalism. To allay the fears of believers, she adds that having such secular schools does not mean that they are anti-religious or atheist.[78] In her personal life, she proved her belief in secularism by marrying a Muslim.

However, the Muslim thinker whose secularism raised a storm of criticism and protest was the Azharite sheikh 'Ali 'Abd al-Raziq (1888–1966).[79] In 1925, he published his book *al-Islam wa Usul al-Hukm* (Islam and the Principles of Government), for which he was tried, dismissed from the circle of *'ulama* and expelled from the *shari'a* (canonical) courts in which he had been a judge.[80] He spent the rest of his life in seclusion.

What incited him to tackle this problem was the Turkish National Assembly's abolition of the caliphate in 1924, after which a congress of Egyptian 'ulama discussed the matter and reaffirmed the traditional opinion that the caliphate was necessary and had both spiritual and temporal power. 'Abd al-Raziq's book was his contribution to the debate.

He started by discussing the necessity of the caliphate. He insisted that not a single Qur'anic verse or Hadith (the Prophetic Tradition) mentions that it is obligatory to have a caliph, although in matters of religion the Qur'an goes into the greatest detail.[81] As for *ijma'* (consensus) which is one of the principles upon which Muslim legislation is based, after the Qur'an and the Hadith,[82] 'Abd al-Raziq finds no proof in Muslim history or in the writings of Muslim scholars of any consensus on this matter. From the days of the first caliph Abu Bakr (d.634) to the present, there had always been factions that rebelled against the caliph, and in every generation caliphs were killed.[83] It is necessary to have a government to uphold worship and the welfare of the community, but, he writes, this government could take on any form, and the upholding of worship and the welfare of the community never depended on a caliph or the caliphate. He then goes a step further when he declares that Muslims do not need this caliphate for either their temporal or for their spiritual affairs, and that, in fact, 'the caliphate was and still is a calamity for Islam and the Muslims, a source of evil and corruption... Our religion, as well as our temporal life, can dispense with this doctrinal caliphate.' As proof, he claims that neither Islam nor the Muslim community suffered after the fall of the caliphate when the Tartars attacked Baghdad in the thirteenth century and murdered the 'Abbasid caliph; nor did the Muslim countries that rejected submission to the Ottoman caliphate neglect their religion nor did they suffer socially.[84]

After dismissing the legitimacy and the necessity of the caliphate, 'Abd al-Raziq goes on to reject the very principle of Muslim political thought, i.e. that a Muslim ruler should have both political and spiritual power. As with the caliphate, to prove this he resorts to the two main sources of Islam, the Qur'an and the Hadith, as well as to the history of Islam. Examining the Prophet Muhammad's life (d. 632), words and deeds, 'Abd al-Raziq finds that even the most basic and elementary attributes of any government, such as a budget, ministries for internal and external affairs and the like were non-existent in the Prophet's day, nor did he mention them.[85] From this he deduces that:

> Muhammad was only the Messenger of a religious message which was purely religious, with no desire for royalty and no claim to a state. The Prophet had neither a kingdom nor a government, nor did he establish a kingdom in the political sense of this word and its synonyms. His primacy was purely religious and his task ended when he died.[86]

Although the Prophet undoubtedly had power and authority over his people, 'Abd al-Raziq assures that this was a religious, spiritual authority leading to God, not that of a political leader which is a temporal authority and has nothing to do with faith. Temporal authority plans what is beneficial for life in this world. He then points out the wide gap between the spiritual and the temporal.[87] There is no better proof of this than the Qur'an itself, he claims. 'Abd al-Raziq goes on to quote all the Qur'anic verses corroborating his view that the Prophet had nothing to do with political rule, and that his sole role was to convey God's message to his people.[88]

However 'Abd al-Raziq did not overlook or deny that many of the Prophet's deeds and sayings relate to worldly, temporal, political matters, such as *jihad*, although he merely sees them as the means to which the Prophet resorted in order to consolidate religion.[89] He also does not deny that the Qur'an instituted many laws concerning everyday life, such as rules for punishment, the army, war, debt, commerce and money-lending, among others. But he insists that all these laws and regulations have nothing to do with forms of government or the systems of a civil state, besides the fact that, taken all together, they constitute only very few of the political principles and laws necessary for such a state.[90] This is because Islam is nothing more than a religious bond through which God sought to unite all the peoples of the world. If religious unity is possible, he insists that political unity is impossible because it goes against human nature and that is why 'God has left people free to administer their worldly affairs, guided by their reason, knowledge, interests, desires and tendencies,' so that they may differ and compete with each other for the advance of civilization.[91]

Thus, although 'Abd al-Raziq's main concern was the separation of the spiritual from the political, he sometimes alluded to *separating it from all worldly matters*, and sees this as a condition for the progress of civilization. Yet, clinging to his faith, he insists that it was God, not man, who ordained this, and the Prophet, who was God's messenger, applied it in his time by leaving it up to each tribe to exercise its own administrative and legal system, never interfering in anything concerning their security or economy.[92] Throughout his life, the Prophet never mentioned an 'Islamic' or 'Arab' state, 'Abd al-Raziq insists, although he was an Arab and the Arabs were the first people to embrace Islam. Had his aim been to establish a state, he would not have died without designating a successor, or leaving laws concerning the form of government he desired, and to which Muslims would have been able to refer.[93]

'Abd al-Raziq then uses the history of Islam to corroborate his ideas. After the Prophet's death, nobody was able to assume his role as leader, therefore every other leadership would necessarily be of a different type, i.e. non-religious, being civil or political. If one considers the way in which his first successor, Abu Bakr, received the pledge of allegiance, writes 'Abd al-Raziq, this can be seen as a political pledge, and his government, like all governments, was established by the power of the sword. Those who opposed him did so for temporal, not religious reasons, because they knew that he and his followers were establishing a civil, temporal government. Yet because in those days several things gave Abu Bakr a certain religious aura, some people imagined his office to be a religious one, in which he was the Prophet's successor. This is how the contention arose that ruling the Muslims was a religious office, and that the ruler was a substitute for the Prophet, so Abu Bakr was named 'successor of the Prophet of God' (*khalifatu rasul Allah*).[94]

After that, the sultans saw that the propagation of this error was to their advantage, and they told the people that to obey the sultan was to obey God, and to oppose the sultan was to oppose Him. They then went a step further, claiming that the sultan was God's representative on earth, and the caliphate became part of Islam; whereas, in reality, neither the caliphate nor any other government office are part of religion. As a result, 'Abd al-Raziq sees that, upon ridding themselves of the caliphate, Muslims should now create new forms of government, based on the most modern principles that human reason has devised, and which the experience of nations has proved to be the most solid basis of government.[95] Here, he clearly seems to be asking Muslims to rely on the modern, i.e. European, political principles set by human reason, and thus break away totally from their political heritage which they based on their interpretation or, according to him, misinterpretation of revealed religion.

Undoubtedly, the main reasons for the fierce attack and punishment 'Abd al-Raziq had to suffer were, first of all, his new interpretation of Muslim history, abolishing the aura of purity, perfection and sanctity it had acquired, and refuting facts that had acquired a religious connotation, such as the political role of the Prophet, the role of Abu Bakr, and the caliphate, as well as his assertion that the Muslim community had been, from the start, a political entity, not merely a religious one.[96] The conservative 'ulama were logically no longer entitled to assert, as they had been doing, that this Muslim past transcended history and was an ideal that had to be emulated in the present and the future. No less a crime in the eyes of the 'ulama was his references to the political thought of such Western political thinkers as Thomas Hobbes (d.1679) and John Locke (d. 1704).[97] These examples showed how highly he valued Western thought in his desire to separate the temporal from the spiritual, including his quotation of Sir Thomas Arnold's (d.1842) words about the caliphate.[98] The 'ulama considered this to be proof of how far he was influenced by 'the enemies of Islam.'[99]

In his defence 'Abd al-Raziq asserted that he had never claimed that Islam was merely a spiritual law, but had said that God sent it only for the spiritual welfare of the people, leaving them free to manage their worldly affairs as they saw fit.[100] Yet he adds that for him 'Islam is a religion that set down laws which, to a great extent, pertain to most aspects of life.'[101] He did not seem to see any contradiction between these two statements, for how were people to be free to manage their worldly affairs if Islam had already regulated most of them?

In his references to the Qur'an and the Prophet's life, 'Abd al-Raziq strresses that which supports the separation of the political and administrative from the spiritual, but clearly underplays everything that pertains to social and everyday life, almost every detail of which neither the Qur'an nor the Hadith omit. This shows that, for all his courage and liberal interpretation of Islam and its history, 'Abd al-Raziq remained a devout believer in Islam as a temporal, and not merely a spiritual, guide for people in their everyday life.

Another interesting aspect of his work is his subjective interpretation of the history of Islam. Why does he consider the Prophet's wars to be a *jihad* to consolidate the religion, while Abu Bakr's wars were political ones to consolidate his power, although Abu Bakr was fighting apostates from Islam?

'Abd al-Raziq was undoubtedly much more explicit than his Muslim forerunners in calling for the separation of the temporal from the spiritual, and, unlike them, went into details concerning aspects of Islam and its history that they had never cared or dared to discuss. Yet all of his secular thought remained within the framework of Islam, never liberating itself completely from religion. For secular thinkers such as 'Abd al-Raziq 'justify their own position by invoking the example of the Prophet, arguing, in effect, that secularism is a valid model because Muhammad himself was a great secularist.'[102]

Taha Hussein (1889–1974)[103], a contemporary of 'Abd al-Raziq, was prosecuted like him and in the same year, for advocating a similar 'limited' secularism. However, for reasons that will be shown in a later chapter, he was not condemned on the same grounds. In advocating the separation of the temporal from the spiritual, Taha Hussein, unlike 'Abd al-Raziq, did not restrict this separation to the political and administrative. He followed in 'Abd al-Raziq's footsteps when he asserted that Islam was a religion and not a political system. 'Had it contained a revealed political system,' he writes, 'the Qur'an would have shown it, and the Prophet would have declared its principles.'[104] Without going into details like 'Abd al-Raziq, he used the same arguments, namely, that the Prophet neither set the basis for a caliphate nor a constitution for the Arabs. This is why after his death, the struggle for power began between the Quraishi emigrants (*muhajirun*) and the Prophet's supporters (*ansar*) in Madina.[105] Like al-Sayyid, Hussein points out that modern governments in civilized countries base their politics on worldly benefits, not on religion.[106] In his view, this applies even to governments that claim to be Muslim. How can the Egyptian government, for example, claim to be based on Islam, be supported by Islam and exist for Islam?[107] If it were really a Muslim government it should eliminate banks, interest and *all other aspects of society* that do not conform to the principles of Islam.[108] For Hussein, this is proof enough of the impossibility of basing temporal affairs on religion in modern times, or even combining them with religion. It is here that we see how his secularism, unlike that of 'Abd al-Raziq, goes beyond politics to encompass the whole of society. 'All that Islam does is to command the Muslims to be just, charitable and good, leaving them completely free to organize their temporal affairs as they see fit.'[109] Thus he does away with all of Islam's injunctions concerning socio-economic relations. As a result, he insists that the Azhar should not be a state within the state, with a special power that can defy and overrule the power of the state, as it does with the existence of the Council of the leading *'ulama*,[110] of which both he and 'Abd al-Raziq were ultimately the victims.

At about the same time, in 1928, a Lebanese Muslim Druze woman discussed the separation of the spiritual and the temporal. Nazira Zayn al-Din (1908–1976)[111] went much further than her Egyptian Muslim contemporaries, while still remaining within the framework of Islam. Her originality and courage lie in the fact that, as a woman, she gives a woman's point of view of the problem, and tackles its social rather than its political aspect. Her book *al-Sufur wa al-Hijab* (Unveiling and Veiling) was a direct response to the demands of the religious clerics who asked the government in Damascus to force women to be completely veiled. Provoked by this, she insists that the government is a temporal power which should apply the temporal laws that hold individual freedom sacred, and that it should refuse to give anyone besides itself the right to restrict this freedom.[112] Here, she is undoubtedly not only seeking to separate the temporal from the spiritual, but to give precedence to the former over the latter in the matter of the veil and laws of personal status.

Following in the footsteps of Muhammad 'Abdu and Ibn Taymiyya (d.1328) before him, in his book *al-Siyasa al-Shar'iyya* (Legal Politics), she clearly separates the principles of faith from those that relate to worldly matters; the former are the only ones that do not and should not change, whereas all that has to do with human life and human relations are based on reason and change with time and the welfare of the population. As proof of this, she quotes the Prophet's words to his people: 'You are more knowledgeable in worldly affairs,'[113] and adds that God Himself changed some of the verses He had revealed in order to suit changing circumstances.[114] She therefore insists that 'religion has the power given it by God, and the world has the power given it by man, and both the spiritual and the temporal co-operate for what is right and good, but each is independent of the other.'[115] Thus, unlike some of the other Muslim men, Nazira does not restrict the separation of the two powers to the political sphere, or, like Kurd 'Ali and 'Abd al-Raziq, avoid expounding the social and legal aspect, for she includes among the temporal customs and laws that she sees must change with changing times,[116] the civil laws designed to protect the freedom of the individual and those that abolish the *'ulama's* monopoly of the laws of personal status. Here, she is fully conscious that changing the laws of personal status might involve changing some of the laws decreed by the Qur'an, such as the laws of inheritance and evidence. Yet instead of avoiding the subject as the others had done, she takes the bull by the horns and says that when the Qur'an decreed that a girl can inherit only half of what her brother inherits, or that the testimony of two women was equal to that of one man, the reason was that *circumstances in those days justified such laws.* But now things are different.[117] To support her point she refers to the Ottoman sultan's having decreed that in matters regarding criminal prosecution and land inheritance,[118] men and women were to be treated equally in their evidence and inheritance rights.[119] Here we see that Nazira Zayn al-Din insinuates that at least the temporal injunctions of Islam are a social phenomena, reflecting the circumstances that gave rise to them, and that they therefore cannot transcend the time and place to which they were linked.

Clearly, here is a woman asking for the separation of powers because this would favour women's rights. From this feminist point of view she sees that the Muslims often separated the temporal from the religious, but *only if it were solely in men's favour.*

> Men have separated from the permanent spiritual principles of religion only the changing temporal ones that concern them, such as those dealing with business transactions, sanctions and certain ways of life. Thus, they altered laws and ways of life to suit their interests; but those ways of life and personal status laws that are not advantageous to women they considered to be part of the permanent spiritual principles of religion that are not to be changed.[120]

Nazira Zayn al-Din insists that the world will not enjoy righteousness, prosperity and happiness unless all of its men and women alike enjoy equal rights, progress and civilization.[121] She goes as far as to eliminate all differences of gender, race and religion, assuring that once every nation and every person become free and independent, peace will reign everywhere, all people and all nations will share ties of fraternity and equality, through one *common law* and one shared government that will rule all nations and individuals, men and women alike, in both East and West.[122]

This might be Utopian, but it definitely is not compatible with many of the principles and laws of Islam. Thus this Muslim woman, without renouncing her deep faith in her religion, took a clearly secular stance with regards to the separation of all temporal from spiritual power, even rejecting what she considered to be temporal in what Muslims in general considered to be part and parcel of the spiritual.

This leads to the next question of how these less secular or wholly secular writers looked upon religion, its role and its clerics.

CHAPTER THREE

Religion and its Role. Anticlericalism

A. *Religion and its Role*

Influenced by the Enlightenment and its belief in reason, logic and science, as well as by the whole of modern Western civilization, Christian writers not only attacked the Church, but even part of the religion itself, or else they reinterpreted Christianity in the light of modern secular principles.

Bustani, for example, says that when Christ asked us, if smitten, to turn the other cheek, what he meant was not giving up our rights or refraining from self-defence, but that we should defend ourselves and our rights without hatred or revenge.[1] This interpretation is obviously influenced by the secular belief in the duties and rights of the citizen. Clearly influenced by secular rationalism, he then severely criticizes all belief in myths and illogicality, enjoining his readers never to accept a theory or principle that is not based on experience or solid proof.[2] This is why in his defence of As'ad al-Shidyaq he says that As'ad accepted only what for him proved to be right, rejecting what the Catholic Church claimed to be right without having any proof thereof.[3] From the arguments he imagined between As'ad and his opponents, it can be inferred that Bustani, also, only accepted what was logical, therefore refusing much of what the Catholic Church believed in, such as transubstantiation, the intervention of saints, the adoration of statues, icons and the cross, and papal infallibility.[4] This belief in logic might also have been a reason for his abandoning the Maronite Church and embracing Protestantism, indicating that his secularism did not lead to atheism. In fact, he, like the other writers, believed that all religions are basically identical, and accentuated the principles and moral role common to all of them, ignoring whatever essential differences there might be between them. To prove this similarity, he quotes the Qur'anic verse 114 from *Al 'Imran* which 'enjoins correct behaviour and forbids indecency.'[5]

His contemporary, Faris al-Shidyaq, was also born a Maronite but became Protestant after his brother's tragedy, though he embraced Islam in 1860 while in the service of the Bey of Tunisia. All of which indicates that he had no deep faith in any one religion, and it will be observed that his attitude towards religion altered to suit the rulers he served as a Muslim.

As a Protestant, he criticized the fasting, prayers and sacrifices the Maronite Church imposes on believers, claiming that none of this has anything to do with Christianity. Nor does he spare the popes and their evil deeds.[6] Then, in a purely secular vein, he makes fun of faith itself and of those who consider Sunday a holy day and do nothing but pray all day, asking ironically how people survived before they had a Sunday![7] Thus he assures his readers that too much worship and faith involve foolishness and insanity,[8] and that the main cause of madness in Malta is exaggerated religious fervor.[9] As proof of this foolishness he cites the way in which believers argue about the number of layers of hell, the length and substance of the devil's horns, and whether there are 105 or 104 steps to heaven. 'Those who claim this are liars who deserve to have their tongues cut and their eyes torn out... because the number of steps is 106,' adds a third party.[10]

Without stopping at that, al-Shidyaq goes on to attack religion itself, poking fun at those who believe in miracles; he then points out all the immoral and unacceptable events recorded in the Bible.[11] He even doubted that religions have ever had any practical value since they have not helped to improve the conditions of the poor and needy, nor cure the sick. What society needs more than religion is education, knowledge, science and art. They are what make people good and humane, without thinking of reward in the hereafter.[12]

God Himself is not spared this criticism when he asks: if even man tries his best to create something beautiful, how is it that God created some very ugly people besides the beautiful ones? Are we not all supposed to be His creatures for whom He cares equally?[13]

Such comments are not only those of Western secularism, but smack of atheism, and his scathing remarks might very well have been influenced by Voltaire and the belief prevalent during the Age of Enlightenment that reason is the only measure of truth and the way to knowledge.

But when al-Shidyaq founded the periodical *al-Jawa'ib* in Constantinople in 1861, he wrote that 'an atheist government can only be just if it believes in religion.'[14] This might be due to the fact that he was directly under the power of the Ottoman Sultan, whereas his previous ideas about religion are to be found in the books he had written while in Europe.

Yet al-Shidyaq admits that religion is sometimes necessary, but only for the common people, since it encourages them to be virtuous and not commit crimes. Intelligent and educated people, however, can dispense with religion, either because they are virtuous by nature, or because the books they have read have improved them.[15] Thus it is their conscience and not their fear of punishment in the hereafter that makes them good.

Another Christian who was not only influenced by Voltaire but actually summarized his philosophy in a long poem, was the Catholic Jubrail Dallal (1836–1892) who was from Aleppo.[16] In his poem al-'Arsh wa al-Haykal (The Throne and the Temple),[17] which he composed while in Paris in 1864, he rejects the Catholic belief in transubstantiation and finds it ridiculous that Christ should be reduced to a piece of bread that is chewed. Like al-Shidyaq, he claims that the Old Testament, if examined by reason, contains errors, untruths and contradictions. Even if what it contains were true, it teaches the most vicious lessons, such as the merciless killing of the vanquished or murdering brothers, the priests of the temples seeming to be God's butchers. The Old Testament also claims that God picked the Jews, of all nations, as His chosen people and ordered them to steal their neighbours' goods before escaping from Egypt. Yet in spite of all the miracles and help they received from God, they were so evil as to murder all their vanquished enemies, men, women and children, as is written in the Book of Joshua.[18]

This poem cost Dallal his life, not only because of its atheistic content, but because in it he attacked the priests and the sultan's tyranny. When he returned to Syria, twenty years later, still speaking openly about the necessity of reforming the Ottoman Empire, he was imprisoned for life, and died in jail.

Another contemporary was the Lebanese Christian Adib Ishaq. Strongly influenced by the ideas of the French Revolution he, too, saw that religion does not contain natural truths, 'although it is a truth we have to admit especially in the East.' Even if there are truths in religion, albeit not natural truths, he, like his contemporaries, could not admit all the myths, superstitions and lies that distort religious truths, and that ignorant people believe to be part of true faith.[19] Since religion did not contain the truths in which he believed, he considered it to be a waste of time to teach children religion in schools instead of science,[20] and like al-Shidyaq, believed that only education and knowledge will improve people's morals. Thus, for example, political education teaches a person his limitations and the meaning of the public interest, so that his actions will not harm society or others. This education is acquired by a thorough study of the conditions of people in the past and present, and of what wise political thinkers wrote. As a result, he insists that morals and political science are inseparable, for without moral virtue neither rulers nor the ruled can be just, and liberty will lead to chaos and eventually to tyranny.[21] Thus, Ishaq did not feel that religion played any role even in improving society, and in his secular thinking, moral virtues were civic, not religious, and were taught through political science, not religion.

Francis Marrash (1835–1874)[22] another Christian from Aleppo, did not agree with this thinking. He insists that the New Testament is what redresses man's nature, laws and life, and makes him virtuous and civilized. His book, *Mashhad al-Ahwal* (A Perspective of Circumstance), in which he points out the injustice of society in its treatment and assessment of the rich and poor, is undoubtedly influenced by Christianity in its disdain of everything material and worldly and its admiration and defence of poverty.[23] Thus he also believes that the Bible is God-given, and if it contains things we cannot understand, that is because our human reasoning is limited. Yet we have to accept these truths like so many others which we fail to understand.[24]

However, being a physician, he cannot but be influenced by rationalism and science, and thus he rejects much of the contents of the Bible. As early as 1870, he expressed disbelief in the biblical story of the Creation, subscribing to Charles Darwin's (d.1882) theory of evolution.[25] He explains scientifically how heat, light, earth and life came into existence, as opposed to the story told in the Book of Genesis.[26]

Marrash then tries to reconcile his belief in religion with his belief in reason and science by claiming that everything that exists must, logically, have someone who brought it into existence, i.e. a Creator. Throughout his book, *Shahadat al-Tabi'a* (Nature's Testimony), he uses his scientific knowledge to describe the various laws and elements of nature and the relationship and balance between them, to prove logically the existence of God 'a Creator with dazzling wisdom and immense power who had looked after these elements with a concern surpassing all understanding' and in which nothing is left to chance and coincidence.[27] Yet when he tries to use this same reasoning to prove the existence of an immortal, immaterial soul, that belongs to man alone,[28] his reasoning is unconvincing. Yet, as though he himself was aware of this, he ends by saying that our limited reason cannot understand such an elevated matter as the connection between body and soul.[29]

The critical views of these Christians concerning religion and other aspects of their work were not subscribed to in writing by any Muslim, even a whole generation later, on the contrary. Al-Kawakibi says that Islam forbids adding to or eliminating anything from Muhammad's prophecy, or using reasoning to change it,[30] and he faithfully abides by this injunction. All he criticizes are the misinterpretations and misunderstandings of true Islam, which he blames on the fanatical or fossilized *'ulama* who fence in contemporary Muslims with endless regulations that have nothing to do with Islam, or opinions that imams issued centuries ago.[31] Even the secular scientific theories he believes in, such as the changes in the earth's crust, the causes of smallpox and Darwin's theory of evolution, he points out that the Qur'an mentioned them all, long before they were discovered in the West.[32] He thus avoids having to disagree with the Qur'anic story of the Creation, for example, or facing the contradiction between it and the theory of evolution. This shows a complete ignorance, not only of the vast implications of the scientific theories, but also of all the research, intellectual progress and philosophy that made them possible. However, al-Kawakibi might also have had a certain aim in mind: to show his contemporaries that modern science is not alien to Islam, and thus encourage them to study it and not restrict themselves to repeating traditional thought as was their custom in his time, for their ignorance of modern science was one of the reasons for their underdevelopment.

The closest al-Kawkibi comes to secularism in his view of religion is when he, like Bustani, does not differentiate between religions, and sees that there are even some atheists who are more intelligent than believers. He claims that it is their incapacity to conceive of the abstract that made them err.[33] Confining the abstract to the existence of God indicates a rather limited intellectual scope, besides the contradiction encountered when, after having considered all religions to be equal, he insists on the superiority of Islam over all other religions because Islam alone, he claims, is compatible with science and progress.[34]

Yet even he admitted that under despotic rule, religion is useless in redressing evil because despotism would have robbed people of all sincerity and honesty, thus they would no longer be sincere even in their faith. But without wanting to abolish religion like al-Shidyaq and Ishaq, he joins them in saying that what is needed is a sound upbringing and education received from parents, teachers, books and life in general.[35] If he seems to be restricting this exhortation to countries under despotic rule, in reality he is talking about all the countries in the Ottoman Empire of his day, which suffered under its despotic rule.

Qasim Amin wrote at the same time but, unlike al-Kawakibi, he did not claim that the Qur'an held modern scientific truths. As Ernest Renan (d.1892) had done, Amin separates the realm of reason and science from that of faith and religion, insisting that faith is not a matter of reason or science, but a pure emotion, and that science searches for the truth, on the basis of exploration and investigation, although this does not prevent the human mind from reflecting on the unknown which surrounds it,[36] and which, he seems to insinuate, pertains to the realm of metaphysics and/or religion. By completely separating the realm of science from that of religion, Amin avoided dealing with any conflict there might be between them, the conflict which his Christian predecessors had so amply discussed.

The Christians of this generation also took a completely secular view of religion, discussing the very principles of faith, agreeing on some points and disagreeing on others. For Zaydan, Antun and al-Shummayyil religions are man-made and not God-given, as Islam is considered to be by the Muslims. This can be deduced from Zaydan's assertion that people believe in religion because they are weak and afraid of natural phenomena that they cannot explain, especially death. Thus religions, like people, are subject to the law of evolution and survival of the fittest, he says, every new religion changing with time to suit the people who adopted it, since people reject what does not agree with their values and customs, and adopt only what suits them. That is why, he and Antun added, Christianity and Islam repeat many of the ancient pagan beliefs and rituals, and why Antun inisists that all religions, Islam included, would have to change if there is to be any progress, just as Christianity changed without deviating from its basic principles.[37] As a result, he welcomes the new Ottoman laws that contradict the religious *shari'a* laws which were no longer suitable for prevailing conditions.[38] All three of these writers saw the relationship between religion and the circumstances that gave rise to them.

In view of the theory of evolution, both Zaydan and Antun believed that in modern times it is not religion but the proper study of science that leads people to even admit the existence of a Great Creator. Therefore *science, not religion, is the means of knowing God*, and scientific truth is the basis of religion.[39] In fact, for both of them, only the natural sciences could teach the truths of every living thing, and they therefore refused any non-scientific explanation of natural phenomena, such as the Biblical story of the Creation, believing that everything in nature follows definite laws, even if not all of them were yet known. One of these definite laws is that matter is the origin of all living things, each creature developing from a previous one, becoming more and more complex in the struggle for life in which only the fittest survive, as Darwin's theory of evolution has shown. Thus, man was not created from a handful of dust into which God had breathed His spirit.[40] However there is a certain ambivalence in Zaydan's attitude towards this problem. In his book *'Aja'ib al- Khalq* (The Marvels of Creation) he tries to reconcile the biblical story with science by saying that both agree to the gradual succession of creatures but disagree as to the time this took, for if we replace each of the six days of the Bible by a very long period, there will no longer be a difference between the Biblical story and the theory of evolution. Yet he tactically avoids saying whether the creatures were created, as stated in the Bible, or evolved, as Darwinism claimed.[41] The reason for this ambivalence might be the pressure of the conservative environment in Egypt for which he had to cater, especially since he belonged to the Christian Lebanese minority living there, and furthermore, he was a journalist who did not wish to loose his readers.

Antun clearly rejected the Biblical story of the Creation not only because it was unscientific but also because it was illogical. He translated Renan's *Vie de Jésus* and *Life of the Apostles* because these books demonstrated rational and liberal ideas, and was interested in Ibn Rushd who valued reason above everything else. Thus Antun says that when enlightened people of all religions examine their religions they find flaws in them and should consequently take a new view of religion, propagating its *usefulness rather than its veracity*. Therefore, if a person wants to keep his/her faith much of what is in religion must be interpreted allegorically to agree with reason.[42] This is why he shows great admiration for those thinkers who refuted the infallibility of the Bible and pointed out the historical mistakes in it.[43]

Both Zaydan and Antun believed that matter has no beginning and that it is the origin of all beings but Zaydan did not take a purely materialistic view of man. He believed in the soul, not for a religious, but for a *rational scientific reason*: for him man, unlike animals, has an emotional life, his actions have a purpose, and he has the concept of perfection and a critical faculty. These and other attributes have the function of making him see the defects of this world, and his concept of perfection makes him deduce, by analogy, that another world exists to continue and perfect this one, although science alone can neither prove nor disprove its existence.[44]

Again referring to logic, not religion, Zaydan tries to prove the truth of resurrection and the immortality of the soul. When one examines the world, he writes, one finds that everything has a reason. Yet one cannot find reasons for the cruelty and injustice that befall many good and innocent people, unless God created a continuation to this world which makes up for this injustice. Since man is the victim of this injustice, he can only be compensated in a second world, i.e. if he is resurrected. Pre-empting the objections of non-believers such as his contemporary al-Shummayyil, he says that if all the secrets of the world we live in have not yet been revealed, how can anything be known with certainty about the hereafter. Thus one can neither deny its existence nor be obliged to believe in it, unless either theory is corroborated by a proof acceptable to our reason.[45] Besides, Zaydan writes, immortality does not contradict the laws of nature, for 'if immortality is a characteristic of original matter from which all things are made, is it impossible for one of its forms, (i.e. the soul) to be immortal?' He reiterates that the immortality of the soul is a necessity in which mankind must believe if human existence is not to be considered futile.[46] Answering al-Shummayyil's criticism of this belief, Zaydan says that since the senses and intellect are limited, he has tried to deduce the existence of the hereafter by analogy, since he is unable to imagine that Creation is purposeless. 'This is only a self-evident feeling for which I claim no proof.'[47] He then adds that although the existence of God cannot be proven, even scholars and philosophers believe in His existence as a self-evident truth that needs no proof, like the other self-evident truths they accept. Just as ordinary mortals cannot grasp many of the truths that are self-evident to scientists, man has no right to deny what the prophets say, just because human reasoning cannot grasp it.[48] It is again by analogy with scientific truth that Zaydan accepts a belief in religious truth.

On the question of the immortality of the soul, Antun disagrees with Zaydan. Antun admires Ibn Rushd for having said that *humanity and not the individual is immortal*, and that, as a result, there was no life after death, nor anything of what the common people say about the hereafter, although Ibn Rushd contradicted this opinion, sometimes believing in the hereafter.[49] Antun may have been the first Christian to call for a reinterpretation of what might appear contradictory to the evidence or to logical reasoning in religion, not only in the Bible but in the Qur'an as well.

Neither Zaydan's nor Antun's secularism lead to atheism, a lack of belief which Zaydan, in particular, severely criticized. Like several conservative, nineteenth-century French philosophers, such as Benjamin Constant (d.1830), Louis-Gabriel de Bonald (d.1870) and Félicité R. Lamennais (d.1854) who criticized the atheism which accompanied the French revolution, Zaydan saw that atheism made the French doubt religion and sometimes become immoral. Like al-Shidyaq, he believed religion to be necessary for the common people who are in need of its constraints to ensure they remain moral;[50] and adds that had all the people been really devout, their rights would have been properly guaranteed and no strong and powerful person would oppress a weaker one.[51] In this he differs from Ishaq who believed in political education, not religion, as a means of safe-guarding human rights and obtaining justice. But like al-Shidyaq, Zaydan considered that for the educated, natural sciences can replace religion, for they contain the origin of moral laws. That is why he advocated teaching young people science before anything else.[52] From this it can be deduced that for him, as for al-Shidyaq and Antun, it was not the educated classes' fear of the hereafter, but their reason and conscience that would make them refrain from wrongdoing.

Antun also considered that religion, like science, aimed at improving mankind and bringing about progress,[53] and agreed with Renan that the conflict between the two can be resolved if they are kept apart, science being the field of the intellect and studies of the world, proceeding by observation, experience and experiment, while religion is the sphere of the heart, based on faith in what its books contain, without examining their sources.

> But science itself does not deny its incapacity sometimes...Thus it cannot deny the 'matters of the heart' because it cannot prove them. Besides the fact that 'matters of the heart' have 'proofs of the heart' just as the intellect has its own proofs... It is better for the intellect to leave them [i.e. the proofs of the heart] alone and not to oppose them. Yet if the intellect desires to investigate them. let it do so, because we do not set limits on its research...Even if it wants to deny them, let it do so because it is completely free to act within its sphere in the way it wishes, but it should not use this freedom as an excuse to attack other people's principles and force them to apply its own.[54]

Thus Antun sees that it is wrong to try applying the proofs of science to religion, or those of religion to science, but insists on the necessity of using reason, not faith, in worldly matters without binding reason by faith and restricting its freedom. And by referring to Ibn Rushd and other Arabic philosophers like him, he wanted to show that this was not an imported Western attitude, but one found in classical Arabic Muslim thought as well. Without being an atheist or defending atheism, he upholds the right of individuals to be atheists if they so choose. Yet, at the same time, Antun did not seek to criticize religion, its principles and values, because he felt that religion and science together could make for progress, and build society on justice, freedom and equality. Therefore he, too, severely criticized the 'materialists' who aimed to destroy religion, as well as Nietzsche's atheism, and those who assert that religion has a devastating effect on society.[55] When Rashid Rida claimed that Antun had attacked Islam in an article he had written about Ibn Rushd, asking 'Abdu to answer and defend Islam',[56] Antun insisted that neither Islam nor any other religion was in need of defence, since they were all the way to civilization and the spirit of people's moral life, and are therefore too strong to be violated by anyone.[57] The aim of all religions, he writes, is to teach virtue, goodness and harmony, and to fight vice, ignorance and hatred. For as long as people are weak, ignorant, greedy and covetous religions are necessary, and the prophets of all faiths aim to encourage people to do good, as Ibn Rushd also believed.[58] It is only people's ignorance of what real religion is that causes religious conflict. In an article, he indicates the essential principles that are common to all religions: 'belief in God, depending on Him and surrendering matters to Him.' This, he believes, is enough to bring all peoples together in a spirit of fraternity and to eliminate all fanaticism and distinction between them.[59] Here, again, lurks the unease felt by someone belonging to a Christian minority in a Muslim world, eager to eliminate whatever might differentiate him from his compatriots.

Ya'qub Sarruf (1852–1927)[60] was another Lebanese Christian contemporary of Zaydan, Antun and al-Shummayyil who, like them, emigrated to Egypt. The scientific periodical *al-Muqtataf* which he edited with Faris Nimr, played a major role in disseminating scientific knowledge and thought throughout the Arab world. One of the scientific theories he endorsed was that of evolution and survival of the fittest, and to which he devoted several articles in his magazine, listing all the services it had performed for science and humanity.[61] Naturally he and Nimr were vehemently attacked by the Jesuit paper *al-Bashir* which accused them of atheism, an accusation which they just as vehemently denied, quoting several clerics who had assured that there was no contradiction between religion and the theory of evolution.[62] Yet Sarruf clearly answers his opponents in the same vein as Antun had answered his, namely, that the editors of *al-Muqtataf* would not let religion thwart or undermine their scientific aim, although all their work was based on the principles of true religion.[63] Among its true principles were love and peace which were not contradicted by the theory of evolution. As proof, he claims that for him war, for example, is not an aspect of struggle and survival of the fittest, for wars are waged to acquire power and profit, not to kill people who are not fit to live or whose life deprives others of their livelihood. There is a law that overrides the law of struggle, that of co-operation which is a necessity in the higher beings and was a main factor in their development, especially the development of man.[64]

Sarruf also tried to prove God's existence and His divine providence scientifically, but he did so differently from Zaydan and Antun; his method resembled that of Marrash, both he and his forerunner from Aleppo being scientists. Sarruf writes that had the elements of which our bodies consist been arranged differently, we would not have been the human beings we are. Life in living bodies therefore necessitates the existence of Someone who gave them this life, and the Someone would exercise divine providence and be concerned that they perform their functions flawlessly.[65]

Depending again on science, not religion, he tries to prove man's immortality, not in the hereafter, but in this world. Science, he writes, had proved that non-existence is impossible. Therefore, if man's mental powers remain in this world after his death, as in the example of the inventions of inventors, his feelings might also linger, and thus man would have another existence after the decay of his body. Science might prove it one day although it has not yet done so, because it considers the whole problem of man's spirit an extremely difficult and complex matter.[66] But when Sarruf had to admit that scientists do not know exactly what life is and how it functions, he resorted to the religious belief in God and His almighty power[67] and added, like Zaydan, that this life would be absurd had there not been another world which perfects the defects of this one.[68.]As for the role of religion, he agreed with all the others that it helps redress morals and combat evil.[69]

The only Christian of this generation whose secularism did not stop at the threshold of atheism was al-Shummayyil. Like Zaydan and Antun he, too, believed that man created religion because of his fear of death and the egotism which made him deny his mortality, and that each religion evolved from a previous one, those that survived were the ones best adjusted to the changing times and societies. Thus he traced their evolution from the worship of idols until 'all the gods were condensed into one abstract God.'[70]

But al-Shummayyil then takes a step further that his secular Christian contemporaries did not take, either out of conviction or out of fear. He claims that there are no sacred God-given laws, as man's ignorance and illusions have made him imagine; all laws are man-made and depend on man's backwardness or his development.[71] Then he goes on to say that all academic theology is nothing but 'senseless jabber which tries to explain the inexplicable, interpret that which cannot be interpreted and apply that which cannot be applied.' This has led many minds astray and prevented them from working, being of no use to society, besides doing it harm and leading it astray.[72] In an allusion to the Islamic reformers and al-Kawakibi, among others, who believed that proper application of Islam would reform society and cause it to progress, he writes: 'Is it not a disgrace for man to neglect the present, busying himself with the past on which he wants to build the future and devoting his studies to uselessness while abandoning what is useful?' He then adds that had men wasted their time in explanations and interpretations in order to prove the secrets of divine revelations the likes of Marconi (d.1937) and Thomas Edison (d.1931) would never have produced their amazing inventions.[73] This, of course, was a direct criticism of the Muslim belief in their God-given *shari'a* law and all the *'ulama's* interpretations thereof, and it is no wonder that Rashid Rida attacked him for being an atheist.[74]

Al-Shummayyil then takes a further step towards atheism when he declares that what people imagine to be religious truths are only delusions, like the belief in heaven and hell, the trinity, the ten commandments and the like that have been taken from previous religions and adapted. The delusion that has been the main cause of man's misery and hardship is his belief in his heavenly origin and that his Creator had banished him from Paradise, but had created for him all that is seen and unseen.[75] Instead of looking up to heaven in search of his origin, al-Shummayyil writes, man should be looking down for it in the place where he was born, grew up and died, for it is both impossible and irrational that the world was created from nothing. Even the word 'nothing' is meaningless, since it has been proved that matter has always existed.[76]

Al-Shummayyil was one of the first Arab thinkers to endorse and explain Darwinism to his contemporaries, doing so as early as 1884 in his seminal work *Falsafat al-Nushu' wa al-Irtiqa'* (The Philosophy of Evolution and Progress). This book was a translation of Ludwig Büchner's (d.1899) commentary on Darwinism, to which al-Shummayyil added an introduction and his own notes and comments. His book provoked very violent controversy which he answered in numerous articles defending his beliefs and pointing out that he did not restrict his theory, as did Darwin, to the realms of animal and man but applied it to all of nature, organic as well as inorganic.

As a doctor, al-Shummayyil believed that the only truth was scientific truth and that which could be proved by reason. Therefore he could *not accept religions*, which are a matter of faith, not reason. He says: 'After believing in religions I started doubting them and then rejected them all.'[77] Referring to faith in God he writes:

How can the intellect accept an existence which is neither a body nor the matter or form of a body... and has no quantity or quality... His deeds emanate from him without emanating from him, are connected to him and, at the same time, separate from him. No doubt only a strong faith can accept this, and where faith begins, science ends. A person is free to have the faith he desires, but faith has no right to oppose the progress of science, and science can do nothing against faith.[78]

Thus, like Zaydan, Antun and Sarruf, al-Shummayyil refuses to allow religious faith to encroach upon scientific freedom, and sees religion and science as two separate realms, but unlike them he refuses to accept what religions say as truths, albeit truths acceptable on the grounds of faith, and considers that the only truths are those of science because, unlike religious truths, they do not contradict reason. As examples, he points out the contradictions between belief in man's free will and the belief that human fate is pre-ordained by God; or the belief in God's justice and mercy when the world He is supposed to have created is full of injustice and misery.[79] Unlike Zaydan and Sarruf who tried to believe in the hereafter so as not to admit the absurdity of this world, al-Shummayyil sides with Antun in denying the resurrection of the soul because there is no scientific proof thereof. Yet whereas Antun avoided details on this subject and clearly criticized all materialistic philosophy, al-Shummayyil insists that the soul is one of the forms of matter which is eternal, with no beginning and no end, and that matter is in constant, everlasting motion. Thus, life and death are merely changes in matter and its forms[80] and nothing that constitutes the living body disappears from the material world, once the body dies.[81] Here, al-Shummayyil explicitly confirms that which Zaydan did not go beyond questioning as a matter open to doubt. For al-Shummayyil, both body and soul were matter which merely took on different forms during life and death. He provided scientific proofs to show that there was no such thing as life in the abstract, free from matter.[82]

Again, whereas all his contemporaries believed that religion had a positive effect on man and society, al-Shummayyil took a purely atheistic stance. He did not believe that religion really improved people; to him people were virtuous only because they feared hell or aspired to paradise. He even went a step further than al-Shidyaq and Zaydan when he assured his readership that only accurate scientific knowledge could reform society because ignorance was the cause of its ills and of man's vices.

> Science has taught man truths and helped him discover and invent things beyond all the miracles that religions claim. Besides this, natural sciences have a genuine social aim, for they consider man the brother of all men, which leads to the friendship between nations, regardless of the frontiers separating countries. Natural sciences *are the true human religion* which teaches what no other religion teaches, i.e. the tolerance and true co-operation that are necessary for civilization, which are built on knowing *right and duty, not kindness and charity.*[83]

Thus the real miracles were not those that religions relate, but those that science had discovered and invented. We know these to be true beyond any doubt. If people were aware of true science and its sound principles their judgements would also be sound.[84] The more science has advanced the better society has become. Consequently, there is a temptation for intelligent people to teach nothing but science, which they consider to be the true religion that fulfills people's hopes as nothing else has been able to fulfill them.[85] Seeing nothing in religion but its negative results, al-Shummayyil believed that *a nation could only improve if religion had no impact on the people*, and the stronger its impact the more backward they were. All he saw in religion was that it prevented freedom of thought, bound science in the fetters of religious belief, was the cause of persecution and torture, and the reason for man's everlasting dread and fear of 'He whom he does not know how to please, because he does not know what angers Him.' Religions are also the cause of fanaticism, bloodshed and wars, and the source of all internal differences in the Middle East.[86]

However, despite al-Shummayyil's devotion to science and reason, contradictions can sometimes be found in his assessment of the value of religion.

Having claimed that it does not improve society, he retracts what he has just said in order to assure his readers that whatever there is in science that contradicts religion, this does not change the importance of religion.[87] He considers that the 'social essence' of all religions is the same, and that they all aim at the general welfare of society, teaching tolerance and love of others, two principles that are necessary for civilization. When asked what he meant by 'social essence' he listed morality, humaneness and virtue.[88] When Lord Cromer accused Islam of being the reason for the backwardness of the Muslims, al-Shummayyil sprang to its defence, saying that Islam had not been an obstacle when the Muslims had created a highly-developed civilization in the past, and that the essence of any religion had nothing to do with the backwardness of a civilization, the fault lying with the *'ulama* who, like the Christian clergy in the Middle Ages, only used religion to promote their own material interests.[89] Although al-Shummayyil blamed the clergy in this instance, this clearly contradicts his statement that the stronger the impact of religion on a people, the more backward they are.

There might be a politico-cultural reason for al-Shummayyil's defence of Islam against Cromer. As an Arab Christian he, like Zaydan and the other Christian secular writers, wanted to distance himself from the foreign West with which their Muslim compatriots associated them, and bring himself closer to the Islamic world.

Another aspect of al-Shummayyil's shifting, or reluctant, atheism is his repetition of Darwin's argument in the face of his critics who claimed that the theory of evolution denied God's greatness. 'If science shows that the various species, including man, were formed according to specific natural laws, does this not add to the greatness of the Power that established these laws?', [90] he writes.

Thus, even the secular writer who came closest to atheism was not a true atheist, in spite of Rashid Rida's accusations. Al-Shummayyil clarifies the reason when he says that 'science does not ask us to be atheists, all it does is reveal the truth.' If science might sometimes lead to atheism this was not its aim, he says. Its aim is to free the intellect from all that hinders it so that it is capable of making independent judgements.[91] The main reason for al-Shummayyil's reluctance and contradictions in this respect was, in the opinion of the author, the pressure of the traditional, conservative and religious ambience around him.

According to Hisham Sharabi 'the main concern of Sarruf, al-Shummayyil and Antun... was to focus men's attention away from religion and metaphysics and back to the problems of the real world'... They were 'sacrificing an untenable truth for a valid new one.'[92]

But no matter to what extent these Christian writers were secular, they all were radical modernists in their assertion that morals were relative and, contrary to what religions preach, there was no absolute right or wrong. Their Muslim contemporary, Qasim Amin, was of the same view, since he was concerned primarily with the social aspect of religion.

As early as the mid-nineteenth century, al-Shidyaq wrote that 'what I consider wrong might be right to others, and vice-versa.'[93] Somewhat later, Ishaq agreed that all moral values are relative: 'Good and bad, righteousness and sin, advantage and detriment are all relative and have no intrinsic value... for good and bad are only so in relation to the person who receives them.'[94] As can be seen, there is no mention whatsoever of what religion says to that effect. Likewise, Amin and Zaydan assert that what is good or bad is relative, and that moral values change with time and place to suit changing circumstances.[95] Zaydan explains this by the fact that man creates and sets these values, for his mind orders him to act according to what his circumstances require, then his will translates them into action, which, when repeated, becomes habit and, with time, habit becomes a moral code.[96] When al-Shummayyil shows that all values, whether moral or not, are not absolute and change with time and place,[97] he also clearly indicates the difference between religion and philosophy in this respect. Philosophy, he says, asserts the liberty of thought and teaches that good and bad are relative values, whereas religions impede reason and teach that good and bad are absolute values. The result is persecution, torture, murder and war.[98]

The closest Kurd 'Ali comes to a secular perspective on religion is in his agreeing with Amin that Islam varies with time and place, for 'everything in the world is subject to evolution, influenced by environment.'[99] He completely disagrees with al-Kawakibi's claim that the Qur'an contained modern scientific theories long before they were discovered in Europe. The Qur'an, he says, is not a book of science dealing with physics, chemistry, astronomy, geography and history, as some people claim. It is merely a law to civilize people and remind them of the Day of Judgement.[100] Although prayer and fasting are two of the five basic principles of Islam, for Kurd 'Ali Islam does not mean to pray and fast, but to be virtuous, for what he cared for most in religion was its essence and its moral teachings.[101] In this respect, like his Christian contemporaries, he believed that the essence of all religions is one, since they all teach people to be good and charitable and to overcome hatred, and they all condemn injustice, theft and war, reminding them of the Day of Judgement.[102] Thus he, too, considered that religion had nothing to do with the truths of nature which only science could discover, the sole role of religion being that of moral guide. Yet even in this, he did not totally believe in the efficacy of religion in improving matters. For one, he says that it cannot reform an immoral person, but only improve a good one; and if a nation wants to reform its temporal, worldly matters in order ensure progress, it is only civic studies (*'ulum madaniyya*) that can ensure this, for religion is not sufficient.[103] In this, he comes close to what Ishaq had written before him.

However, Kurd 'Ali did not take a further step towards secularism, as did his Christian contemporaries. He never agreed with them that religion could be dispensed with, nor that religions were man-made, since like all Muslims he believed the Qur'an to be God's revealed word. Like his Christian contemporaries, he considered that some of the content of religion, such as the hereafter, cannot be explained through logic and reasoning, but he did not reject such content, as did Antun and al-Shummayyil, or try to explain it scientifically, like Zaydan and Sarruf. Kurd 'Ali accepted a belief in the hereafter as part of his faith. Like the others, he separated the domain of faith from that of reason, but insisted that a true interpretation of religion cannot contradict reason, something the great Muslim thinkers of old had also believed. If people found themselves incapable of interpreting religion logically, they should accept certain matters on the grounds of faith and allow the scientist to be completely free to follow his own path without let or hindrance.[104] Thus, like Amin, in keeping religion and science completely apart, he avoided dealing with the relationship between religion itself and freedom of thought and research. In this, he was unlike the earlier writers al-Shidyaq and Dallal, or his contemporary al-Shummayyil.

Lutfi al-Sayyid disagreed with the abovementioned writers who believed that civil education could sometimes be more effective than religion in redressing the ills of society. He insisted on basing all *moral education on religion, any revealed religion*, since all religions teach people to be good, refrain from evil and believe in the Day of Judgement:

> I am not one of those who insist that a religion or a specific ethical system should be taught for its own sake. But I say that general education must have some principle which should guide the student from beginning to end, and this is the principle of good and evil.
>
> There is no doubt that theories of good and evil are numerous, and disparate, but each nation should teach its sons its own beliefs in the matter. Since for us Egyptians the principle of good and evil is grounded in belief in the essence of religion, it follows that religion, seen from this ethical point of view, must be the basis of general education.[105]

Thus Lutfi al-Sayyid does not believe the moral teachings of Islam to be better than others, or even better than non-religious moral systems, and accepts the relativity of moral values, since each nation should teach its own beliefs. This is a modern secular outlook on the moral value of religion.

As a result, al-Sayyid strongly opposed fanaticism, and like the other writers, he claimed that it had nothing to do with Islam.[106] When Lord Cromer accused the Egyptian Muslims of fanaticism, al-Sayyid insisted that fanaticism was unknown to them, for did not Muslims and Copts study and work together?[107] (In spite of this assurance he had to combat the disputes between Muslims and Copts which came to a head with the murder of Butrus Pasha Ghali in 1911.[108]) This was based on his firm belief in the necessity and possibility of reconciling the different religions, and on his conviction that whatever transformation Islam had undergone in later centuries had been the result of the depravity and tyranny of the rulers in the Muslim world, just as the Christianity of the popes in the Middle Ages was very far removed from that of Christ and his disciples.[109]

A common factor between Kurd 'Ali and Lutfi al-Sayyid is that neither of them directly addressed the principles of Islam, as did the Christians when dealing with Christianity, which demonstrates a difference between the secular Christian and the secular Muslim. When insisting that the essence of all religions is the same, they stressed the moral role of religions, thus diplomatically avoiding the deep divides between the various religions. This could be due to the fact that both Kurd 'Ali and al-Sayyid were journalists and nationalists, as will be shown in a later chapter, and as such they felt it their patriotic duty to stress unity as opposed to dissent.

There is a striking difference between all these Muslim writers and Taha Hussein. Unlike them and even unlike most Christians, Hussein sometimes insists that only with time might people's morals improve.[110] This appears to insinuate that religion, as such, has no real effect. He even asserts something that contradicts religious morality when he defends prostitutes, claiming that God is above blaming people for the way in which they earn their living;[111] or when he criticizes charity as being a way of feeling superiority over the poor and seeks to replace it by the belief in justice and equality between people.[112] Therefore it is not religious virtue that Taha Hussein seeks to promote, but the secular civic virtues of the West. In this, he resembles the Christian secularists of previous generations. That is why he insists that it is the university's duty to instill in students love and mutual respect and a belief that duty comes before right. He believes that people should have self-respect and refrain from being base and vile. He considered that the university could promote these values by organizing cultural and sports clubs.[113] There is no mention here of religion or its moral guidance or religious reformers.

Hussein also takes a purely secular stand vis-à-vis the Bible and the Qur'an when he writes that one can study and analyze these religions without being a believer because they contain an artistic beauty that is independent of their religious content. Therefore every one should have the right to express an opinion regarding these texts from the points of view of art and science which have nothing to do with their religious importance. Westerners have gained this right, he claims, and they write freely about the results of their studies, regardless of whether they approve or disapprove of the religious texts. In the Umayyad and 'Abbasid periods, the Arabs also enjoyed this freedom to a certain extent, but when they lost their political power, they became ignorant, stagnated and lost their freedom as well. In modern times, political power exploits religion for its own purpose and this, Hussein sees, can only result in disaster.[114]

Undoubtedly Hussein is commenting here upon what had happened to him two years earlier, in 1925, when he published his book *Fi al-Shi'r al-Jahili* (On Pre-Islamic Poetry). His book was banned and he was prosecuted as was 'Abd al-Raziq in that same year. As early as 1923, he wrote a sarcastic essay criticizing those who, like Muhammad 'Abdu and Sheikh Muhammad Bakhit (and al-Kawakibi among our writers), tries to prove that the Qur'an contains modern scientific truths and that its contents in no way contradict modern science.[115] He declares the *'ulama* to be the enemies of history because the conflict between religion and science is natural, since science is linked to reason, whereas religion is linked to the heart, influenced by the imagination and capturing the emotions. When liberty is opposed in the name of religion, this is an aspect of the conflict between the new progressive forces which are based on reason and science and the forces of conservatism and reaction. Such a struggle happened in Europe during the Middle Ages.[116] In this, he appears to be influenced by August Compte's (d.1857) positivism that considered the religious world-view to be one of the earlier phases of history.

In his book on pre-Islamic poetry, Hussein clearly differentiates religion from scholarly interpretations of the Qur'an itself for the first time in modern Islamic thought. Firstly, he shows that it is the Qur'an and not pre-Islamic poetry which reflects the political, social and intellectual life of the period. Judaism and Christianity were widespread among the Arabs before the advent of Islam, but the Arabs embraced Islam because it suited their nature perfectly,[117] not because it completed and perfected the previous religions as Muslims believe. Here, Hussein sides with the Christian secularists in believing that people embrace the religion that suits them and their circumstances. This is also corroborated by his pointing out the great social improvements that Islam introduced,[118] and from which we can also infer, first, that he regarded religion as a social phenomenon reflecting a certain phase in history and in people's evolution, and second, that the Qur'an is a literary text reflecting its time, just like any literary text. Here, he never alludes to its being God's revealed word. In fact, it is said that he had told his students that the Qur'an could be analyzed like any other literary text, and in doing so one can differentiate between the primitive style of the Meccan suras, full of harshness, violence and lacking in logic, and the Madina suras that are in the calm, sober style of the legislator, reflecting the more civilized society of Medina which had been influenced by Judaism.[119] Thus, Hussein not only completely separates religion from science, as did Amin, Kurd 'Ali and al-Sayyid, but also examined religion scientifically, as did his Christian predecessors.

Then, taking a further step into secularism, Hussein dared to doubt the veracity of some of the facts stated in the Qur'an:

> Both the Bible and the Qur'an may mention Ibrahim and Isma'il, but the fact that they are mentioned in the Bible and Qur'an is not sufficient proof of their historical existence, or that the story of Isma'il's emigration [from the south] to Mecca is true... We are obliged to find in this story a sort of stratagem to prove the relationship between the Jews and the Arabs on the one hand, and between Islam, Judaism, the Qur'an and the Bible on the other.[120]

Hussein explains the reasons for this stratagem as being the socio-political conditions of the time. Because of the fierce enmity between Arab paganism and Islam, the latter needed to prove that it was closely related to Judaism and Christianity, the two older monotheistic religions in the area. On the other hand, the Arabs needed to find a bond to unite them politically against the Persians and Byzantines. This, too, he believed is why Quraish adopted the legend that the Ka'ba was founded by Ibrahim and Isma'il,[121] both of whom were biblical figures.

The fact that Hussein treated as a legend the Muslim belief in their holiest shrine, and as stories, doubtful historical facts and stratagems that to believers were God's revealed eternal truths, shows to what extent he had been influenced by the Western secularists' examination of their own sacred books. Unlike the Christians Zaydan, Antun and al-Shummayyil, Hussein only questioned the veracity of historical events and incidents mentioned in the Qur'an, but not that of beliefs concerning the essence of faith, such as immortality, the Day of Judgement and man's relationship with God. An explanation for this could be found in his saying that the East's religious view of the universe was the reason for its lagging behind the West which had a rational outlook.[122] Although he insisted that Islam was a rational religion, we see that he felt the rationalism of the East, as well as his own, were restricted by faith, whereas Western rationalism had no restriction except logic.

Hussein's secularism, like that of almost all the other writers, did not lead to atheism because, for him, reason and science are limited, since all of man's knowledge and intelligence cannot protect him from natural disasters. He extolled the virtues of men such as Louis Pasteur (d.1895), who believed in both religion and science, for he claimed that religion brought hope and preserved people from despair in the face of adversity, while science contributed to the quality of life.[123]

Hussein also separated reason from faith, as did Amin, Zaydan, Sarruf, Antun and Kurd 'Ali before him. When defending himself against his prosecutors, he claimed that as a Muslim he believed in the existence of Ibrahim and Isma'il and in all that the Qur'an says about them, but that as a scientific researcher he had to doubt their historic existence.[124] Thus he saw that the only way to eliminate the conflict between religion and science was by keeping them completely apart.[125] That is why in his introduction to his semi-fictional biography of the Prophet he says that many of the stories he would be telling might be rejected using reason and logic because they contradict scientific thought. However, in relating them, he was not addressing the intellect but the heart, feelings, emotions and imagination of simple believers. 'And there is a big difference between addressing the intellect with these stories and claiming they are scientific truths that can be properly investigated, and the way in which they address the heart and feelings in order to encourage them to do good and refrain from evil.'[126]

Hussein therefore sides with the abovementioned writers in their belief in religion's positive effect on morals and society. When he also confirms that the Qur'an is revealed,[127] in contradiction to his earlier stand, and devotes his last years to writing Islamic books, a certain regression appears in his secularism. Was this due to age? Or was it due to the fact that he now held high office that he wished to retain, not wanting to arouse public opinion against him as he had done in 1925? Or was it due to his belief that religion still had the strongest impact on his compatriots and he therefore considered it to be the best way to implement whatever reforms he tried to introduce? Perhaps his religious books were 'attempts to re-tell the story of Islam in ways which would appeal to the modern Egyptian consciousness,' as Hourani suggests, since he 'presented the Prophet as a hero in the modern sense, 'Uthman as the symbol of human weakness and 'Ali as the scrupulous Muslim ruler.'[128] Whatever the reason, Hussein's attitude to religion clearly changed after the 1930s.

Nazira Zayn al-Din, like the other 'secular' Muslims, believed that the essence of Chritianity and Islam were the same since they are both revealed religions, and she insisted that Muslims and non-Muslims are completely equal, as both Muhammad and Christ had taught.[129] This, of course, contradicts Islam and the *shari'a* that do not treat them at all as equals. Like her predecessors, she avoids all the basic differences between these two religions. Nazira greatly admired Western knowledge and science, having been educated in European missionary schools in Beirut. She therefore severely criticized a sheikh who wanted to humiliate Christians and Jews, and showed great admiration for those '*dhimmis*' who conquered the world and nature, free of all restraint, and progressed in knowledge and science, so unlike the Muslims.[130]

Influenced by her education, she insists on using reason to examine and study the Qur'an and the Sunna (the Prophet's sayings and deeds) and in analyzing the interpretations and opinions of the *'ulama*, and thus judging the truth or untruth of these opinions and interpretations. The Prophet himself had said, after all, that 'a person's religion is his intellect' and those with no intellect have no religion. Therefore, for her there was no contradiction between religion and reason, and if anything in the scholarly books of the *'ulama* contradicted reason the fault lay with their misinterpretation of Islam.[131]

Unlike Hussein, who dared to doubt the truth of facts revealed in the Qur'an itself, Zayn al-Din only doubted the veracity of the interpretations by the *'ulama*. However, using reasoning, she had the courage to doubt the authenticity of even some of the Prophet's Traditions (*Hadith*) as handed down by Bukhari (d.870), the most reliable transmitter of these traditions, because she finds that he is liable to make mistakes like any other human being, or be influenced by certain factors. She thus rejected, for example, what he claims the Prophet had said about women lacking intelligence and faith, and asserts that many of the traditions attributed to the Prophet are not true.[132]

In order to avoid any views of religion that were more secular she, too, insisted that religion and science be kept completely separate. Benefit can only be derived from religion, she says, 'if free scientific research is independent of restricted religious research.'[133] But when she severely criticizes those who believe in Darwin's theory of evolution instead of the Biblical and Qur'anic story of creation,[134] she does not seem to realize that she is contradicting herself and letting religion encroach upon scientific research and restrict it.

No matter what shortcomings are found in some of these writers' secular approach to religion, their role should not be underestimated in their desire to restrict religion to its moral message, prevent its interference in politics, learning and education and thus be a cause for stagnation, underdevelopment and fanaticism.

B. *Anticlericalism*

No matter how much or how little these writers differed in their opinion of religion and its role, they all severely criticized the clergy, regardless of religion or sect.

Naturally, it was the Lebanese Christian Bustani and the Syrians Dallal and Marrash who blamed the clergy for causing the differences between the various Christian sects from which their countries suffered. Dallal, for example, accuses the clergy of charlatanism, and says that the factions they formed were the cause of all the evil and calamity from which the world had suffered throughout history.[135]

There were several reasons for this, in their opinion, the most important being *fanaticism*. All the writers, whether Christian or Muslim, Egyptian, Lebanese or Syrian, severely attacked the fanaticism of the priests, pastors and sheikhs. Al-Shidyaq neither spared the Maronite priests and patriarch, nor the Protestant High Church in England. He claimed that the Maronite Church excommunicated and even executed anyone who disagreed with their opinion,[136] while the Protestant High Church refused to marry or baptize those who did not belong to it, and belonging to it was the only means of obtaining employment or wealth, as did being a member of the Catholic Church in other countries.[137] Even scientists and reformers like Jan Huss (d.1415), Jerome of Prague (d.1416), Galileo (d.1642), and William Harvey (d.1657) were excommunicated, persecuted by the Church or burnt at the stake, explained Marrash.[138] Dallal also attacked the clergy, alleging that they stole the money of those they claimed were heretics and even burnt them alive,[139] while Azoury stated that the clergy encouraged fanaticism for material or personal gain, since the common people feel that a difference in confession is of no importance.[140] Since the clerics of any faith believe that all the truths of their religion are absolute, Farah Antun criticized their claim that a person is an atheist if he/she does not believe in the prophets, the Trinity, resurrection, heaven and hell, and God's omnipotence and omniscience. Thus they instigate fanaticism, hatred and war. Otherwise people belonging to different religions, confessions and sects would agree and work together towards one goal, namely, the common good, including the struggle against all the vices and atrocities in the world, no matter what their origin.[141]

Qasim Amin, a Muslim, also said that because the ignorant *'ulama* decided that 'what a few legislators had laid down was the eternal truth, nobody had the right to oppose it.'[142] Kurd 'Ali added that due to the way in which the Muslim clerics stuck rigidly to traditional ideas, they rejected all reforms and any new opinions and interpretations of Islam, while their fanaticism drove them to fight and kill each other.[143] Those same fossilized *'ulama* were severely attacked by Nazira Zayn al-Din because they used accusations of heresy and atheism against anyone who wanted to use his/her reason to return to the real sources of religion in their desire to progress and reveal the truth. She insisted that unless their writings were supported by the Qur'an, the Sunna, and modern reasoning, not all that the theologians (*fuqaha'*) had written was true. Even in the days of the Prophet, she writes, many of these theologians invented false beliefs and sayings that had nothing to do with Islam.[144] Kurd 'Ali accused fanatical religious clerics of having caused the downfall of Arab philosophy and science after the twelfth century, since they accused all philosophers and scientists of heresy.[145] Thus, it is not surprising to read Taha Hussein's severe attacks on these 'doctors' of religion in Egypt who used their power and influence to combat all liberal thought, even before they prosecuted authors like him and 'Abd al-Raziq, and banned their books.[146]

Linked to their fanaticism was the clergy's *ignorance*, something that was also severely attacked by all these writers. Al-Shidyaq criticizes the extreme ignorance not only of the ordinary clergy, but even of the Patriarch himself, and believed that all those who have neither knowledge nor employment became monks in order to guarantee themselves livelihood. One of the things that infuriated him most was their complete ignorance of Arabic, and the illiterate language which they used in their published religious books.[147]

The Muslim writers also unanimously criticized the extreme ignorance of their *'ulamas* which had repercussions on Islam itself and not only on the faithful, as was the case with the Christians. First of all, Kawakibi, as well as Amin, Hussein, and Nazira all criticize the ignorance of those doctors of religion whose knowledge is restricted to useless linguistic exercises, philology and jurisprudence, and who know nothing of history, geography and modern science,[148] i.e., of secular subjects. It was Taha Hussein who most severely attacked their institution of higher learning, al-Azhar in which he himself had been a student, and said that its teachers and graduates do not even know its history, nor that of the mosques, and understand nothing of the artistic beauty of the Qur'an.[149] He therefore strongly advocated reforming al-Azhar by introducing modern subjects and science into its curriculum,[150] reforms that Sheikh Muhammad 'Abdu had tried to introduce in vain.

The ignorance of the *'ulamas* had serious repercussions for Islam, as is clearly shown even by the Christian al-Shummayyil. Since these ignorant *'ulamas* controlled Islam, reasoned Kawakibi, Kurd 'Ali and Nazira Zayn al-Din,[151] they misinterpret it. Al-Din, al-Shummayyil and Hussein also claimed that with their fossilized mentality the *'ulamas* only repeated what the ancients had written, slavishly imitating them and rejecting all change and progress.[152]

Another perhaps less serious result of their ignorance, were the *superstitious beliefs* they spread among the people, such as buying indulgences to guarantee them a place in heaven, belief in magic, fortune-telling, amulets and other such old wives tales, for the sheikhs themselves practised magic and used charms and amulets, claiming they could heal the sick or help people to resolve their problems. These were all aspects that Dallal, Zaynab Fawwaz (1860–1914)[153], Kawakibi, Antun and Kurd 'Ali severely criticized.[154]

These authors considered that the spread of these superstitions was closely related to the religious clerics' *greed and love of money*. Al-Shidyaq claimed that they were even willing to praise prostitutes in return for a bribe; al-Kawakibi also accused the *shari'a* judges of accepting bribes, and the rulers of being flattered by the *'ulama* who misinterpret religion in order to gain money and position. Fawwaz, Zaydan, Antun, Shummayyil and Kurd 'Ali made similar accusations.[155]

This caused al-Shidyaq, Dallal and al-Kawakibi to attack the *hypocrisy* of the religious clerics. Dallal called them 'wolves in sheep's clothing squirting out their poison.'[156] He also accused them of immorality and of being liars and charlatans.[157] The Christian writers claimed that their clergy were full of hatred and jealousy, showing how far they were distanced from the teachings of Christianity.[158] This caused al-Shidyaq and Antun to claim that mankind could easily dispense with the clergy, especially if the people were intelligent and educated.[159] So long as the clergy retained the power they had over the people by instigating hatred and religious strife, controlling their minds and feelings, both al-Shidyaq and al-Shummayyil considered that the people would remain ignorant and backward.[160]

This criticism of the clergy was closely tied to their belief in the individual.

CHAPTER FOUR

The Individual

These writers' more-or-less secular attitude towards religion naturally influenced their opinion of the individual's relationship with God, pre-destination and fate.

In the period under review, both Muslim and Christian Arabs believed in divine decree and surrendered themselves to their fate. It is true that the Qur'an asserts belief in pre-destination, but it also refers to man's free will, and early Muslim philosophers, such as the Mu'tazilites, stressed man's freedom of choice and responsibility. Yet it was the belief in fate and destiny that dominated people's faith in general. Their lives were governed by a transcendental perspective, in which the individual was nothing more than a passive pawn. This is one of the things that the secular writers, among others, tried to overcome, directly or indirectly expressing a belief in *individual autonomy and free will*.

Al-Shidyaq strongly criticized people's belief in fate and divine decree which, he claimed, caused indolence and ignorance, and said that if, people were determined to achieve something they could do it. Marrash also clearly stated that people have an independent will and the capacity to forge their own destiny, for they are not mere instruments for performing God's will.[1] If France had attained such a high level of freedom and civilization, this was due to her belief in reason and free will.[2] However, being a staunch believer in religion as well as in 'a God above human reason, from Whom all life flows,' Marrash seems to contradict his own belief in man's autonomy when he asserts that 'God is the cause of all motion, the origin and end of all being' and in His never-ending concern for the world, plans it and all creation, including man's existence, linking all its parts in a chain to which all submit. Since Marrash also believed in pantheism[3] which eliminates all differences and contradictions between beings, the contradiction between man's autonomous will and God's omnipotence would also be eliminated since, he claimed, both would melt and unite in a single Whole.

Indignant at the apathy and inertia of the Egyptians over the centuries, Ishaq pointed out repeatedly that it was in the hands of the people to change their destiny, just as the French had changed theirs when they revolted against tyranny, injustice and poverty, and obtained the liberty and equality they desired. Success depended solely on the nation's will.[4]

The Muslim writers of this generation were just as disgusted as their Christian contemporaries by people's blind reliance on destiny. Al-Kawakibi, for example, says that one of the reasons for the Muslims' backwardness is their blind fatalism, blaming destiny and fate, instead of their despotic rulers, for their all their woes.[5] He fully believes that if people unite and desire progress, persevering in their striving for improvement, they will succeed. It is only the people themselves who can liberate themselves from despotic rule.[6] Zaynab Fawwaz also believed that civilization and knowledge flourished thanks to human determination and 'were it not for the firmness of the human being's will then the slightest stumble would have forced him to retreat from his aims.'[7] However, neither she nor al-Kawakibi believed in man's existential liberty because their deep faith in Islam prevented them from asserting the complete independence of man's will from that of God. That is why Zaynab Fawwaz urged people to 'be content with what God has decreed necessary for them to live by.'[8] And although one can understand that here she might merely have meant satisfaction with material things, it is difficult to separate the material from the intellectual in life and civilization.

Qasim Amin, on the other hand, is completely secular when he insists that 'the independence of man's will is the most important moral factor in his advancement.'[9] The Qur'anic verse 'Allah never changes the grace He hath bestowed on people until they first change that which is in their hearts,'[10] which is often quoted by the Muslim writers, does not demonstrate man's autonomy, although it indicates his responsibility, as did the Mu'tazilite philosophers. Therefore the autonomy in which Qasim and later Muslim writers believed originates in Western secular influence. To this effect, Kurd 'Ali clearly states that the people learnt from the West that it was in their power to gain their rights, change their conditions and impose their will.[11]

Thus, the belief in man's autonomy and his individual liberty to be found in the writings of Zaydan, Farah Antun, Sarruf and al-Shummayyil is due to their Western culture and particularly to the influence of writers such as John Stuart Mill (d.1873), Herbert Spencer (d.1903) and Aldous Huxley (d.1895), whose ideas they often quoted. Besides Western influence, the Christians needed to rely solely on themselves, since they could rely neither on a just government to guarantee their rights, nor on a society in which they were a small minority. All that they achieved in their lives was due to their reliance on nothing but themselves and their willpower.

Thus, Zaydan insisted that a person should depend solely on himself, and this is why he stressed the importance of common sense in all that a person does.[12] His whole autobiography proves that it was only due to his will and dependence upon himself that he obtained what he did. On the other hand, he asserts that man only *imagines* that he acts out of free will, yet it is not God who restricts this freedom, in his opinion, but scientific and worldly factors. Thus, Zaydan assures us that in reality, man's actions are governed by three main factors: heredity, environment and education. Man has no choice in the genes he inherits, nor in the place in which he was born and where he lives. Although the mind strives for improvement through education, yet the mind is also affected by the same factors of nature that affect everything else. These natural phenomena (storms, floods, earthquakes, heat, cold, etc.) are like irrevocable fate that can neither be warded off nor changed.[13] Therefore, it is not God's will that seals man's fate here, as Marrash, al-Kawakibi and Fawwaz believed, but scientific, natural and material factors. Yet due to his education and his own life experience, Zaydan cannot but believe in man's responsibility and free will on which, according to him, the social order and laws depend, and without which our whole existence would be futile. Thus he shows that, although the mind is affected by external factors, it still retains some kind of independence in its activity. For example, the mind struggles all through a person's life against the body's carnal appetites, without the mind's convictions changing. This shows that the mind contains something other than matter, and this gives it some kind of independence and makes it responsible for its actions.[14] Here, too, Zaydan depends on scientific phenomena and not on religion.

The previous chapter alluded to Antun's admiration of Ibn Rushd for having written that humanity, rather than the soul, was immortal. In evaluating August Comte's philosophy, Antun writes that its greatest merit was 'its reverence for humanity and complete respect for the human being.'[15] Just as Comte had replaced the idea of divinity with that of humanity, Antun, too, replaced a religious absolute with a secular one, finding man's fulfillment in mankind, not in religion, and independently of God.

When Sarruf translated *Self-Help* into Arabic, it was to convince his compatriots that man forges his own destiny through hard work, perseverance and will-power, and that a human being makes his own success and should not rely on external powers, such as luck, destiny and the like.[16] By 'the like' one might infer that what he meant was God's will. Al-Shummayyil, who came closest of all to atheism, also could not but believe in man's complete autonomy. When he writes that man is capable of controlling nature and changing it for his own good, and that man's discoveries and inventions have taught him that nothing is impossible,[17] his belief in man's complete autonomy can easily be deduced, for in his opinion it is man, not God, who controls nature, and man, not God, for whom nothing is impossible.

The Muslim writers of the following generation also had a completely secular belief in man's autonomy. Al-Sayyid declares openly that 'man is born free... He has a free will, is free to act or not, and is free in everything.'[18] Therefore, a dependence upon destiny is a retrograde step.'[19] This faith in man's free will and autonomy is transferred by him to the realm of politics when he assures the Egyptians that they should rely on nobody but themselves in their struggle for freedom and independence from British rule,[20] and that it is in their power to overcome many of the disadvantages of British occupation, for this was not a catastrophe they can do nothing about.[21]

Likewise, Kurd 'Ali believed that nothing is impossible for man. By using intelligence, willpower and perseverance, he can overcome any and all problems.[22] Therefore, he repeatedly and severely attacked his countrymen's dependence on others or on the government, pointing out that this was the major difference between themselves and Westerners. Even the educated among his countrymen flatter and bribe, he says, in order to obtain a government post, even when they have the means and opportunity of practising an independent profession.[23] The government's sole duty is to safeguard security, enforce justice and facilitate work, everything else, including agriculture, industry, education, construction, etc. is up to the people.[24] However, neither al-Sayyid nor Kurd 'Ali raised the problem of man's free will in relation to God's will, thus avoiding a potential conflict with their religious beliefs.

Likewise, Julia Tohme Dimashqiyya believed in God's omnipotence, but also insisted that 'God helps those who help themselves,' and that it is within people's power to achieve their goals, no matter what difficulties they face. Thus 'our future is what we desire it to be, happy and successful, or unhappy and a failure.'[25] Even virtues are only acquired by training and the will to be virtuous.[26] Her Muslim compatriot, Nazira Zayn al-Din, also believed in the individual's free will, autonomy, liberty and freedom of choice,[27] and considered that freedom could only be achieved through willpower, resoluteness and determination.[28] However, unlike her two Muslim contemporaries, she does not avoid the question of the individual's relationship with God. Pre-empting any contradiction with religion that her belief in man's free will might involve, she says that God's glory would not be diminished if man took his destiny into his own hands, pursuing what would benefit him and others in this world and the hereafter.[29] She does not take the next step, however, which would be to discuss the relationship between God's omnipotence and the autonomy of the individual.

Having seen the evidence of Taha Hussein's liberal, secular attitude to religion it is hardly surprising that he, too, should believe in man's autonomy and willpower, and put much of the blame for Egypt's cultural and intellectual backwardness on the people's lack of willpower, laziness and dependence on others.[30] Yet, on the other hand, we find him believing in a certain transcendental social and historical determinism, arguing that the causes of social and historical change are beyond man's control.[31] This determinism, however, was not religious, but was influenced by the sociological philosophy of his teacher, Emile Durkheim (d.1917) who considered that society is relatively stable whereas the individual changes and perishes. Furthermore, he held that society regulates individuals, since social rules are imposed on them as if they were not of their own making, while individuals internalize society since they are its constituent and without them society disintegrates. On the other hand, it is this collectivity which civilizes the individual and becomes the basis of any higher thought.[32] Thus, even when reconciling his belief in man's free will with his belief in a Supreme Power to which his freedom is subjugated, it was in secular Western philosophy that Hussein sought his inspiration, and not in religion, and that supreme power was human society rather than God.

A natural result of man's free will is his *responsibility*, whether in the private, social or political sphere. Since nothing in Islam or Muslim heritage contradicts this, it was mainly the Muslim writers who insisted on individual responsibility. The Christians seem to have taken it for granted, since the only two who mentioned the importance of the individual responsibility were Zaydan and Dimashqiyya. One of the virtues Zaydan most admired in Europeans was their sense of responsibility,[33] while Julia Tohmi Dimashqiyya wrote that knowing one's duty and doing it were the most honorable virtues and the basic factors in civilization and progress.[34]

The Druze, Nazira Zayn al-Din, insisted that a free and conscious woman is a responsible person who is accountable for her deeds and actions.[35] She pointed out, however, that whereas the Sunnis believe in destiny and that good and evil are sent by God, the Shi'a believe that man is the cause of good and evil and is therefore responsible and accountable for his actions.[36] Whether she is right or wrong, it should be remembered that the Druzes are a Shi'a sect, and all the Sunni Muslim writers can be seen to insist repeatedly on the individual responsibility, which shows that they had to contend with a deep-rooted lack of responsibility and dependence on destiny. Both Kawakibi and Kurd 'Ali, for example, wrote that the people of the Middle East were solely responsible for their plight, so they should not blame others or fate for it.[37] Therefore neither of them blames the European colonizer but the Muslims themselves, pointing out their faults and weaknesses in order to change them so that they might improve. Kurd 'Ali specifies: 'If the peasants in Syria are ignorant and uncouth, the fault lies with the notables, the religious clerics, the landlords and the educated class, for they are all responsible for the backwardness of the people'.[38] Qasim Amin also believed that the individual is responsible for his own backwardness or progress, and that he is capable of changing all bad habits that hinder progress, since if people want to change for the better they can do so.[39] Bahithat al-Badiya (the pen-name of Malak Hifni Nasef)(1886–1918),[40] an Egyptian Muslim woman defending women's rights like Amin but writing one generation later, also repeatedly insists on individual responsibility for everything a person does, including the choice of a marriage partner, bringing up children or making a marriage last.[41] She ends by declaring that people are responsible for their unsatisfactory situation, for other people give a person the status that he/she has chosen, and as long as a person does not respect himself or herself, one cannot expect respect from others.[42]

A generation later, Lutfi al-Sayyid and Taha Hussein continued to insist on individual responsibility. When writing about the 'cultured' human being, al-Sayyid defines him as a person who, among other things, refuses to follow others in unlawful behaviour, and who holds himself responsible for every one of his thoughts, words and deeds, and develops his mind by learning whatever he can about science and the arts, also learns to do his duty to others.[43] As can be seen, religion plays no part in al-Sayyid's definition of a cultured person. Al-Sayyid also stressed that every individual should be accountable and responsible for his deeds and words. He claims that the Egyptians did not feel this accountability and responsibility for everything they did. For example, those who ran in elections only thought of whatever personal glory and profit they could reap; those who spoke never felt accountable for their words, and therefore became hypocrites, changing their words to suit the person they were addressing.[44] He did not even spare the Egyptian peasant, claiming that the latter's poverty and plight were due to his belief in fate and destiny, instead of trying to foresee, assess, and estimate matters, and maintaining a sense of his own responsibility.[45] Since al-Sayyid belonged to the landed gentry in the feudal system of Egypt that prevailed in his time, he refused to hold the class to which he belonged responsible for the peasants' plight, and blamed the unfortunate peasants themselves.

Hussein also considered that it was mainly the Egyptians themselves who were to blame for their intellectual and cultural backwardness, although European colonialism could not be held guiltless. Yet the responsibility to develop and progress was that of the people themselves as well as of the state.

It was the duty of the rich and the industrialists, for example, to contribute to the development of knowledge, science and the arts.[46]

It was natural to stress, however, that a person's responsibility could not be separated from hard work and perseverance. Al-Shidyaq admired the way that Europeans bring up their children to do work of any kind,[47] and Marrash believed in the necessity of struggle, work, ambition and emulation in order to improve society.[48] Thus, al-Kawakibi insists that 'fate and destiny are aspiration and work... All that is on earth is the work of human beings,' while Bahithat al-Badiya says that her people should learn from the Europeans their love of work, perseverance and energy.[49] It was natural for Christian emigrants like Zaydan, al-Shummayyil, Sarruf and Antun to believe in hard work and perseverance, since only through hard work and dependence upon themselves did they manage to achieve so much. Thus, al-Shummayyil considered that progress was the result of man's cumulative work through the ages, and that the rise and fall of nations was not a matter of destiny, but the result of work and strife.[50] Antun points out that it was Europe's and America's energy and strength that made them conquer the world, and asks bitterly:

Of what use is our sheepish, oriental submission, our philosophical tranquility, our Buddhist apathy, our Confucian meditation, Muslim faith and Christian charity? What do all these negative virtues do in the face of the positive qualities of the West whose aim is to conquer the earth [by energy and force] mentally and physically, regardless of the individual's feelings and strong religious faith.[51]

He not only thus denies any positive influence religions might have, but assures that they are destructive and hinder all progress and civilization, for these are only the result of man's will-power, work and perseverance.

Muslim writers were no less convinced, however, of the importance of work and perseverance. What Kurd 'Ali admired most in the Swiss and the Germans was their work ethic, diligence and perseverance, which were the reason of the high morals of the Swiss; and, he insists, the main reason for a nation's economic, social, political and intellectual development is the hard work of its citizens.[52] He therefore considered that the solution to his country's social problems was to educate people to depend on themselves and to improve themselves through hard work and perseverance, 'as did our forefathers at the dawn of Islam,'[53] lest anyone should think that hard work was alien to Muslim heritage and culture.

In Egypt, Taha Hussein also insisted that continuous hard work was the only way to progress, and severely criticized Egyptian laziness.[54] Lutfi al-Sayyid laid the heaviest stress on the importance of hard work and perseverance. Like many of his contemporaries, he believed that they were the secret of Britain's strength, and quotes Gustave Lebon (d.1931) who claimed that what made the early Romans great were their qualities of patience, will-power, perseverance, self-sacrifice to attain a goal and the respect of the law.[55] When he writes that he translated Aristotle's *Ethics* so that the Arabs could benefit therefrom,[56] he gives the reader the impression that he considered that his Islamic heritage was not sufficient in itself to arouse his countrymen from their lethargy, and he therefore resorted to secular European moral values. Thus, like the other writers, he took secular Europe as an example in propagating even such universally accepted virtues as diligence and perseverance.

Another very important point on which these writers insisted was the *individual's right to freedom of belief and thought.*

Since each monotheistic religion considers itself to be the sole purveyor of absolute truth, the claim that every person had the right to believe or not believe in whatever he/she wanted, was taking a secular approach to faith. Here, again there is a marked difference between the Christian and the Muslim writers.

It was shown in the preceding chapter that both Christians and Muslims severely criticized the fanaticism of the clergy. The Christian Lebanese and Syrian Muslims also attacked the fanaticism of the *people* since their countries had been victims of civil war fought on the grounds of religion. When Bustani wrote a whole book recounting in detail As'ad al-al-Shidyaq's torture and death at the hands of the Maronite Church, he clearly states that neither the clergy nor anyone else had the right to punish or torture a person because of his beliefs, or force him to believe in something he did not want to believe in. He therefore encourages Christians to freely express their personal beliefs.[57] It is not surprising that As'ad's own brother, Faris, defended people's freedom of belief and their right to interpret religion freely, even if that interpretation contradicted what the Church itself taught, and he also insisted on their right to change their religion or even become atheists.[58] While living in Malta, he admired British religious tolerance of other faiths.[59]

Thus, too, we find Ishaq, al-Shummayyil, Antun and Kurd 'Ali, for example, agreeing that religious fanaticism was one of the reasons for their compatriots' weakness and discord,[60] Ishaq rightly pointing out that this disunity makes them dependent upon foreigners who are thus free to exploit their country. He criticizes religious fanaticism in Europe as well, saying that rulers encouraged it for fear of loosing their power.[61] Al-Shummayyil realised that it was ignorance that breeds religious fanaticism which causes bloody wars, and that only education and knowledge could eradicate it. When writing about the Ottoman Empire, he claims that fanaticism is the worst thing that can befall it because of all the different faiths practised within it and adding that the fanaticism which led to the murder of Ottoman Christians and Jews is contrary to the principles of Islam.[62] Antun, however, criticized the fanaticism among the Christian sects themselves as well as their attitude to the Jews,[63] and showed that Christian as well as Muslim fanatics had persecuted and killed philosophers and scientists.[64] Although Kurd 'Ali also advocated tolerance and criticized religious fanaticism, he boasts of Muslim tolerance throughout history, and insists that the Arabs were among the most tolerant nations towards those of different religion, race and language, comparing between them and the fanatical Christians who reconquered Spain.[65]

In addition to nationalistic reasons, Zaydan had personal reasons for criticizing religious fanaticism, since he had been a victim of it as a Christian, being forbidden to teach a course on Islamic history at the Egyptian university. He was also severely attacked by Muslim revivalists in *Manar*, a periodical, and had his books on Arabic literature and Islamic civilization completely ignored by others.[66]

Al-Shummayyil did not merely oppose religious fanaticism but fanaticism of all kinds, whether religious, social or political, for he believed that chauvinism, like religious fanaticism, was the cause of wars and division, and that unity could only be obtained if there was complete freedom, especially freedom of thought and belief, involving the separation of the temporal from the spiritual.[67] Due to his insistence on absolute freedom of belief, he severely criticized the French government for persecuting religious associations in France,[68] although he himself was an atheist. Clearly, it was mainly the Christians, as a religious minority, who suffered directly or indirectly from the religious fanaticism of the majority among whom they lived and wrote, causing them to criticize the fanaticism of the people in general, and not only of the religious clerics.

However, religious tolerance and freedom of belief were not advocated solely by Christians such as Ishaq, Antun and al-Shummayyil,[69] but also by Muslims such as Amin, Kurd 'Ali and Nazira Zayn al-Din. All of them clearly expressed their belief in a person's absolute right to freedom of belief. In this respect, Nazira quoted the inaugural speech of the missionary Bayard Dodge (d.1972) at the American University of Beirut,[70] reinforcing it with the Qur'anic verse that 'There is no compulsion in religion.'[71] Amin took a particularly courageous stand when he even declared a person's right to repudiate belief in God and His prophets.[72] This same secular tendency can be detected in Kurd 'Ali's admiration of 'French thought in the days of Voltaire and Montesquieu (d.1755) that spread the ideas of religious tolerance, social justice, truth and humanism throughout the world.'[73]

The individual's *freedom of thought* is related to his autonomy and freedom of belief and this, too, is a secular attitude. Muslims and Christians alike strongly defended the individual's right to freedom of thought in religious as well as in other matters. Bustani vehemently defended As'ad al-al-Shidyaq's right to criticize the Maronite and Catholic Church,[74] for 'freedom of thought is most important in order to acquire knowledge and achieve the truth,.'[75] while al-Shidyaq sees that one of the reasons for Great Britain's prosperity is the freedom of the press to discuss any subject.[76] This same freedom of the press was considered by Marrash, al-Shummayyil and Bahithat al-Badiya to be the main reason for the advancement of all culture and civilization.[77] As journalists, Ishaq, Zaydan, Antun, Kurd 'Ali and al-Sayyid insisted primarily on the freedom of the press to criticize, fight ignorance and lies, create national awareness, and, in a word, spread the truth.[78] In an open letter to 'Abdülhamid in 1896, al-Shummayyil details the dangers of prohibiting press freedom, and the advantages to be gained from such freedom, as had been proved by the improvements in the quality of life that Egypt had enjoyed ever since the British occupation had permitted this freedom.[79] In 1913, al-Sayyid was still insisting on the importance of freedom of the press as the means by which people could learn and evaluate what was happening in the world and through which they could improve their condition. He saw press freedom as a necessity in civilized societies, one with which the government had no right to interfere.[80] Kurd 'Ali attacked Arab governments for banning books and journals out of fear of their critical attitude, insisting that hiding the truth never did the ruler or the ruled any good.[81]

These writers defended freedom of thought in general. Bustani, al-Shidyaq, Marrash, Ishaq, al-Kawakibi and Bahithat al-Badiya all strongly defended the individual's right to freedom of thought and speech,[82] Ishaq believing that tyrannical rulers killed people like Socrates because they feared their free independent mode of thought.[83] On the subject of Spain, Kurd 'Ali asserts that the Jesuit persecution of all freedom led to the national decline, as a result of which Spain had no philosophers during the Inquisition, just as the Muslim *'ulama* had persecuted free thought, claiming to be the sole purveyors of truth, leading to the decline of Arabic thought. If he admired German universities it was because they granted their students complete freedom of thought thanks to which Germany has produced such a great number of philosophers.[84] Kurd 'Ali adds that the freedom of thought Westerners had enjoyed since the seventeenth century had led to the existence of a group of erudite scholars who were not afraid to tell the truth and contradict what people were accustomed to believing.[85] When writing about the freedom of thought in the West, he demonstrates how and why the West triumphed over the repression it had faced in the past. This was unlike the situation in the Eastern countries that had enjoyed freedom of thought in the past, a freedom that was now being repressed. As a result, these Eastern countries had become backward.[86] Kurd 'Ali does not show why this happened in the East as opposed to the West, however, probably feeling that this would lead to making a connection between Islam and freedom of thought and inquiry, a subject he preferred to avoid, especially since, as has been shown, he believed that there was no contradiction between science and religion.

Another aspect of freedom of thought was the freedom of scientific research. Al-Kawakibi also believed in the freedom of scientific research, and considered that the safety of science and its applications should be guaranteed.[87] He did not tackle the problem of a possible contradiction between this freedom of scientific research and the principles of Islam, however, since he was a believer.

Naturally, Christians were not faced with such a dilemma as is clear from their attitude towards religion. In his autobiography, Zaydan shows great admiration for the Syrian Protestant College because it trained its students to think and talk freely, and this had influenced the development of the country, for he firmly believed that freedom of thought and speech are the first step towards progress.[88] Scientists like al-Shummayyil and Sarruf both insisted on the necessity of free, rational thought and objective scientific research. This was the aim of *al-Muqtataf* as its articles asserted.[89] al-Shummayyil asked people to liberate themselves from the influence of other people's thoughts, seeking to be rational and independent in the questions they were asking in their search for truth and basing themselves solely on experience, experiment and scientific research.[90] The main reason for Antun's arguments in favor of a civil, secular government was his belief that, once such a government had rid itself of all religious power, it could guarantee every individual's freedom of thought.[91] He advocated freedom of research, thought and speech in religious, as well as in all other subjects. Thus he shows great admiration for the Declaration of Human Rights because it is designed to prevent the repression of any ideas, even those dealing with religious matters, and guarantees complete freedom of speech and the press. What the Eastern writer needed above all was freedom of thought and the press; if he enjoyed these he would be able to be honest and fair in what he wrote,[92] according to Antun. Accordingly, he believed that the basis of any reform in the East was:

... complete freedom of thought and the press so that truths and principles can gradually be revealed. Although this freedom is a basic principle in science and literature, people are not and will not become used to it unless their rational compatriots propagate it.[93]

In the next decade, the two Christian writers, Azoury and Samné, reiterated the belief in tolerance and free thought. Azoury saw them as the result of education, a slow evolution and an indicator of civilization,[94] while one of the reasons for Samné's opposing Faysal's rule of Syria was his belief that it would not guarantee the Syrians freedom of thought which the French would maintain if they ruled the country, for liberalism and freedom of thought had to be the watchword of Syria.[95]

The Muslim writers of the next generation did not differ in their belief in an individual's right to freedom of thought, and criticized the clergy and their own Muslim past for having opposed it. Thus 'Abd al-Raziq says that because the caliphs wrested power and kept it for themselves by pure armed force, they were against freedom of thought and inquiry, and did all they could to closely control institutions of learning. In the name of religion, they had prevented people from studying political science, or even religion itself. No doubt political science is the most dangerous science as far as kings are concerned, he writes, since it deals with the different forms, systems and characteristics of government. This is the reason for the lack of Muslim books on politics.[96] While he was on trial, he insisted that it was the duty of any scholar ('alim) to search and investigate so as to arrive at the truth, and that both religion and the laws gave people the right to discuss and argue about any scientific study or investigation.[97]

It is therefore not surprising that Taha Hussein, al-Sayyid and Nazira should also be staunch supporters of an individual's right to freedom of thought. Hussein's great admiration for ancient Greece and its culture is mainly due to Greek teaching freedom of thought,[98] and it was Socrates, he says, who taught people that freedom of conscience and freedom of thought and speech are what make a real human being.[99] His great admiration for Voltaire who fought for freedom of thought, speech and the press, and whose struggle influenced France, Europe and humanity in general is part of the same belief.[100] But Hussein also wanted to show that Islam itself guaranteed this freedom since the Qur'an states that 'No compulsion is there in religion',[101] consciously extending the meaning of the Qur'anic verse to include freedom of all thought, not only that of faith. However, when using his right to freedom of thought in his study of Pre-Islamic poetry it is not the Qur'an he invokes, but the method of René Descartes (d.1650) in searching for truth by eliminating all preconceptions and/or accepted ideas,[102] insisting that one should doubt everything people believed about literature and history, possibly even refuting it, or doubting facts that one was forbidden to doubt, for this was the only path to true knowledge and scholarship.[103] That is why he severely criticizes the Egyptian government and religious clerics for repressing freedom of thought and the press using the excuse of defending virtue, whereas in reality what they were doing was encouraging vice.[104] Unlike Kurd 'Ali, who only blamed the rulers and religious clerics for banning freedom of thought, Hussein saw that it was also the deeply religious feelings of the people that were an impediment to complete freedom of thought.[105] In this, he was influenced by Comte's positivism which considered that the religious view of existence was more primitive and predated rationalism, science and the complete freedom of thought that must, of necessity, accompany them.

Al-Sayyid also repeatedly insisted on the importance of freedom of thought and speech, and that it was modern civilization and its accompanying philosophy that revived them, once the despotism of the Middle Ages had ended.[106] The modern civilization and philosophy to which al-Sayyid refers are undoubtedly those of the modern secular West. Nazira makes no secret of her admiration for Western culture and civilization as being the product of free thought. Freedom, she believes, is the basis of any cultured life.[107] She addresses the fanatical sheikhs who attacked her for admiring foreign schools and education, as follows:

> The best schools you could found would be in the spirit of Western universities such as Oxford, Cambridge, Columbia, Princeton and Harvard, where the minds are free to pursue science to the end, liberated from the stagnation and useless traditions that are the calamity of the East.[108]

Yet, consistent with her own personality and her deep belief in Islam, she insisted that this Western civilization and the freedom upon which it was based were completely compatible with the Qur'an and the Sunna.[109] Thus, in adopting it Muslims would not be distancing themselves from their religion and culture but, on the contrary, they would be applying that which their religion required but which they had neglected. This, of course, shows to what extent Nazira blinded herself to whatever runs counter to complete freedom of thought that exists in all religions.

The Muslims had another problem to contend with, namely the right and freedom of the individual to reinterpret Islam, which the Sunni *'ulama* forbade. Muhammad 'Abdu rejected an imitation of the ancients, whereby their hidebound interpretations of Islam were mindlessly repeated, and had worked towards reapplying independent judgments in legal and theological matters. In this respect, he was followed by many liberal Muslim thinkers. Here, too, there is a difference between a late nineteenth century writer such as al-Kawakibi, and the writers of the first third of the twentieth century.

Al-Kawakibi criticizes many of the ancient interpreters of Islam, noting how they disagree on issues relating to prayer, and pointing out the shortcomings in the interpretations of even famous imams such as Abu Hanifa (d.767) and Shafi'i (d.820).[110] He therefore asks Muslims not to follow the traditional interpreters of their religion. In reinterpreting Islam, however, al-Kawakibi separates the purely spiritual from the worldly, as Muhammad 'Abdu had done before him. In the former, i.e. the principles of faith and prayer, Muslims must restrict themselves to imitate (taqlid) what the Prophet, his companions and the Orthodox caliphs had determined. In all that relates to everyday life and society, however, the 'ulama should be free to use their reasoning to reinterpret Islam to suit the changing times.[111] However, he does not show how and why what pertained to everyday life had been and continued to be considered part and parcel of the principles of Islam.

A quarter of a century later, 'Abd al-Raziq, Hussein and Nazira Zayn al-Din also severely criticized the way in which the 'ulama stuck to imitating the ancients and rjected the freedom to use reason in order to reinterpret Islam.[112] But whereas al-Kawakibi had insisted that reinterpretation was the sole right of the 'ulama, the three later writers adopted a more secular stance. When 'Abd al-Raziq writes that their tyrannical rulers misused religion in order to prevent the Muslims from studying and truly understanding their religion, they paralyzed the people's intellect.[113] When he also criticizes those who refuse to use reason in dealing with religion and reinterpreting it, as if it were static and impervious to progress,[114] it might be inferred that he does not give the 'ulama the exclusive right of reinterpretation.

Hussein is more explicit. He says clearly that neither Christianity nor Islam contain anything that condemns freedom of thought. However, as soon as those in power felt themselves threatened by philosophy or science, they resorted to religion in order to combat this freedom.[115] Besides, there is no clergy in Islam, nor any religious power monopolized by the 'ulama that gives them the right to judge who is a believer and who an atheist.[116] Therefore, they have absolutely no right to prosecute or punish anyone who disagrees with their fossilized traditional interpretations, for God has given people brains so that they may think and analyze both religious and worldly matters. Thus it is clear to him that any person has the right and freedom to interpret Islam, even if this interpretation is wrong, and it is the government's duty to guarantee this freedom, and to protect people from persecution and punishment for believing in ideas that are generally considered false.[117] Although this is clearly in accord with his belief about separating the temporal from the spiritual, with the former having the upper hand, in this, too, he feels that Islam confirms his opinion, for it is 'a religion of freedom, science and knowledge.'[118] This is in spite of the fact that no religion admits complete freedom of thought, or is a source of science and knowledge, as he himself proved when discussing the historic veracity of certain facts in the Qur'an. It is in Western culture and civilization and not in Islam that he sought science and knowledge, as will be shown.

Nazira Zayn al-Din also felt that freedom was held to be sacred in the Qur'an, and that Islam was a religion based on freedom of thought, will, speech and deed. To prove this she quotes a number of Qur'anic verses. Accordingly, she, like Hussein, considers that every individual has the right to reinterpret Islam, to follow freely what his/her reason tells him/her is for his/her good or for that of society, and in this a person is not accountable to man but to God alone. She adds that while studying the ideas and interpretations of other religious scholars one should use one's intellect to decide whether what they had decreed agrees with the Qur'an and the Sunna, otherwise it should be refuted.[119] In advocating a person's right to freedom of thought and interpreting the Qur'an she goes a step further by quoting the Prophet himself who had said that diversity in belief is a good thing. This, she explains, is because it encourages people of every creed to expand their knowledge and perform greater deeds, leads them to better interpretations, emulating each other, each one hoping to outdo the others in virtue, justice and goodness.[120] Thus for her, as for the others, freedom of thought even in religious matters, could only lead to a better society.

Yet, as can be seen, no matter how much the Muslim writers believed in freedom of thought, they always remained within the framework of Islam itself, using religion as a reference point to justify their secular belief in absolute freedom of thought, unconscious or oblivious of the contradiction this might involve.

CHAPTER FIVE

The Status of Women

The status of women in the second half of the nineteenth century and first third of the twentieth century was the subject of much attention and controversy in the purely patriarchal society of the Middle East, and not only in Muslim circles. Some writers included the liberation of women and a change in their status as part of the liberation of the individual in order to change the whole of society. Since all the personal status laws in the Arab countries were, as they still are, religious rather than civil laws, the status of women was regulated and supervised by religious clerics with a patriarchal, conservative mentality in anything pertaining to the female sex. The status of women thus falling into the socio-religious context, their liberation was very often seen as part of a national problem, and was fought against by those who claimed that changing the condition of women was unpatriotic and played into the hands of the Western colonizer. For example, when the Committee of Union and Progress proposed its democratic reforms in 1908, declaring all citizens of the Ottoman Empire to be equal, the religious clerics in Syria opposed it. To rally support, the *'ulama* of Damascus seized upon the women's dress code, winning over many influential personalities who joined them in opposing the Committee.[1] The status of women thus became politicized, in addition to being a social, religious and moral matter. The change in the status of women was an integral part of the effort to secularize both thought and society in the Middle East.

The local women were mostly illiterate, the Muslims veiled and secluded, except in the countryside, and all were completely under the autocratic rule of the male head of the household, whether the father, husband, brother or even a son. The Christian writers al-Shidyaq and his successor Zaydan, for example, criticized men's despotic treatment of and disrespect for women. Al-Shidyaq claimed that girls were prisoners of their fathers, and after marriage they became prisoners of their husbands, their victims and slaves; he severely criticized the injustice and humiliation of women at the hands of men and society in the Middle East, for they always blamed women for everything, even when the man was really to blame. Zaydan asserted that men considered women to be defective in 'mind and faith'.[2]

It was mainly the Muslim writers, however, who were disgusted by the status of women in their society. Before the renowned women's champion Qasim Amin published his two books *Tahrir al-Mar'a* (The Liberation of Women) in 1899 and *al-Mar'a al-Jadida* (The New Woman) in 1901, Zaynab Fawwaz, a Lebanese Shi'ite émigré to Egypt, had written articles about women's plight and rights and which were collected in 1882 in her book *al-Rasa'il al-Zaynabiyya* (Zaynab's Letters). Here she, too, strongly attacks man's injustice to and enslavement of woman, and the way in which men used all their military, literary and legal might to subjugate and chain women, humiliating them as creatures 'defective in mind and faith'. This is supposed traditionally to have been said by the Prophet, but Zaynab, as well as later defenders of women, insisted that it was falsely attributed to him.[3]

Qasim Amin linked women's situation to the political setup in Muslim countries and tried to show that the reason for this injustice was the despotic rule under which each person tyrannized the person weaker than himself. Thus, men who were stronger oppressed and despised women who are weaker, keeping them ignorant, using them solely for their pleasure and to satisfy their lust, treating them as slaves who have to submit to their every whim, divorcing them for no reason, refusing to allow them any activity and keeping them imprisoned in the house until the day of their death.[4] Amin summarizes woman's plight as follows in *al-Mar'a al-Jadida*:

> From the day she is born until her death, woman is a slave because she does not live independently and for herself, but through man and for him. She needs him in everything that concerns her, and only goes out when guarded by him... She thinks only through his mind, sees through his eyes, hears through his ears and wills through his will.[5]

Those same aspects of man's tyranny and injustice are shown by Nazira Zayn al-Din,[6] and described in detail by Bahithat al-Badiya who adds the injustice of polygamy, pointing out that man's despotism very often caused women to become hysterical or even go mad.[7] With clear insight and an unusual feminist feeling for her time she perceives that men who fight for the liberation of women are just as despotic about liberating them as they were about enslaving them.[8] That is why both Zaynab Fawwaz and Nazira warn women that only through their own hard struggle will they be able to obtain their rights and to resist the men who deny them these rights.[9]

True, no religion actually endorses tyranny and injustice, but on the other hand, neither the Bible nor the Qur'an treat men and women as equals. Verses 3, 7 and 9, for example, of chapter 11 of Corinthians I say that 'the head of the woman is man,' and man 'is the image and glory of God: but the woman is the glory of man. Neither was the man created for the woman; but the woman for the man'. And although the Qur'an stipulates that faith alone is what puts one person above another, and several of its verses call for just and kind treatment of women,[10] it definitely does not consider women equal to men, for example, in the matter of polygamy, inheritance, or bearing witness,[11] and it clearly states that 'Men are in charge of women, because Allah hath made the one of them to excel the other, and because they spend of their property (for the support of women). So good women are obedient'.[12]

It is therefore the secularism of certain Christian and Muslim writers that makes them insist on complete *equality between men and women*. Bustani says that women are just as intelligent as men, while al-Shidyaq writes that men are not superior to women in anything;[13] and in his symbolic story *Ghabat al-Haq* (The Forest of Justice) Marrash makes the king refute his wrong decisions thanks to the queen's wisdom,[14] demonstrating his belief that woman is just as intelligent as man, if not more so. Dimashqiyya also insisted that women were equal to men in intelligence, ambition and the desire to create and excel, and were not there for the sole pleasure and satisfaction of man.[15] The Muslims Fawwaz, Amin, Bahithat al-Badiya, al-Sayyid and Nazira Zayn al-Din all repeatedly insisted on the intellectual equality between the two sexes.[16] In a long article, Fawwaz refuted all the Islamic verses and sayings quoted by a certain Abu al-Mahasin to prove the superiority of men, giving him examples from religion, society and history to prove him wrong.[17]

As for Nazira, true to her belief that many of the Qur'anic verses were linked to the time and place in which they were revealed, she indicates that the verses favoring men over women did so for social and historic reasons, and not because Islam considers women to be inferior. For example, polygamy in pre-Islamic times had no limits, and Islam limited it to four wives. There was a danger that Arabs might reject the whole religion had it imposed monogamy, although Islam clearly prefers the latter to polygamy. She then quotes the Prophet's sayings that prove women's intelligence, faith, equality and respected position in Islam,[18] choosing from only those sayings that suited her purpose, and not doubting their authenticity the way she had done with the sayings that reflected his disrespect for women. She repeatedly insists that women are equal to men in intelligence and faith, in their right to education, independence, freedom of thought, free will, speech and deed, and in their right to vote and interpret the Qur'an and the Hadith.[19] All this shows how far she had been influenced by Western secular thought, for Islam never mentioned the right to vote, for example, whether for men or women, and in her time most of the women in the West still did not have that right.

Hussein likewise insisted that women were completely equal to men,[20] but he did not go into details, since the logical result of such an attitude would be a belief that women's status and rights are equal to those of men, and need not be discussed any further.

It is surprising, however, that fundamentally secular thinkers such as Zaydan, al-Shummayyil, Antun and Sarruf, all four of them Christians, vehemently denied the equality between men and women. Al-Shummayyil, the scientist and doctor, tries to prove this scientifically by saying that since a man's brain weighs more than a woman's, the brain being the center of intellect, it follows that man is more intelligent than woman. Besides, had woman been equal to man, why did she let him get the upper hand, and set laws that were unjust towards her? And although she might improve if better educated, her constitution prevents her from learning what men learn, and therefore she could never become equal to men.[21] Antun and Zaydan also insisted that a woman's place is in the home, that her husband was the natural head of the family and that it was her duty to please and obey him.[22] And although Sarruf encouraged women to learn, and admitted that many European women had become writers or played an important role in politics, he insisted that woman's first and foremost duty was not to emulate men and become famous for great deeds, but to bring up her children properly.[23]

Here one might ask the reason for this traditional, non-secular attitude of otherwise secular Christian writers: were they driven by fear of being even more stigmatized as Westerners by their Muslim contemporaries, and thus tried to show their rejection of the Western mentality which claims equality between the sexes, and which to them as men was much less important than the political equality they demanded in a democratic state?

What Kurd 'Ali writes to this effect even later might be the answer to this question. On a visit to Europe, he noticed that Western women shared the social, civil and political rights with men, but said that a wise person would not ask Eastern women to do the same, to share in politics, mix with men and devote their lives to science and humanities, for this did not suit 'our customs, traditions or religion'. All he asked for was that women receive a good elementary education so that they would be better mothers and wives.[24]

Zaydan, Antun and especially al-Shummayyil showed some ambivalence in their attitudes towards women's equality and rights. Antun wrote later that he admired the French thinker Jules Simon (d.1896) who supported a woman's right to work, adding that he himself was not against female independence;

while Zaydan expressed his admiration for Eastern women who participated in public and political life.[25] al-Shummayyil seems to have felt more comfortable after noting his Muslim compatriots' defence of women. In an article he wrote deploring Bahithat al-Badiya's early death, he states that all religions treated women unjustly because they were created by men. He strongly defended a woman's right to freedom, which is one of nature's laws, comparing between Arab societies in which women are uneducated and imprisoned in their homes and the developed societies in which women are educated and free.[26]

When writers insisted on the equality between men and women, they went on to demand that women have equal rights with men. Bahithat al-Badiya, Amin, al-Sayyid, Dimashqiyya and Nazira all fall into this category. The Muslims tried to support their case by referring to Islam, while ignoring anything it contained that contradicted their modern secular stand. Amin, for example, insists that Islam gave women as well as men the right to pass judgment and deliver legal opinions,[27] and established complete equality between men and women in matters of personal status, with the sole exception of polygamy, which had been decreed for important reasons concerning lineage.[28] Nazira insists that women have exactly the same rights as men, and that there should be no difference between them in either temporal or in religious matters.[29] She then shows that the reason for the existing differentiation between them is that all the laws were promulgated by men with women having absolutely no say in them, and that many such laws contradict the teachings of Islam. To prove her point she lists several of these laws.[30]

The first right demanded by all the secularists was a woman's right to education. Some women in Egypt had had access to elementary education since the days of Rafa'a Rafi' Tahtawi (d.1873), yet in 1917 only 2% of the Egyptian female population was literate, and even as late as 1910 the Egyptian state guarded 'against too much education of an impractical nature [for girls] which would divert them from their natural vocation'. Girls were excluded from higher education and training in modern professions.[31] The Lebanese Bustani was the first Arab to claim the need to educate women in exactly the same way as men, doing so as early as 1849. In his famous speech, Ta'lim al-Nisa' (Teaching Women), he expounded all the reasons for the importance and necessity of educating women, insisting that a society can never be civilized unless its womenfolk are educated.[32] Yet whereas al-Shidyaq, Marrash and al-Kawakibi believed in educating women because it would make them better mothers, they only demanded an elementary education for women.[33] On the other hand Ishaq, Fawwaz, Bahithat al-Badiya, Amin, Zaydan, al-Sayyid, Dimashqiyya and Nazira, all insisted on a girl's right to receive the same education as boys, while also pointing out the importance of having an educated mother bring up children.[34] The influence of Western secular thought in this is made clear by Bahithat al-Badiya's constantly alluding with admiration to the equal education given to boys and girls in the West, resulting in the excellent way in which Western children are brought up by their mothers. When al-Sayyid participated in founding the Egyptian university, he insisted that it must accept women, although he had to do so in secret for fear of arousing public opinion, which was hostile to the idea of girls mixing with boys.[35]

With the exception of Zaydan, these writers also wanted girls to be educated because education would help them to become *free and independent*, both in thought and deed. This conflicts with the demands of religion that requires women to be submissive and obedient. Bustani clearly states that among the advantages a woman gains by being educated is the acquisition of the ability to think independently, no longer being obliged to obey her husband unquestioningly. He contradicts himself in that same speech, however, when he states that he still believes a woman must obey her husband 'for woman's status with regard to man's is known and should not be overstepped'.[36] Later Bahithat al-Badiya and Dimashqiyya, for example, asked women to use their intellect and to debate,[37] to act according to what they believe, not according to tradition and what others think, 'thus loosing their freedom which is their life's spirit'.[38] al-Sayyid assures women that they have the same right as men to personal freedom, claiming that until a woman is an independent individual, free to dress, learn and go out as she pleases, she will be unable to bring up free men, for 'a slave does not bring up free men, but slaves like herself'. The best way to bring up a girl is to prepare her to be free and independent from the day she is born.[39] Thus he, like Amin before him, saw the close connection between woman's status and politics, and this, too, is why liberating women became a political issue and not merely a socio-religious one.

Freedom for women was insisted upon even earlier by Qasim Amin and Bahithat al-Badiya, as well as by al-Sayyid, all of whom were obviously influenced by Western ideas. After asserting her belief in the equality of boys and girls, Bahithat al-Badiya severely criticizes the practice of giving boys a better education and allowing them freedom in everything, when women were not even allowed to leave the house. In a long essay, she compares the Egyptian girl, adolescent and woman and her European counterpart, pointing out the great difference between them, because in Europe, unlike Egypt, from the moment they are born girls are given the same rights and the same care as boys.[40] Qasim Amin explicitly declares that he finds no 'objection to the way in which Europeans have preceded us, since we see that European civilization is advancing day by day' because European women enjoy freedom and all their rights.[41] Dimashqiyya also sees that true education is the way to liberate women from the past, and enable them to acquire new morals and customs. She says that she aims in her journal at 'breaking the despotic fetters with which ignorance has bound women, so that they, like men, can enjoy freedom'.[42]

Nazira Zayn al-Din did not rely on the European model but on Islam itself in her campaign for women's freedom. 'The Muslim woman is free according to the Qur'an, the Sunna, the Shari'a, the law and the loftiest principles of society and human rights'.[43] It is the misinterpretation of the Qur'an and Sunna, she claims, that have led to her enslavement, because the *'ulama* who interpreted them were prejudiced against women; therefore women, not men, should be the interpreters of the verses that deal with women's rights and duties because they would understand them better.[44] She ends by declaring that freedom is the source of all good in human beings, and the basis of morality, honour and self-confidence and independence, in women as in men, is the most important factor in self-advancement.[45]

Naturally, one way to achieve this independence was by working and having an independent source of income. There are many examples to show that women, rather than men, were the strongest advocates of a woman's working outside the home. One of the few men of the first generation to insist on a woman's right to work outside the home were al-Shidyaq and, surprisingly, Kawakibi,[46] whereas both Bustani and much later Zaydan, only accept a woman's working if her husband is incapacitated and she is in need to raise her family.[47] Since both Zaydan and Kurd 'Ali insist that a woman's natural duties are in the home, Kurd 'Ali finds that when women in the West go out to work like men they become immoral, and Zaydan adds that the real reason for the spread of immorality in Paris was the liberation of women. making them equal to men and allowing them to earn a livelihood like men.[48]

While, on the other hand, a Muslim woman such as Zaynab Fawwaz, writing much earlier, encouraged women to work outside the home – as the Egyptian female poor had in any case been forced to do – because women's work is very beneficial to society, ensuring that a working mother is a role-model for her children, and even if she is veiled, the veil should not prevent her participating in public life.[49] Likewise, Bahithat al-Badiya strongly defended a woman's right to work outside the home. To those who objected, claiming that women were born to stay at home, she retorted: 'Where did God decree such a law?' and insisted that even child-bearing and delivery should not be an excuse to prevent them from practicing a profession, for do not men also absent themselves from work because of illness? Besides, she sees that no matter what profession a woman practices outside the home she will never forget or neglect her children. On the contrary, the more enlightened a woman is, the more responsible will she be. Bahithat al-Badiya then shows that the division of labour is purely arbitrary, since, for example, in some primitive tribes it is the men who stay at home and sew clothes for the family while the women go out to work in the fields. To prove her point she gives examples of women who fought, ruled or mastered various arts in the same way as men.[50] That is why she greatly admires the economic independence of Western women and their hard work in and outside the home, and wishes Egyptian women could do the same.[51] The women that both Zaynab and Bahithat al-Badiya have in mind here are the middle-class Egyptian women, for the lower-class urban and peasant women were all working outside their homes in the fields, shops, bakeries and factories and sometimes running their own businesses.[52] Accordingly, it is the middle class of whom Amin is also thinking when he sees that only the Egyptian woman's ignorance and lack of education prevent her from activity in science, the humanities and fine arts, commerce and industry, like her European counterpart, and that women should be brought up to be independent and should not be the property of a man and the mere object of his pleasure.[53]

A very contemporary note is struck by Dimashqiyya when she deplores the fact that all the work that women do in the home and in bringing up their children is not valued and considered when calculating the national income, and that housewives are considered to be 'unemployed', although, economically, if the income of their work were counted, it would be greater than that of the menfolk.[54] Of course, this does not mean that she does not repeatedly insist on the importance of a woman's being economically independent and working outside her home at no matter what job,[55] and going as far as to say that although marriage is every girl's dream, unless a woman finds something really attractive in marriage she should gladly dispense with it in favor of all the job opportunities open to her by which she could earn money and be independent.[56] But she shows that a working woman can at the same time be a perfect mother and housewife.[57]

Nazira also insists on woman's right to independence and freedom, but a freedom within the Shari'a, just like that of men,[58] and advocates a woman's right to work, pointing out that Islam has given women the right to interpret the Shari'a, be judges and give legal opinions, be guardians, as well as the right to trade and ownership. She concludes: 'Women's and men's rights are equal in all dealings, transactions and actions'.[59] However, unlike Zaynab, Bahithat al-Badiya and Dimashqiyya she repeats that a woman's role is that of housewife and mother,[60] an attitude which is surprising in someone who elsewhere expressed very liberal ideas.

Another aspect of these writers' secular stand concerning women is that they assert women's right to engage in politics. Again, Zaydan, while admiring European women who are active in politics and mentioning the names of Arab women who were influential in politics in former times, refuses to allow women to participate in public and political life, since he sees their natural place as being in the home. He makes fun of 'some crazy English women who went to such extremes as to ask for the right to vote'.[61] In the first part of *al-Saq 'ala al-Saq* (The Leg Over the Leg), al-Shidyaq also objects to women participating in politics, but in the second part he has his wife say that men's selfishness has made them seize and monopolize all power and influence, and that it would have been a better world had women been in the influential positions held by men.[62] Could it be inferred from this that he later agreed with her, since he does not refute her comment? Women writers are more direct and open. Zaynab Fawwaz, Bahithat al-Badiya, Dimashqiyya and Nazira all insisted on women's political rights.[63] Dimashqiyya sees that the result of male domination of world politics is war, destruction and bloodshed, whereas if women were in control, there would be peace, happiness and order, and all mankind would be better off.[64] Nazira asks about the logic and reason behind allowing ignorant and even depraved men to have the right to vote, whereas even educated women are deprived of that right.[65]

Qasim Amin and Lutfi al-Sayid also approved of giving women all their political rights, and Amin shows the advantages of having granted them these rights in parts of the United States, and having them share in the judiciary and other public offices.[66]

An issue closely associated with that of liberating women was that of the *veil*. Naturally this was addressed only by Muslim writers. Although the peasant women and lower class urban women were neither veiled nor secluded, Leila Ahmed points out that the veil became the symbol of backwardness in Muslim and Arab civilization and societies, an attitude disseminated by Western colonizers and certain Muslims who espoused their views.[67] These included Qasim Amin, Lutfi al-Sayyid, Kurd 'Ali and Nazira Zayn al-Din.

Verse 31 of the Light Surah in the Qur'an specifies only that women should 'draw their veils over their bosoms'. However, custom had them completely veiled and virtually imprisoned in their homes. This is what these Muslim writers revolted against. Both Bahithat al-Badiya and Nazira were against complete unveiling and wanted to apply the *'shar'i* veil' imposed by the Qur'an, and preserve women's freedom to come and go as they wish. However, Bahithat al-Badiya was cautious. She was wary of Western ways and believed that the mixing of men and women in the West was the cause of immorality. Although she believed that uncovering the face was not harmful as such, she saw that veiling women completely was better in Egypt's present state because the men were corrupt and degenerate, for even though women were veiled, men stared at them insolently and brazenly in the street. That is why she sees that women should first be educated and the men well brought up before women can enjoy the freedom of uncovering their faces.[68] She thus rightly criticizes the men in the first place and holds them responsible for whatever is amiss in a patriarchal society. She was thus in favour of gradual innovation, but this innovation had to be part of a general change in society, including both men and women, for it to have positive results. She insisted, however, that complete veiling should not keep a woman imprisoned in the home and prevent her from going out.[69]

Nazira, writing a generation later, was more radical, although she still favoured the legal Islamic veil.[70] Her first book *al-Sufur wa al-Hijab* was her reaction to the Syrian government forcing women to remain completely veiled, as has been shown. In it she wrote:

When the West brought in the spirit of freedom, it was reflected by our embracing the light of freedom and that of science, and these banished the darkness of ignorance and despotism. We became educated, saw all the wisdom and nobility in religion, and realized that it was contrary to how it had been represented to us. We discovered that religion wanted us to expose our faces to the air and light, just like everybody else, and wanted us to use the faculties God gave us, the way every one else does. This is proved by the Qur'an, the Hadith and their great scholars and interpreters.[71]

She then discusses the problem of the veil in the context of the Qur'anic verses and the Sunna as a whole, with their various linguistic interpretations.[72] Unlike Bahithat al-Badiya she does not see that the West was immoral because its women are unveiled and mix with men, quite the contrary:

If we look at the countries in which women are unveiled we find free minds, free women and developed countries. The reason for their progress is that they have freed themselves from tradition and freed women...

Woman's freedom is the basis of a nation's progress, and the first step toward progress is doing away with the veil, because the veil paralyzes half the nation and if half the nation is paralyzed it cannot compete, overtake and win.[73]

Although she, too, believed that proper upbringing based on high principles and virtuous conduct was the way to safeguard a woman's honour, she refused to see that the veil was that safeguard for the present, as did Bahithat al-Badiya. She even went a step further by saying that veiled women could perform the most immoral and dissolute acts, because they could feel safe in the knowledge that no one would recognize them behind their veils, and that what gave the Westerners their high morals was the way in which they mixed together, for mixing socially improves the morals of both men and women.[74] In answer to those religious clerics and conservative men who severely criticized her, accusing her of being influenced by Christian missionaries, she retorted that if Muslim women adopted Christian dress, which is healthier and more practical, this does not mean that they were adopting Christianity, just as Muslim men had adopted Western dress and yet remained Muslim.[75] In defence of her position, she quotes many examples from the dawn of Islam of devout Muslim women who were not veiled and who mixed socially with men without sullying their impeccable morals.[76] Although Nazira still believed in retaining the Muslim legal veil, she took a big step towards secularism when she agreed that if women so desired they could discard the veil completely, and she claimed that the fact that women could mix freely with men encouraged morality.

This same step towards secularism was taken much earlier by Qasim Amin who, in his *Tahrir al-Mar'a* urged the adoption of the Islamic veil instead of veiling a woman completely.[77] In his second book, *al-Mar'a al-Jadid,* however, he insisted that the veil was a remnant of human savagery, and that the first step towards liberating women is by tearing the veil and *eliminating all trace of it*. He then pointed out all the negative and bad effects veiling had on women, children and family life in contrast to the advantages of unveiling. When he describes the complete freedom and liberty of Western women he stresses their impeccable morals, in spite of their liberty, and the solid family life they enjoy,[78] thus completely disagreeing with Zaydan, Kurd 'Ali and Bahithat al-Badiya. He then insists that veiling women is the reason for the East's decline, and not having them veiled in the West was the cause of its progress.[79]

That same secular stand is also taken by Lutfi al-Sayyid and sometimes by Kurd 'Ali who often contradicted himself. The former severely attacks imprisoning women in their homes and veiling them, considering them to be 'a blemish to be strangled under the veil'. This cannot help woman to be a free, complete human being, and a responsible person able to bring up children properly.[80] While Kurd 'Ali, after quoting all the traditional and religious arguments in defence of the Islamic veil, resorts to Darwinism, stating 'that the removal of the veil has triumphed, due to the influence of modern civilization and nature which decrees the survival of the fittest'. However, he strongly attacks Western women for shamelessly baring parts of their bodies, dancing and mixing with men, judging them as immoral and dissolute.[81] That Kurd 'Ali should apply the theory of evolution only to the veil but to nothing else in women's status, shows to what an extent the veil was the symbol of backwardness in Muslim society, as Leila Ahmed has pointed out.

Woman's inferior status in religious marriage laws was another problem that these writers had to tackle. Al-Shidyaq may have been the most liberal in this respect when, contrary to all religious injunctions, whether Christian or Muslim, he advocates complete sexual freedom for women. He asserts that if a man really loves his wife, he should let her enjoy whoever she loves, and that a woman should leave her husband if he does not satisfy her sexually.[82] In view of the fact that even today, the mere mention of sex is still taboo in Arab societies, and women's sexual satisfaction hardly ever taken into consideration, it is astonishing that al-Shidyaq should have raised the question in the mid-nineteenth century.

Ishaq's secular approach is different. He asserts that marriage is a natural law desired by human beings due to their animalistic nature, and natural laws to which human beings submit are independent and separate from all religious laws.[83] From this, it can be deduced that as far as he is concerned, marriage has nothing to do with religion, and therefore should not be regulated or controlled by religious laws or clerics.

Secular Muslim writers had to contend with two main problems, that of polygamy, which is sanctioned by Islam as a sole male right, and the divorce laws. Although Islam grants women the right to divorce, they have no such right in reality.

Naturally, Qasim Amin was against polygamy and cited the Qur'anic verses that discourage it.[84] He claimed that the Islamic legal system grants women marriage rights similar to those given to men, and that it insisted on love and compassion in marriage.[85] This is not quite correct. Islam does not grant women the same right to divorce as men, nor do they have custody of their children in the case of divorce, for example. When the Qur'an clearly tells husbands that as for the wives 'from whom ye fear rebellion, admonish them and banish them to beds apart, and scourge them',[86] it does not mention equal rights for the wives. Amin can thus be seen to be taking a secular view of marriage, the more so when he insists that marriage is a *spiritual* relationship between husband and wife, based on mutual love, respect and understanding,[87] something that is not confirmed by the above Qur'anic verse.

Women did not try to overlook the difference in the treatment of men and women in the Qur'an, since it is they who suffered from it. They therefore took a completely secular stand in this respect. Zaynab Fawwaz criticized the injustice of men being free to divorce their wives at any time, as well as their right to have more than one wife at a time,[88] both of these being granted in Islam exclusively to men. Bahithat al-Badiya attacked polygamy most vehemently since she had been its unsuspecting victim. She severely criticizes the marriage customs in Egypt whereby people marry before even having met. She claimed that this leads to misery and unhappiness, but adds that what facilitated these customs was the fact that Islam permits polygamy and divorce. In her comments on the Qur'an's enjoining a man not to differentiate between his wives, she appears to be speaking from her own bitter experience when she says that treating them equally and giving them the same material things cannot eliminate the deep sense of humiliation a woman feels, nor the deep wounds it leaves in her heart. Furthermore, polygamy is the source of jealousy between brothers of different mothers, jealousy between the different wives, and hatred of the husband. Polygamy, she concludes, is a woman's worst enemy. As far as women are concerned, it is much better to be divorced than live as a second wife, since 'an unhappy free woman is better off than an unhappy prisoner'.[89] Commenting on polygamy, she says that civilization and enlightenment forbid it, although they claim that religion permits it.[90] She knew full well that religion indeed permitted it, but was afraid that society would accuse her of being hostile to Islam. In reality, except for polygamy, she never questioned Islam's marital laws, on the contrary, she criticized Western marriage customs which permitted men and women to mix before marriage, saying that this could lead them to flit from relationship to relationship without marrying at all.[91]

Kurd 'Ali, on the other hand, took a very ambivalent view of polygamy. In his earlier writings he criticized it, as he did concubinage, which Islam also permits,[92] but later on, in 1934, he began defending it, showing its advantages and pointing out that some Christians, such as the Mormons, practice it and are perfectly happy with it, while other Christians take mistresses, which is nothing more than a hypocritical form of poligamy.[93] This contradiction might be due to Kurd 'Ali's taking a defensive stand against the West, for France now ruled his country and undoubtedly considered the veil and polygamy aspects of Muslim backwardness.

Regardless of the writers' views of women's status, all agreed that it was closely linked to the nation's standard of civilization, and that the progress of a nation depended, to a large extent, on that of women's condition.[94] Amin puts it in a nutshell: 'The nation cannot improve unless woman's condition improves'.[95] This shows that all these secular writers were, to varying degrees, conscious of the fact that the problem of women was part of the wider social, national and religious problems, since they all felt the need to reinterpret Islam and attacked the fossilized *'ulama*.

What the Muslim writers said about women's work, economic independence or even unveiling the face was in complete agreement with Islam, as Muhammad 'Abdu himself had shown. This they could and did prove by quoting verses from the Qur'an or the Hadith. Nevertheless, they were subjected to very fierce opposition and criticism. Zaynab Fawwaz was strongly criticized because she advocated equality between men and women and demanded that women have the right to higher education and work.[96] Although Qasim Amin's first book was very cautious in the reforms it suggested, it raised a storm of protest. This made him all the more radical in his second book. Bahithat al-Badiya was indirectly attacked by no less a person than Muhammad Rashid Rida because she asserted the intellectual equality between men and women and demanded rights for women.[97] This was despite the deep faith in Islam which permeates all her writing. It is true that Nazira could be considered the most secular of writers since she even questioned the inequality between the sexes in inheritance rights, which is something that is laid down in the Qur'an. Her first book, caused the same sort of furore as Amin's, although she was writing at a much later date. She responded to the antagonism in her second book. Yet even Nazira still admitted that men, if virtuous, 'are in charge of women, because Allah hath made the one of them excel the other,'[98] as the Qur'an had stated.

The opposition faced by these writers was merely due to the very conservative customs and traditions of a society that remained unwilling to change. In all the reforms they demanded, the Muslim writers were very careful not to defy the Qur'an, and to question only those sayings in the Hadith the authenticity of which could be doubted. As for the ancient *ulama's* interpretations, they could never be considered binding by any religious consideration, since there were disagreements between them on many topics. Yet is is clear that writers like Amin, in his second book, and al-Sayyid were totally in favour of women adopting a European life-style, while all the others refused to abandon their Muslim heritage, and chose from it whatever suited their modern circumstances, or reinterpreted their heritage to fit their modern ideas.

CHAPTER SIX

The Role of Education and Knowledge

Whatever the Arab attitude towards the West in general, Western science and knowledge was greatly admired. The Arab world felt the necessity to acquire these skills, although for different reasons and with different goals in mind. This chapter examines to what extent did the writers that are the subject of this book realize that secularism was a pre-condition for adopting this knowledge and its rational system of thought.

The Christian Lebanese were the first to realize the importance of keeping education free from any religious influence, although what they mainly had in mind was to combat the fanaticism and disunity of which their country was the constant victim. Thus when Bustani lists the subjects taught in *al-Madrassa al-Wataniyya* (The National School) which he founded in 1863 he does not mention religion, although he says that religious instruction was available for who ever wanted it and that it was taught by teachers of the pupils' own faith. The teachers were chosen for their knowledge and ability, regardless of their religion, for Bustani's aim was to develop love of their country in his students and to instill in them the principles of that love and unity, regardless of the religion or sect to which they belonged. This is also what Samné insisted upon, although at a much later date.[1] In this same vein, al-Shidyaq criticizes the fact that children are taught the psalms in schools, without even understanding them, while their teachers are ignorant of all other branches of knowledge, such as arithmetic, history, geography and even the Arabic language.[2] From this it can be deduced that, like Ishaq, he wanted children to be taught secular, non-religious subjects. Ishaq claimed in his writings not to be opposed to religion, but said that he found it of no use to teach children religion in school instead of science.[3]

Naturally, secularists like al-Shummayyil, Sarruf, and Antun were very clear about their wish to have all teaching in the schools free from any religious influence.[4] Sarruf severely criticizes those universities in the United States whose only criterion for appointing a principal was that he should be a practising Christian minister, even if such a person knew nothing of the science subjects taught in the institution, or was even fanatically opposed to them.[5] He therefore insists that one of the most important roles of the university is to teach objective knowledge, devoid of any religious fanaticism, adding that, unfortunately, this was no longer done by the Syrian Protestant College in Beirut, a reference to the troubles caused by Dr. Lewis's mention of Darwinism in a lecture, as a result of which the teachers and students who supported him were suspended.[6] Julia Tohmi Dimashqiyya also insisted that schools should be free from any sectarian or religious bias, and did not want religion taught in schools.[7]

Even Muslim writers who believed in the importance of religion as a guarantee of morality did not rule out the possibility of replacing it with a secular education. Thus al-Kawakibi writes that the role of religion can be replaced in schools, using textbooks on ethics, economy and history, and even home economics, novels and plays, all of which, he adds, the Muslims lack completely.[8] When writing about the education of women, Amin insists that they should learn the scientific laws of physiology, health, and child psychology,[9] with no mention at all of religion, while Kurd 'Ali sees that true knowledge is that which is free of all political and religious influence. He favoured a quest for knowledge no matter where it was to be found and from whatever viewpoint.[10] This is clearly a purely secular stand, since secularism is against the monopolizing of culture and education by religious institutions. That is why he severely criticizes his contemporaries who believe that knowledge of religion and language is enough.[11] He explains that educational reform in Germany came about when the government took over from the Church the organization, supervision and diffusion of knowledge, after which the Church no longer had anything to do with education and learning.[12]

When Lutfi al-Sayyid and his friends founded the Egyptian University they insisted that its aims were purely scientific, and that it should be free of any political or religious affiliation.[13] Thus, what all these writers have in common is their desire to take education out of the hands of the clergy, sheikhs and political parties and hand it over to secular specialists in the field.

With their belief in the importance and necessity of secular education, how far did these writers adopt the *rational system of thought* on which secularism is founded? Rationalism and the belief in reason are not new to Arabic thought, for the Abbasid Mu'tazilites and later Ibn Rushd, were among the rationalists who depended upon reason in their thought and analyses, and many verses of the Qur'an itself encourage believers to use their reason. These writers appear to have promoted reason and logic in their books, however, not because they were part of their heritage, but in order to combat the superstitions and fossilized reasoning of their contemporaries and also because they were influenced by the ideas about which they had read in the works of the philosophers of the Enlightenment. Their attitude was reinforced by their own experiences of the West. Kurd 'Ali, for example, states clearly:

> The Easterners' spirits and minds were, consciously or unconsciously, influenced by the West, thanks to the knowledge their universities, schools and societies... spread every day, and thanks to what they [i.e. Westerners] had discovered, invented, produced and corrected in the field of science, the new ideas they had propagated and subjects they tackled. Thus, their circumstances changed ours, and our concepts were replaced by theirs, as our ways of thinking... talking and wanting were changed.[14]

The writers under review started with a vehement attack of the *traditional system of education* used in schools, a system that was a reflection of the socio-political establishment built on the absolute authority of those in power; the students had to learn by rote, accepting blindly everything said by the teacher. They were neither taught nor encouraged to think, analyze, discuss and criticize. As has been shown in a previous chapter, these writers believed in the individual's right to freedom of thought, and for them education was a way in which to train people to think for themselves. What they aimed at was the liberation of the individual's reasoning from all authority except that of his/her conscience and reason.

Al-Shidyaq strongly condemned the way in which children were not educated to use their reason. They were taught to read without understanding what they read and he accused both the political and religious rulers of using this as a way of keeping the people stupid and ignorant. Children were also brought up to believe in superstition, demons, ghosts, spirits and the like, something he ridiculed while claiming that it also did much harm. Marrash and, later, Kurd 'Ali also severely criticized[15] these same widespread superstitions and beliefs in magic, djinns, demons and so on, although the Bible often mentions people being possessed by evil spirits and the devil, and the Qur'an repeatedly refers to the existence of the djinn. Comparing education in Europe and the East, al-Shidyaq says that in England, children are taught to think and understand things from earliest childhood, and because their rulers are just, the children grow up to be courageous in thought and deed. By contrast, people in the East fear their unjust rulers as well as their religious leaders, therefore children are brought up in fear, are taught to fear demons, bad spirits and the dark, thus as adults they are only brave because they believe in fate and divine decree.[16]

This same connection between the traditional system of education and despotic rule can be found in the writings of al-Kawakibi. In his book *Taba'i' al-Istibdad*, al-Kawakibi sees that people whose will is constrained and whose hands are tied by despotic rule cannot properly guide and educate children since they live in constant fear. Therefore the greatest disaster in the East is the lack of education based on training the mind to differentiate between things, to explain and convince. Al-Kawakibi believes that enlightenment and knowledge could destroy this fear and are the means of overthrowing tyranny.[17] Unlike the Christian al-Shidyaq, however, al-Kawakibi blamed the tyrannical political rulers alone for the faulty system of education, and not the religious clerics, although they served as the teachers in the Qur'anic schools that were widespread at the time. Could the reason be the tyranny his country suffered from which was his main concern? Or was he was afraid that the rationality and freedom of thought he advocated would not be the sole way to political enlightenment, but would also undoubtedly lead to an analysis of that which was inexplicable and unconvincing in religion?

No such religious constraints faced Marrash and Ishaq who were both greatly influenced by French culture and the secular principles of the French Revolution. Marrash says that it is thanks to their reasoning that the French were able to conquer nature, and reasoning reached new heights thanks to their schools, libraries and museums.[18] These schools developed the mind by teaching science, art and the humanities.[19] Ishaq, too, severely criticizes the way in which children are educated in the East where schools stress learning by rote, forbidding them to think and discuss, even if they wanted to prove something right, killing in them freedom of thought and the capacity to judge, corrupting their minds and thus perpetuating illusions and mistakes.[20] Taking a lesson from Europe and the United States where he saw the beneficial results of compulsory secular education, he insists that this kind of education for boys and girls is one of the government's duties and the main reason for a country's success. This belief was shared by Zaydan, and later by Kurd 'Ali, Lutfi al-Sayyid and Taha Hussein and put into practice by Hussein when he became minister of education.[21]

Amin, on the other hand, criticizes the ignorance of the people in general. He severely attacks all superstitions, seeing in them as a sign of ignorance, and insists that Islam enjoins Muslims to use their powers of reasoning,[22] saying that he himself refuses to believe the truth of any opinion that is not based on sound proof.[23] This, undoubtedly, leads to the deduction that for him the truth is to be found only in science and any other secular branch of knowledge which is based solely on reasoning. This shows the influence of Comte's positivism, in that Amin sees that science is the only valid foundation of truth, and its value is in its usefulness in eliminating the power of the church, introducing constitutional government, liberating the slaves and making radical changes to the status of women:

> The new scientific discoveries in Europe liberated human reason from the power of delusion, assumption and superstition and made reason its own guide, showing it the road it has to follow, a road in which science started investigating everything, criticizing all opinions, only accepting what proved to be for the greatest general good, and culminating in the abolition of the power of the clergy.[24]

It is clear that the knowledge Amin is referring to here is purely secular knowledge. For him, secular sciences such as psychology, anatomy, history, mathematics and natural science were even necessary to properly understand religion and its jurisprudence, for 'all knowledge is one' and aims at obtaining the truth of everything that exists.[25] However, when inciting his countrymen to seek knowledge for the sake of knowledge, for the love of obtaining the truth, he gives as examples the scientists, writers and philosophers of the West,[26] and not those who sought to explain the religious truths, probably because he might have felt that these 'truths' were not always based on reason or sound evidence.

Not surprisingly, knowledge and education were purely secular matters for Zaydan, Antun, al-Shummayyil and Sarruf. Zaydan and Farah Antun severely criticized superstitious beliefs in demons and other such charlatanisms.[27] All four of them insisted on the importance of teaching children to use their reasoning in order to investigate, discuss and critically analyze whatever they were taught, and to be independent and free in their thinking.[28] Moreover, all four of them, and particularly al-Shummayyil, were undoubtedly influenced by Huxley's complete belief in scientific rationalism, refusing any conclusions that were not demonstrated or demonstrable. The spectacular discoveries and inventions in the field of science in their day made them believe science to be the sole judge of truth. Thus, Sarruf writes that had scientists not analyzed and investigated what were thought to be scientific truths, people would still be believing in many falsehoods.[29] Sarruf's main merit may have been to have helped, through his publication al-*Muqtataf*, to introduce the Arabs to new inventions and discoveries in the field of science and technology and to scientific reasoning that is independent of all other factors. His student Isma'il Mazhar says that by introducing the Arabs to the theory of evolution, for example, Sarruf paved the way to eliminating the ancient thinking of the East,[30] a role also played by Zaydan's *Hilal* and Antun's *Jami'a*. Both Antun and al-Shummayyil say that those who use their reason to investigate, discuss and form independent judgments cannot possibly be fanatics.[31] On the contrary, they urge people never to accept anything without closely examining it first to make sure of its veracity. For example, Antun says that a closer examination of history shows that there is no such thing as history, merely different opinions that a person should examine in order to see which one is more likely than the others to be correct, with no proof of any being really true.[32] al-Shummayyil says that science progressed only because people refused to accept any preconceived ideas, otherwise they would have claimed that everything science mentions exists in religion, and whatever religion does not mention they do not need.[33] Although he realizes that the intellect is not really free but works according to certain laws, he insists that these laws are not those of religion and faith but are part of the general laws that govern nature as a whole. Just as nature follows the law of evolution, so the intellect changes of necessity, the result of this change being improvement. This improvement, he says, could not take place if the intellect were governed by an illusion or a teaching that rejects all change.[34] This undoubtedly refers to religions that are unchanging and that he also considered to be an illusion. Al-Shummayyil goes overboard, however, when he attacks all the literature, philosophy, law and linguistics that were currently being taught, claiming that they were useless or harmful, and seeking to replace them with the study of science and technology. In his opinion, the natural sciences, which are 'the mother of all real sciences and should be the mother of all human studies' were the only worthwhile subjects to be taught. Once natural science was introduced in all teaching, he believed all the branches of learning would become properly understood and taught.[35] This shows to what extent al-Shummayyil believed in reason and reason alone, since natural science is based on reason and whatever derives from it, although he retracted later on and explained that he did not want to abolish the study of the humanities, but only meant to criticize his contemporaries' study of nothing else.[36]

Bahithat al-Badiya also repeatedly criticized ignorant women's belief in magic, spells, charms and demons,[37] which shows how widespread these superstitions were. She also urged the acquisition of European knowledge and methods in teaching and education, and although she did not specify the methods to which she was referring, it can easily be deduced that they were those based on reason, for the knowledge she urged her compatriots to acquire was that of science. Unlike Amin and his Christian contemporaries, Bahithat al-Badiya advocated a cautious, limited adoption of only that which is necessary and useful, Egyptianizing it to suit the local customs and lifestyle. 'For the sake of honour and independence, we should not merge with the West and thus loose to the West's formidable and overwhelming power whatever little power we have.[38] Here, too, she never explained what she deemed 'necessary and useful,' though she was probably referring to knowledge and science that could eliminate the backwardness of her society.

Kurd 'Ali and Nazira Zayn al-Din did not have Bahithat al-Badiya's reservations, although their countries were under Western occupation just like hers. Nazira says that truth cannot be really arrived at unless one is allowed to search for it without any hindrance and no matter what method is used.[39] Kurd 'Ali attacked the methods of learning practiced by the Arabs, and as minister of education he tried to impose modern methods of education, criticizing the ancient ways of teaching in the Qur'anic schools (kuttab).[40] Like Amin before him he pointed out that even the study of Muslim jurisprudence was built on methods that did not improve the intellect, for the jurisprudents memorized the Qur'an without understanding it, and without investigating the Hadith, analyzing and criticizing it in order to separate the authentic from the false.[41] When visiting Europe he admired Anglo Saxon education because, besides the curriculum, it teaches children hard work and to depend on themselves,[42] and he saw that no where did learning and education spread as it did in Saxony and North Germany where Protestantism appeared and with it freedom of research and investigation.[43] Thus he also highly praised Paris 'because she was among the first to extol reason, even deify it, preferring reason to everything else and honoring the men of reason among her citizens,' and because she is the city of Descartes, Voltaire, Comte, Denis Diderot (d.1784), Simon, Montesquieu, Victor Hugo (d.1885), Blaise Pascal (d.1662), Renan and hundreds like them. Here he expresses his great admiration for thinkers who were not only secular, but even atheists, insisting that in their research the Westerners were under nobody's influence, unlike the people of the East,[44] insinuating that these were under the influence of the religious clerics and/or politicians. Therefore he felt that adopting Western civilization which is based on rationality and free thought was the only way to advance and, contrary to Bahithat al-Badiya, the only way to defend his nationality and safe-guard it,[45] since progress led to independence and political freedom. As early as 1909 he declares that if people acted according to the law of reason and profited from the experience of other nations, the material and moral power of their country will attain that of a country which is really alive.[46]

Dimashqiyya, who taught for many years before marrying and founding her periodical al-Mar'a al-Jadida, also worked to change teaching methods in schools and ensure that they were based on the quest for true knowledge.[47] The way to seek true knowledge obviously meant to her free, secular thought, independent and critical rational judgment, perseverance, objectivity and all the other characteristics of research that make true knowledge possible.

Al-Sayyid and Taha Hussein were more concerned with changing antiquated methods of teaching since they both held responsible positions in the field of education, and both believed that a sound, proper education was the basis that would enable Egypt to gain its freedom and independence.[48] Therefore they, too, severely criticized the traditional, methods of teaching used in the Qur'anic and other schools in which the students learn by rote, repeating other people's thoughts, never being encouraged or trained to think for themselves, understand and have personal, independent ideas, or be creative in any way.[49] As a result, al-Sayyid criticized the ignorant sheikhs who only inspire fear in the children they teach, as well as the teachers in foreign schools who educate the children to be submissive, stifling their personalities and suppressing any freedom.[50] The government, he feels, is equally unfit to take over responsibility for education because it would force its policy and politics on the students. Instead of educating them to be free, independent thinkers, it would train them to be obedient, submissive government employees and civil servants.[51] As a result of this attitude, when, in 1932, the ministry decided unilaterally to remove Taha Hussein from the university, al-Sayyid resigned from its presidency.[52] This hostility towards government interference might have been influenced by Herbert Spencer's *The Proper Sphere of Government*. Al-Sayyid therefore advocates handing over the education of children to specialists in sociology and psychology,[53] both of these branches being modern and secular. This same hostility towards government interference is also voiced by Hussein but only regarding the university curriculum.[54]

It is thus obvious that the teaching methods advocated by al-Sayyid and Hussein are purely secular Western methods based on free, independent and rational thinking, by which the teachers guide the students to discover and deduce truths without imposing any preconceived ideas upon them, and developing in their students the desire to read, research, discover and form their own personal independent opinions, no matter what its consequences.[55] For Hussein believes that:

> in every civilized country it is the rational people who are the source of its real strength because they are the ones who think, evaluate matters, plan and manage them. They formulate the ideas that are put into practice in various fields. This is what happens in every country that enjoys freedom, no matter how small a measure of freedom there is.[56]

Unlike Kurd 'Ali, who completely avoided the subject, Hussein blamed the religious faith of the Muslims, although not Islam itself, for suppressing freedom of thought and causing his country's backwardness at the time.[57]

Hussein, therefore, explicitly insists on introducing European study courses and education methods in order to shape young people in the European mould, with European minds, thought patterns and value judgements.[58] When setting the curricula for schools, he insisted on the need to teach certain compulsory subjects, such as history, geography, Arabic and Egypt's political, social and civic system, all of them secular subjects, while he repeated that religion need not be compulsory and could be left to the parents to deal with.[59] In his day, al-Azhar trained Arabic teachers for schools, but Hussein considered that al-Azhar should merely become a centre for religious studies and Arabic should be taught by secular teachers who would apply modern language teaching methods. The teaching of religion in schools could be optional, but he insists that Latin and Greek be compulsory subjects in all state-run schools because they are necessary tools of learning.[60] Realizing that it was useless to acquire Western scientific knowledge without its philosophical origins and spirit, Hussein explained that they sprang from Greek and Latin philosophy, since they contain the rational philosophical principles of correct thought. Hussein's advocacy of the teaching of not only secular subjects but even pagan philosophy, at the expense of religion, shows how westernized and secular his mindset had become. Thus, the leaders of thought who were the subject of his book *Qadat al-Fikr* (The Leaders of Thought) were Homer, Socrates, Plato, Aristotle, Alexander the Great and Julius Caesar.

When he pointed out that adopting the European learning, education and mentality does not mean casting Islam aside, for in the past Muslims adopted Persian and Greek learning and civilization without any decrease in the influence and power of Islam,[61] it is clear that even when opting for purely Western secular methods of education and curricula he sought to link this philosophy with his Islamic heritage.

For all their faith in reason, did these writers believe its power to be limitless? They all realized to what extent knowledge had progressed, and even as conservative a secularist as Bahithat al-Badiya, for example, insisted that knowledge and learning were limitless, while Hussein pointed out that because research in all branches of science and knowledge is endless, everything they contain is subject to change and open to more research.[62]

Only the purely secular writers Antun and al-Shummayyil believed in the limitless power of reason. This is a secular stand, since according to theology, human reasoning is finite and can never fathom all the secrets of the universe or understand God's wisdom. Both these writers not only asserted that there is no end to knowledge or progress, but also that 'in these days the mind knows no limit to its quest, and if a limit is set it will choke and kill it.' If obstacles are put in the mind's way it will dismiss them completely, no matter how strong they are, with the result that some principles disappear, in order to be replaced by new ones.[63] Both writers thus insinuate that neither religion nor anything else can limit the freedom and power of reason, as the progress of science and knowledge has proved.

Other writers, whether Muslim or Christian, admitted that reason could not fathom the essence of the soul or the secrets of God's wisdom. Marrash, al-Kawakibi, Amin, Zaydan, Kurd 'Ali and Sarruf all made this admission when they dealt with religion, but other writers avoided the subject completely. Hussein also stated that he believed the power of reason to be limited and therefore incapable of fathoming the miracles that God worked through His prophets.[64] Although he explicitly states this in his later Islamic works, there is a trace of this thought even in his courageous book *Fi al-Shi'r al-Jahili* . For example, he refers to the Sura of the Djinn in the Qur'an which tells of the djinn who listened to the Prophet and believed his message. Hussein does not question the existence of these djinn in the same way that he had questioned the historical existence of Ibrahim and Isma'il.[65] Hussein first studied at al-Azhar, and no matter how secular his thought had become, the effect of that early religious education appears to have left a trace.

Another principle that enabled Western science to progress was that knowledge was often sought for its own sake, regardless of the practical applications that might result therefrom. Amin, Bahithat al-Badiya and Dimashqiyyah were among the few writers to insist on the fact that knowledge could be sought merely for its own sake, regardless of any practical purpose.[66] Antun, al-Shummayyil and Hussein concurred with this view, while Antun shows great admiration for a French thinker who said that:

> the only aim of science is the search for truth for truth's sake regardless of its practical results, whether these be good or bad. I believe that anyone who is influenced in his research and in the results of his research, whether it be for patriotic, religious or moral reasons, does not deserve to have a place in the great institution of science which needs integrity and honesty more than proficiency.[67]

Taha Hussein writes that knowledge should be sought for its own sake and not to gain a means of livelihood or a better standard of living.[68] In fact, he insisted that science could only exist, progress and yield the practical results that it had if knowledge were sought for its own sake.[69]

Did the other writers realize that real scientific knowledge and its mentality cannot be acquired and developed unless knowledge is sought for the sake of knowledge, regardless of its practical aims? Be that as it may, the sorry plight and backwardness of their respective countries drove all these secular writers to care more for the practical results of education and knowledge than for their mere intrinsic value. Marrash states clearly that knowledge and science are useless unless they are put into practice.[70] Much later, when al-Sayyid participated in founding the new Egyptian university, he wrote that its aim was to make new discoveries in scientific fields that could be usefully applied in exploiting the forces and resources of nature.[71] This, too, might be a reason for their being influenced by Comte's positivism in which education and knowledge were supposed to pave the way for social and political reform. Thus, whether they were Christians such as Bustani, al-Shidyaq, Marash, Sarruf, Zaydan and Dimashqiyya, or Muslims such as Amin, Kurd 'Ali and al-Sayyid,[72] they all insisted that education was a basic factor in improving their compatriots' morality, without referring to religion as also playing a major role. Marrash, for example, writes that through the power of reason the French had 'vanquished the kingdom of falsehood and error',[73] while Amin insists that without knowledge, morality could exist but would not be stable. He gives as examples and proofs of the close link between morality and knowledge the fact that in the enlightened West, a scientist gives up the comforts and pleasures of life, preferring to solve problems and understand causes; while a rich and powerful statesman deprives himself of rest in order to find ways to improve his nation; and a rich man gives thousands of pounds to charity or good works, the profit from which goes to his country or to the good of mankind.[74]

If they believed that religion, too, could also be a factor in improving morals, as was shown in a previous chapter, they found no role for it in creating political and social awareness or helping towards socio-political improvement. Like Comte, they saw that this was the role of education and knowledge alone. If people are educated, writes al-Shidyaq, they will know their rights and duties,[75] while Marrash, al-Kawakibi, Samné, Sarruf, al-Shummayyil, Zaydan, Antun, Kurd 'Ali, Bahithat al-Badiya, Dimashqiyya, and especially Ishaq, al-Sayyid and Hussein believed that modern knowledge and education were the only way to create social and political awareness in people, make them reject obsolete customs and traditions, tyranny and injustice, in order to attain their liberty, freedom and independence.[76] Hussein writes explicitly:

> We cannot aspire to real independence unless we have the freedom of thought that foreigners enjoy in their own countries and unless we apply modern European methods of education and learning, and this can only be done in an atmosphere of freedom of thought and tolerance.[77]

This spirit of tolerance which, in their opinion, only knowledge and education could instill, was regarded by both Hussein and al-Sayyid as a precondition for national unity between the Muslims and Copts in Egypt. Al-Sayyid asserts that it is education that spreads the spirit of tolerance in personal and political matters. It should have two aims in Egypt, namely, to restore to the Egyptians the cohesive society they had lost during long years of tyranny, and to gain the science and knowledge which would enable them to compete with others in their country on an equal footing in scientific, technical and economic matters.[78] It will be seen that no mention is made of the religious preaching of either social virtues or the spirit of tolerance. It was mainly the Lebanese Christians who insisted on the importance of spreading education and knowledge as the *sine qua non* for creating a spirit of tolerance and unity, since their country bore the scars of intolerance and religious fanaticism. That is what Bustani, Zaydan, al-Shummayyil, Antun, Samné and Dimashqiyya stressed, for only by educating people could fanaticism disappear, the people unite and the nation progress, writes Zaydan.[79]

It will thus be seen that most of these writers could not separate scientific truth from political and practical concerns. Al-Kawakibi, Amin, Kurd 'Ali and even Hussein, all of whom were Muslims, refused to separate rational principles from Islam. As long as intellectual activity remained hidebound by political, religious and even practical considerations, a truly scientific mentality was out of reach. What the secular writers were really advocating when they urged the introduction of modern education and knowledge, was progress and change, as opposed to pure scientific research. Their recognition of the underdevelopment and backwardness of their countries is what provoked most of their writing. The problem of this underdevelopment will be discussed in the next chapter.

CHAPTER SEVEN

Change, Progress and Civilization

It has been clear from the previous chapters that the greatest concerns of the writers who are the subject of this book were the political weakness and the cultural, economic and social backwardness of the countries in which they lived. They sought through their action and writings to find the means that were required to achieve change and progress.

Two Muslim writers from two different generations realized that the deterioration of Islamic culture was partially to blame for their country's sorry plight. Al-Kawakibi believed that the Muslim decline was due to the confusion caused by the variety of opinions expressed by the various imams as well as their excessive rigour in religious matters, just as this same excessive rigour had caused the decline of the Jews, Catholics and Greek Orthodox in the past. It was the zealotry that had led to Protestantism which eliminated the additions and severity that are to be found nowhere in the Gospels.[1] This caused him to say that 'Easterners do not think of the near future, as if all their concerns were concentrated on the hereafter.'[2] Obviously, it was not Islam itself he blamed, but its imams and ignorant, stupid *'ulama*. He insisted on the need to introduce reforms similar to those that Christianity had experienced, reforms that would eliminate all the false ideas that had been added to Islam, restoring it to its pure origins.[3] This, he considered, was the way to progress. Likewise, Kurd 'Ali believed that if the Muslims studied their religion in the same way that it had been taught at the dawn of Islam they would overcome their backwardness which was caused by the ignorant, stagnant *'ulama*.[4]

In their opinion, one outcome of this misunderstanding of Islam was an exaggerated dependence on destiny. People believed that their present plight was their fate, about which nothing could be done. This blind dependence upon destiny was condemned by both Muslims and Christians, as has been shown previously.

There is a difference, however, between the Christian criticism of the reliance on destiny with regard to progress and civilization and that of a

Muslim. Kurd 'Ali shows that belief in fate has a positive side, since it was one of the principles of his religion. Thus he says that, thanks to their belief in destiny, the Muslims of the past were able to face death and conquer territory, but they had never exhibited an exaggerated reliance on destiny, for they used reason in their interpretations of the holy texts, and their belief in fate never prevented them from working and searching for the cause of the situations they faced.[5] A blind belief in fate and complete dependence on destiny and nothing else had become one of the causes of Arab weakness and backwardness.[6]

In blaming the backwardness of the Muslim countries on the misinterpretation of Islam by ignorant imams and *'ulama,* al-Kawakibi and Kurd 'Ali were acting as mouthpieces for Muslim reformists and other socio-political activists who believed that by applying the true teachings of Islam and reviving a distant past the present social and political ills could be overcome and the lost glory of that past could thus be restored. They believed that Islam represented the whole of history and was valid for any society, since it is God's revealed word. None of these revivalists admitted that there was a relationship between religion and the circumstances that gave rise to it.

The rational principles underlying secularism, however, made some Muslim writers realize that clinging to or reviving the past was an illusion, as was their belief that this past was a social and political Utopia.

The Christians were naturally more reticent than the Muslims in their attack on the attempts to cling to a past of which Islam formed an integral part. They merely voiced generally critical remarks without going into any details that might provoke their Muslim compatriots. Ishaq, for example, only criticizes the way in which people clung to their customs and traditions, believing the old ways to be perfect, and, as a result, remaining backward and stagnant, rejecting all the new ideas which were the reason for the progress of the West.[7] For all Zaydan's admiration of the traditional Arab virtues, he sees that they were no longer compatible with a modern civilization based on equal rights and duties, rather than on the traditional Arab virtues of generosity, forgiveness, clemency, munificence, undauntedness and succour.[8] Shibli al-Shummayyil was more direct and aggressive, demanding: 'Of what use to civilization is it to have our interest centered on investigating a dead past and a history that is full of contradictions and, for the most part, full of lies?'[9] Here al-Shummayyil not only refuses to revive the past, but also insists on eliminating from it the halo of sanctity with which the Muslim revivalists endowed it, showing that what they imagined and pictured to be their past was nothing more than an illusion. Without actually saying this overtly, Dimashqiyya shows that even religious beliefs are not embraced out of faith and conviction but only because they are passed down by the forefathers, and those who do not believe in what the forefathers said are immediately condemned and accused of atheism. She therefore urges people to free themselves from all traditions, received opinion and other social fetters that are futile and harmful and are handed down from generation to generation, and advocates forming independent beliefs and principles.[10]

Al-Kawakibi merely sought to eliminate the misinterpretations of Islam which ignorant imams and *ulama* had introduced in the past in their quest for fame. He believed that the free, enlightened contemporary thinkers could not be compared to those writers of the past Dark Ages.[11] The change he sought was therefore limited and within the framework of Islam. Although writing a generation later, Nazira Zayn al-Din still mainly criticized the way in which past misinterpretations of Islam were stubbornly maintained, pointing out that the ancients, with their limited understanding, could not properly grasp the essence of religion which modern enlightened minds are more apt to do, by using reason, freedom of thought and respect for others.[12] She blames the *ulama* who cling to imitation for having caused the East to become stagnant, because they 'deadened our thoughts and drugged us with their invented myths which have concealed the light of our religion...The principles of true Islam are lost today.'[13] For her, as for al-Kawakibi and Kurd 'Ali, a return to the true Islam was guarantee enough for liberating the Muslims from their backwardness.

Brown summarized the problem as representing 'a tension between principles of stability and of flexibility, between the authority of the past and the exigencies of the present'[14] Yet it was the exigencies of this present that made all the writers under review insist on the necessity for change, regardless of what they considered the best means for such change to be. This was not new in Arabic thought. Before them, the Egyptian Tahtawi and the Tunisian Kheir al-Din were two among many who had sought change, fully realizing the backwardness of the Muslim East compared with the European countries they had visited.[15] Even earlier, Ibn Khaldun (d.1406) had drawn attention to the cycles of history.[16] The philosophers of the Enlightenment and Comte also strongly influenced the writers under review and encouraged them in their pursuit of change for the purpose of progress.

Qasim Amin was much more liberal and secular in his attitude towards the past, even though he was a generation older than Kurd 'Ali and Nazira. Without going to al-Shummayyil's extreme, he rejected not only the previous misinterpretations by the *ulama*, but the whole Islamic civilization which he criticized as being far from perfect and which he considered to be unfit for the present.

> We do not want to deny the merits of our forefathers, but we do not want
> to cheat ourselves by imagining that their civilization was so perfect that it
> cannot be surpassed.[17]

He then goes on to prove, using examples from history, that Muslim
civilization, for all its merits, was far from perfect. Throughout its history, the
Muslims had suffered from tyranny and internal strife; morally, their society
was tainted by depravity, hypocrisy, debauchery and other vices, from which
he concludes that Muslims should fight the habit of clinging to the past,
because this leads to underdevelopment and regression.[18] Amin realized the
difference between Islam as a religion and historical, sociological Islam,
therefore, unlike al-Kawakibi, Kurd 'Ali and, occasionally, Nazira, he did not
ignore the relationship between religion and the circumstances that gave rise
to it, his sole aim being to improve the society in which he lived. With this in
mind, he looked objectively at his past history and liberated himself from all
preconceived ideas of an ideal past to be revived. That is why Farah Antun
shows great admiration for Amin's courage since 'he seemed to put the
scientific, social and literary ideal above the religious ideal' when he pointed
out the ills in Islam's past history, urging his countrymen to seek perfection in
the future, not in the past.[19]

A generation later, these writers still had to contend with that same
idealization of a past which the Muslims wanted to revive, seeing in it a remedy
for all their ills. When Kurd 'Ali visited Europe in 1913 and saw with his own
eyes the great difference between Europe and his country, he could not but
criticize the Muslims' boasting about their past and considering it an ideal for
progress. 'Unfortunately we want to live in the twentieth century the way they
lived in the tenth, and to our misfortune we believe that remembering our past
and ancient glory is enough to enable us to forever lead a good and reasonable
life.'[20] Attacking his stagnant contemporaries who clung to the past, never
bothering to understand or acquire anything new, he cites as an example their
insisting upon seeing the moon with the naked eye in order to determine the
beginning and end of the fast of Ramadan, instead of depending upon
astronomy which could determine the dates a long time in advance. 'Truly we
are stagnant to the point of ridicule,' he says, 'neither ridding ourselves quickly
enough of that which is ancient and obsolete, nor adopting that which is new
and useful.[21] Here Kurd 'Ali differentiates between Islam and its history, which
contradicts his having claimed that applying the true religion of the dawn of
Islam was a guarantee of progress.

The first steps the Muslims had taken in liberating themselves from the
burden of the past were continued by Hussein and al-Sayyid. In accordance
with Comte's positivism, the former refused to accept that the past is better

than the present, and that time regresses instead of advancing. In an objective evaluation of this past, he says that the ancients were neither better nor worse than his contemporaries, but they made more mistakes 'because reason in those days was not as developed as it is today, and the methods of research and criticism that we have now had not been discovered.'[22] al-Sayyid agrees that the present state of regression is due to their having clung to the ideas of their 'worthy ancestors'. Therefore the only issue left to them is to do away with the ideas, customs and values that were the cause of this backwardness, and to start changing and progressing so as to be able to compete in the arena of civilization.[23]

For the Christian writers, change was a normal process that was taken for granted. The Darwinist al-Shummayyil sumarized their attitude when he declared that the laws of society were like those of nature, always evolving and progressing, even if they were sometimes stationary or even regress, although civilization was progressing faster than it ever did in the past.[24] The Muslims, too, not only insisted on the necessity of change, but also considered it unavoidable, as can be deduced from what has been quoted before from the writings of Kurd 'Ali, 'Abd al-Raziq, Hussein, al-Sayyid and Nazira. Yet even al-Kawakibi believed that only the principles of religion should remain unchanged, whereas everything else should change according to time and circumstance.[25] What that 'everything else' was he did not specify, but he was probably referring to social customs and traditions, or the Islamic tents that covered worldly matters and which had been interpreted, or according to him, misinterpreted, by imams in the past, still believing that a correct interpretation of them would prove Islam to be fit for all times and places.

Qasim Amin, who was of the same generation, was more explicit. In his earlier book, *Tahrir al-Mar'a,* Amin was still writing cautiously, avoiding any conflict with Islam. He thus proved the necessity for change by basing himself on Islam itself. Just as Islam had caused people to abandon the beliefs and values of their forefathers, thus, too, he says, contemporary Muslims should realize that the only things that are not susceptible to change are the Qur'an and the Prophetic tradition. Otherwise, all the traditions and procedures should change with the changing times and social conditions.[26] He then asks: 'Can the Muslim contradict God's laws of creation, God who has made change a basis for life and progress, rather than stagnation and inflexibility which are characteristics of death and backwardness?'[27] In his second book, *al-Mar'a al-Jadida,* he becomes more radical and no longer relies upon Islam as much as he does on Western secularism. Even in his first book, he had cited Darwin's theory of evolution and survival of the fittest as well as Edmond Demolins' (d.1907) *The Secret of National Progress* and *The Secret of the Anglo-Saxons' Progress* which had been translated into Arabic by Fathi Zaghlul (d.1914). Both books were very popular in Egypt at the time.[28] In Darwin's theory Amin had seen the reason for Europe's strength and progress. He thus states in his second book:

> Change is the law of the Europeans' progress. Anyone who studies history since the previous century will see that they have changed everything in their lives: their government, language, sciences, arts, laws, dress and customs. And all these are still subject to the criticism of scholars among them and liable to further change from time to time.[29]

Although Bahithat al-Badiya also agreed that all ideas and customs change with time, and that people should not cling to the old ways, she also insisted on making a choice, stating that only harmful customs and habits should change. Of these harmful customs she only cites those connected with marriage,[30] probably because they were the ones from which she herself had suffered the most, not realizing that all ideas, values, customs and traditions are interlinked, and that changing one involves a change in all.

Nazira insisted that change is necessary and progress inevitable, whether one likes it or not, for one cannot prevent new ideas emerging in science and society.[31] And she became more specific when assuring that:

> ... every belief, religion, custom, tradition and dress code has evolved with time according to the development of reason and understanding, the loftiness of ambition and resolution, and the strength of will. This is what has brought humanity to its present level of civilization and perfection.[32]

In her mention of religion she did not want to give the impression of having deviated from Islam. Therefore she adds, like Amin before her, that Islam itself has ordained change in matters regarding human relations to suit what is best for people and changing times.[33] Just like al-Kawakibi and Bahithat al-Badiya, she makes a distinction, here, between the unchanging and unchangeable basic principles of Islam, and the verses that deal with worldly matters. Thus we see that for these Muslim writers change and progress had to remain within the confines of Islam, and that their secularism remained within their religious, and sometimes historical, heritage. Yet, in their reinterpretation of their religion, it is clear that even they were unconsciously influenced by Western secularism.

No matter how these writers differed as to the causes of underdevelopment, the means of reform and the paths to progress, they all agreed that *education, knowledge* and *science* were a *sine qua non*, since they believed that ignorance was one of the main reasons for their backwardness. In this, too, they were undoubtedly influenced by the philosophers of the Enlightenment. Marrash states clearly that the East became backward when 'reason was murdered...until people's minds sank in the sea of ignorance.'[34]

In his introduction to his encyclopedia, the first volume of which was published in 1876, Bustani states that the reason for his having undertaken this expensive and arduous task was his belief that the Arabs needed it in order for their countries to 'develop whatever leads to their evolution, civilization, wealth, affluence, science and knowledge,' so that they could become able to provide for themselves what they now depend on developed countries to provide them with, for they themselves lack the modern means of mastering agriculture, industry, commerce and other branches of modern civilization.[35] This encyplopedia was the first to be written in Arabic, it occupied him till his death and was then continued by his sons, but never finished. It is full of articles on science, medicine, engineering and the liberal ideas of the West, which shows how far he believed the acquisition of Western knowledge and its liberal concepts to be the basis for his countrymen's progress.

Perhaps the writer who was most strongly influenced by French culture and the Enlightenment was Marrash. He repeatedly asserts that civilization was the result of knowledge and science,[36] and his symbolic novel, *Ghabat al-Haq*, shows that only through reason and science can progress be achieved.

It was not only the Christians of this generation who firmly believed that progress and civilization depended on the acquisition of Western knowledge. Amin insisted that perfect civilization is based on science, and since Islamic civilization reached its zenith in the past, and Europe went on to develop science, the Islamic past cannot be taken as a model to be emulated.[37] He considers the only treatment for the ills of his society lay in a knowledge of all the branches of European civilization and its principles, for 'no social reform can take place if it is not based on modern science.'[38] It will be seen that Amin does not call for the adoption of European civilization and its sciences alone, but its principles as well. The previous chapter had shown his belief in reason as the sole guarantee of truth, proving that he had accepted the secular philosophical attitude and principles which made these sciences possible, and that he was convinced that progress was impossible without them. For a Muslim of the turn of the nineteenth century to take such a stand shows how big a step towards secularism some writers had taken.

This advocacy of secularism was not a problem for the Christians Zaydan, Sarruf, al-Shummayyil and Antun. They all agreed that progress depended solely on the adoption of European science and its values.[39] Both al-Shummayyil and Antun stated clearly that religious observance was a handicap to progress. Al-Shummayyil, for example, states that if a society had a less developed system of science and medicine, the reason was religion and the moral teachings of the past that had affected the laws and systems of that society and influenced the people.[40] He asserts that it was the liberation of thought in Europe that was the reason for its scientific, industrial, agricultural and economic progress.[41] As a devout believer in the absolute value of science, he adds that it was only when science developed and spread, especially after the theory of evolution became accepted, that Europe progressed.[42] Through his belief in education and science, al-Shummayyil deduced that another condition existed to enable society to evolve and progress. Egotism, he says, is a natural instinct but the more educated a person is the more he realizes that his happiness depends on co-operation with others. Co-operation is the only way to improve civilization, and co-operation can only be achieved if the people accept conduct that improves their dealings with each other, and this in turn can only happen if they know their rights and responsibilities, something that can only be discovered through true science.[43] As a physician, he compares a developed society in which its members cooperate with a living body in which even the smallest organ functions in its own interest while simultaneously working in the interest of the whole, while the whole also works for the good of each part. Since man is intelligent and can control his environment, thanks to science, co-operation is able to replace the struggle for existence that is to be found in nature.[44] Yet al-Shummayyil contradicts himself and his belief in co-operation when he applies to society the theory of struggle for existence and survival of the fittest, and as a result sometimes defends wars since their outcome will prove that only the fittest deserve to conquer.[45]

Antun disagrees with this perspective, believing that Darwin's theory only applies to nature because what counts in nature is physical strength, whereas in society it is intelligence that counts. Therefore society cannot do without scientists, since it is they who guard and preserve order and try and teach the meaning of love, kindness and harmony to those who fight each other for material things. Like Huxley, who considered science to be the new religion, Antun says that it was scientists who brought a new religion into this world after the guardians of the old religions had become corrupt and false, and it is thanks to science and its discoveries that agriculture, industry and commerce developed.[46] In this he is clearly influenced by Comte and Renan as well, especially when he states that 'once nations have become civilized their progress does not depend on religion but on science,' and heathen nations such as the Japanese, who pursued science and the natural laws, have became more civilized than nations that follow the precepts of the New Testament and the Qur'an without pursuing science.[47] Tracing the slow progress of civilization, he writes in a completely Comtian vein:

In the beginning, science was weak and religion was the influential factor in conquering territory, propagating good and fighting evil. But when societies developed, they saw that religion was no longer enough to unite a nation, and that, in addition to unity, order and organization were required, and these could not be implemented by faith and goodness alone, but needed practical virtues as well, based on various sciences and arts. It was then that science sought to wrest power from religion. After a long and bitter struggle between them, science triumphed, thanks to the wonderful inventions and discoveries of great men who alleviated the misery of mankind and increased their well-being and comfort.[48]

Thus, Antun clearly believes that science and knowledge are the way to progress in all fields, political, social as well as moral. This shows that he considered society to be a whole, consting of interdependent parts in which changing one entailed changing them all. He and al-Shummayyil were among the few to realize that underdevelopment was due to a combination of various causes, and that the elimination of all of them through science and its principles was the way to progress. This can also be deduced from al-Shummayyil's statement that changing people's thoughts and all that results from them and is based on them might lead to the invalidation of the whole social system.[49] That is why he believed that change should come gradually through evolution which would be the result of the people's desire and acceptance of change. Although revolutions are sometimes necessary, they would only have positive results if they expressed the people's will, so that in fact they are the result of a slow process of evolution.[50]

Kurd 'Ali's attitude towards progress contains contradictions which might be due to the fact that he wrote in different periods. After the French occupation of Syria, he wrote that if Muslims were to study and apply Islam correctly, they would overcome their backwardness, as was shown above. While Syria was still under Ottoman rule, however, he had repeatedly insisted that if the Arabs wanted to progress they would have to learn Western science. He claimed that the history of the European countries as well as that of Japan proved that their progress was due to the minds that guided, created, invented and planned, and that Egypt's progress began when it started following in the footsteps of the West, thanks to the European scholars and those Egyptians who studied at Western universities.[51] However, since he believed in the complete separation of the domain of reason and science from that of faith, he did not raise the question of how Western scientific knowledge might conflict with his belief in Islam, although he seems to have felt that underlying Western scientific knowledge and research were moral and intellectual principles that differed basically from those prevalent in the East:

> The Westerner kills animals and might expose human beings and even himself to danger in order to advance science and inventions. Western civilization knows no mercy when aiming at the advance of science which will benefit mankind, whereas an Easterner might kill his brother for a trifling matter but would never put his life in danger for the sake of some great deed.[52]

Here he voices his admiration for secular values that have nothing to do with religious principles such as mercy, but he naturally avoids alluding to other values since they might conflict with the essential principles of religion although they were undoubtedly at the base of the West's scientific progress.

Considering Hussein's strong faith in the importance of education, it is not surprising that religion plays no part in his belief that 'culture, education and learning are the source of a country's civilization, strength and wealth.'[53] Comte's positivism, with its belief that intellectual and scientific progress are the bases of society's evolution, is clear here, too. Hussein therefore asserts that the whole human race is capable of progress, and that life in a democratic system is forever changing and evolving, both materially and spiritually.[54] For Hussein, this progress clearly depends on 'following the path of the Europeans so as to be equal partners in civilization, in its good and evil, its sweetness and bitterness, what can be loved or hated, what can be praised or blamed.'[55] Unlike Bahithat al-Badiya, Zaydan, Kurd 'Ali and al-Sayyid who believed that one could pick and choose from Western civilization, selecting only that which was good and/or useful,[56] Hussein rightly considers civilization to be a unit in which the material aspects cannot be separated from the intellectual, emotional or spiritual factors that created it and caused its progress,. He believed that the only way for Egypt to progress was by emulating this situation, 'to learn the way the Europeans learn, to feel the way they feel, judge the way they judge, work the way they work and understand life the way they do.'[57] Hussein does not deny the religious element in civilization, but he stresses the secular basis and outlook. This, too, is evident in what he believes is the drive to ensure such progress, i.e. the Promethian spirit which was the reason for all that Europe achieved and was still achieving, the eternal dissatisfaction with what had been achieved hitherto and the belief in man's limitless capacity to reach unheard-of goals. 'Fertile unrest and anxiety are at the base of all productive progress, whether in our intellectual or in our material life.'[58] This is an expression of a completely secular faith in man's ambition and capacity that has nothing to do with the resignation and contentedness with one's lot encouraged by religion.

Al-Sayyid also demonstrates a completely secular attitude when he jeers at the people of Bukhara who, in order to repel a Russian attack, resorted to prayers and reciting the Hadith, naturally to no avail, not realizing that every effect had a cause, and that there were specific means by which to attain a goal, and that weapons and power are the only means of self-defence.[59] Thus it is not religion, but logical, scientific thought and action that are necessary in order to face life's tribulations; in other words, learning and education. In this respect, al-Sayyid's approach is similar to that of Hussein for both insisted that progress was inevitable, and that learning and education were the way forward to progress and development, although the results were not immediately visible because a nation's progress is never a matter of fate or chance, but the result of struggle and hard work in order to acquire the knowledge and education which would permit the nation to compete in life.[60] This learning and education could be acquired from Europe, for

> In our present situation we need to adopt European civilization and imitate that which is useful, and with time what we imitate will become egyptianized and become part of our language, religion and morals, just as the civilization which the Arabs took over from the Persians and Greeks became stamped with their characteristics and became a Muslim civilization.[61]

Hussein had avoided the problem of egyptianizion by trying to prove in his book *Mustaqbal al-Thaqafa fi Misr* (The Future of Culture in Egypt) that Egypt had always been part of Europe, a theory al-Sayyid obviously disagreed with. That is why al-Sayyid also realised that since the methods of education change like everything else, he agreed with Bahithat al-Badiya that of the European methods of education only those which suited Egypt should be chosen. Since 'we in Egypt are Europe's pupils, we have to understand all their methods of education so as to choose the ones which suit us best.'[62]

On the other hand, al-Sayyid asks the Egyptians to adopt the principles of modern civilization, besides its science and methods of teaching and education, and to develop in themselves its various moral, economic and political capacities.[63] Yet he did not seem to realize that the principles he asks the Egyptians to adopt include secular ones that could never be compatible with religion, even when 'egyptianized'. By developing in themselves the various moral and political capacities of Europe, they might also create a clash with some of their own morals. Thus Hussein's thought was more consistent when he avoided these contradictions by trying to make Egypt part of Europe.

Nazira Zayn al-Din strongly criticizes the fanatical sheikhs who attacked Christian missionaries. She insisted that it was the missionaries who established schools and institutions of higher learning in Egypt, and made no secret of her belief that the only way to progress was by acquiring Western knowledge.[64] That this progress is based on secular knowledge seems clear to her when she compares the foreign universities that have given the world great men, and the al-Azhar and al-Najaf religious institutions that had given the Arab world nothing but regression.[65] No matter how much she claimed that the cause of this regression was misinterpretation by the religious clerics and their false teachings of Islam, she undoubtedly realized that the teaching in those Western universities she so admired was purely secular. However, in order to remain consistent with her faith in Islam, she claimed that Western civilization, its freedom and the bases of its society, were fully compatible with the Qur'an and the Sunna, and therefore if the Muslims followed in the West's footsteps they would achieve Western progress, even without deviating from their religion.[66] This was to overlook the fact that the basis of Western civilization is fully secular, and that many of its aspects are in complete contradiction to the Qur'an and the Sunna.

All these writers nevertheless realized that civilization and progress were also due to *material and economic factors*, and were very often aware that these lay behind all progress. All were disgusted by the social and economic injustice which existed in their countries as a result of the feudal system. From what has been mentioned above about Bustani's encyclopedia it is clear that he believed that improvements in agriculture, industry and commerce were essential for the advancement of society.

Al-Shidyaq was influenced by the Christian Socialists, a movement that emerged in England in 1848, the year of his arrival there.[67] Under their influence, he attacked the social injustice in England, whereby the farm labourers and workers slaved all day but still remained poor because the rich exploited them, enjoying the fruit of their labours and remaining idle. He stated that the rich were more in need of the poor than vice versa, and that giving the poor workers and farm labourers less work and more money would not encourage them to become feckless and lazy, as was often thought. He takes up a whole chapter of *al-Saq 'ala al-Saq* he describes the wretched lives of the ignorant poor and the dissipated lives of the rich. Under the influence of Frederick D. Maurice (d.1872), the prophet of Christian Socialism who denounced the fight for equality among the social classes, al-Shidyaq, nevertheless insisted that it was normal to have rich and poor in the world, but that what he found unacceptable was the extreme poverty of the poor.[68] However, he, too, was aware that a solid economic system was the basis of all political strength, 'for nothing makes a country as rich and powerful as mastering industry and commerce.'[69]

The writers of the following generation were just as revolted by social injustice in their countries, influenced this time by secular, not Christian, socialism. The principles of socialism are obvious in Marrash's saying that 'he who does not work does not have the right to eat'[70] and, had it not been for the labour of the poor, the rich would never have been rich.[71] But this does not mean that Marrash is against private enterprise for, without actually declaring it, he advocates restricted capitalism. This could be deduced from his statement that the government should outlaw anything that could hinder commerce and its development, and should encourage industry and agriculture. In the case of the latter, the injustice of the tithe collector and monopoly holders should be removed.[72] Ishaq insists that 'a person should receive only the equivalent value of what he produces.'[73] He then attacks the whole economic system in Egypt, whereby the poor destitute peasant was the victim of the feudal lord and his stooges, and the worker was the victim of the police who robbed him and the ruler who exiled him, and even the merchant was a victim of the cruel tax-collector. He regarded the whole prevailing socio-economic system to be based on theft, exploitation, injustice and bribery.[74] Under the influence of socialism, he also attacked the notion of charity and did not glorify poverty, as Christianity does, but showed that it leads to theft and crime.[75] While being fully aware of the secularism of Western thought, Ishaq urged his countrymen to seek guidance in that thought in order to reform their commercial treaties, agriculture, internal regulations, rules and bye-laws.[76] Clarifying what he means by Western thought, he insists that the faltering economy of the country could only be corrected by introducing liberty and equality,[77] the two famous slogans of the French Revolution. In view of his great admiration for the French Revolution and the impact its slogans had on him, what he probably means here is political, rather than economic freedom, believing that political reform was the basis for economic progress, contrary to the assertions of the next generation of secularist writers.

Al-Kawakibi was just as disgusted as his Christian contemporaries by the economic injustice in the society in which he lived, and praised the countries that seek to achieve economic equality in society,[78] while criticizing the capitalist system 'that subjugates people, as in civilized Europe which is now threatened by anarchists because the people have lost hope in their ability to fight against the capitalist despotism there.' However, al-Kawakibi finds that Islam contains the principles of socialism and the solution to all economic injustice, claiming that poverty would disappear if the Muslims observed the precepts of their religion as regards financial contributions, such as alms, expiations and the alms tax (zakat).[79] Thus al-Kawakibi not only overlooks the social and economic reasons that gave rise to socialism and which exclude its being found in Islam, but also completely ignores the fact that some of the precepts of Islam contradict the basic principles of socialism. These include Islam's acceptance of slavery and the inequality between men and women, rich and poor, Muslim and non-Muslim.

Qasim Amin shared this attitude to economic problems. From the fact that a Pasha, for example, is not ashamed to receive a poor man in his home, Amin deduces that all classes in his country can mingle freely, and claims that Muslim society does not discriminate between social classes or between rich and poor. He then goes on to say that the alms tax, which is one of the five basic principles of Islam,

> has regulated the distribution of wealth, and enables the poor to participate in owning the money of the rich, thus solving a social problem with a unique kind of socialism... This socialism is nobler and more practical than the one spoken of in Europe, which is obviously defective and difficult to apply.[80]

Amin may have been defending Islam against the Duke of Harcourt's accusations and this could have blinded him to the fact that the alms tax had not solved any social problem and had never led to the poor having a share in the wealth of the rich. It may also have been because he was himself a member of the upper middle class and did not fully realize the tragic plight of the poor. Or perhaps he subscribed to Islam's world-view which accepted class, ethnic and religious discrimination, and was thus unable to see how this contradicted the tenets of socialism and how it was certainly no 'nobler'.

Be that as it may, the social inequality that preoccupied him and that he strove hardest to change was that of women and he never dealt in detail with the necessity for radical economic change. That task was left to the Christian writers of the following generation, Zaydan, al-Shummayyil and Antun. Unlike his Muslim contemporaries who strongly clung to their religion's worldview, Zaydan believed in the scientific theory of evolution and survival of the fittest and it was this that prevented him from accepting the principle of equality between the social classes, for he considered that there were and always would be some who were stronger or more intelligent than others.[81] He thought it normal that people should be divided into two main classes, the elite and the masses, tending to disdain the latter,[82] although he severely criticized injustice in society and the exploitation of the poor by the rich.[83] Yet he did not consider that the theories of socialism or communism were the way to reform these ills, due to his belief in the survival of the fittest, and he claimed that all attempts to overthrow this law of society had been unsuccessful. As example he cites Charles Fourier (d.1837) and other socialists who failed to overthrow the social system and replace it with an artificial one because of the injustice and corruption they had witnessed. Had they aimed at merely reforming society while preserving the existing system, they would have been more successful.[84] The communists, Zaydan continues, wanted the people to have a share in all of the country's wealth, industry, land, etc., but these theories and aims are incompatible with human nature and habits. This is why they, too, have failed. Socialism also aimed at replacing the existing social structure, but this resulted in merely reforming society in general. Zaydan provides examples of the ills and injustices of society that the socialists wished to cure.[85] Although he praises socialism in this respect, he finds that it cannot be applied, because private ownership is the norm and it is just, while competition is necessary for progress. He thus recommends state-regulated capitalism which would safeguard the workers' rights.[86] This controlled capitalism would enable agriculture, industry and commerce to develop and progress leaving economic power in the hands of the people, whose wealth the government needs, rather than their being dependent on the government.[87] Thus Zaydan insisted that real independence is economic independence, and he rightly felt that a political system such as democracy is the result of economic factors, for it was thanks to their economic power that the new bourgeoisie in England had succeeded in participating in government.

Zaydan's belief in capitalism might also be due to the influence of Spencer who advocated the free market and evolution, as well as to the works of Demolin and Lebon,[88] since both were great admirers of England's economic and political system. His own circumstances might also have led to his advocating competition and free enterprise, for he, like his Christian contemporaries, had only themselves to depend on in order to succeed, which led to their believing in hard work, competition, initiative and risk, all of which pertain to capitalism.

Al-Shummayyil and Antun took the opposite view, as the real champions of secular socialism, realizing that social injustice was the result of a class conflict within society caused by the economic system of capitalism. Both severely attacked the exploitation of the masses and the injustice in society,[89] blaming this injustice for lies, theft, murder and other vices since it punishes honesty and deprives people of the necessities of life. This is why they believed that punishment, no matter how severe, never reformed society, but on the contrary actually made criminals worse.[90] Thus al-Shummayyil considers that those who should be punished as criminals are not the poor but the rich who manage to remain above the law.[91]

Contradicting and severely criticizing Zaydan's defence of survival of the fittest, Antun asserts that applying the theory of the struggle for existence and survival of the fittest to human society is egotistic, savage, inhuman and contrary to all moral and religious principles.[92] He indicates all the injustices of the capitalist system which exploits the workers, keeps them poor, with absolutely no social or medical security, although they are the majority of the population and are the source of all the agricultural and industrial production.[93] Of the writers under review, Antun was the most virulent in his attack on capitalism. In a series of articles in *al-Jami'a,* he criticizes the capitalists who monopolize industry and agriculture, reap excessive gains from the stock exchange without doing any work themselves and cruelly exploit the people.[94] This severe criticism increased during his short sojourn in the United States. Although showing great admiration for America's political and educational system, he severely attacks its ruthless capitalism, a system under which millionaires like Rockefeller live happily in a country whose masses often crave a piece of bread, exploited by industrialists and other capitalists. It is a country, he writes, in which individuals struggle bitterly and destroy each other for the sake of money and power; a country which values nothing but money and anyone who advocates a principle, idea or moral quality is considered to be naive and gullible.[95] His novel *al-Din wa al-'Ilm wa al-Mal* (Religion, Knowledge and Money) is a critique of the ruthlessness of capitalism.

As regards a solution to this injustice and how change and progress can be introduced in order to save humanity and society, both he and al-Shummayyil consider that the solution lies in secular socialism, as the only way to change the whole existing social order. Al-Shummayyil clearly states that he is a socialist, devoting several articles to the defence of socialism,[96] for he does not consider it to be just another social doctrine, but an intrinsic part of any thinking person's attitude to society, 'since we find the principles of socialism in the writings of all philosophers and all reformers throughout the ages.'[97] That is why he declares that socialism is inevitable, and is the key to progress since it applies the correct laws of society and thus redresses everything in it, for it endorses virtue and discourages vice, with the result that socialism prevents the decline of society and encourages rapid progress.[98] Antun agrees that

> ... neither religious reform nor civil reform can produce the desired results; that is, neither of them can create a newly virtuous humanity, except after *generalised social reform* to eliminate poverty, oppression, iniquity and ignorance among the people. This is a practical social, political course of action, not a religious one.[99]

The rules of a just society that socialism applies, in al-Shummayyil's opinion, are co-operation between people in their general interest, because socialism considers the individual to be necessary for the masses and the masses obliged to consider the interests of the individual. Socialism enables the masses to benefit from the abilities of each individual and the individual from his own abilities.[100] Likewise, in his novel *al-Din wa al-'Ilm wa al-Mal*, Antun reiterates his belief in co-operation and unity as the sole hope for the future of mankind. Whereas Antun preaches moderation and co-operation between workers, capitalists and religious clerics in this novel,[101] al-Shummayyil calls for co-operation of the common people only between themselves and is convinced that revolution is the only solution. As early as 1899, he forsaw a revolution which, unlike the French bourgeois revolution, would revolt against *the social order and its laws*, a revolution of the workers against the capitalists:

> ... against the injustice of the laws and the capitalists' monopolization of everything, their exploitation of the minds and work of the people, giving them hardly anything in return. Unfortunately the so-called 'democratic' governments are blind puppets in the hands of the capitalists.[102]

The social revolution in which both al-Shummayyil and Antun believe aims at reducing human misery, guaranteeing the common people the necessities of life, protecting their rights against exploitation, improving their status in society and teaching them that everyone deserves to be rewarded for their labours. It is the government's responsibility to ensure that this comes about.[103] Since in al-Shummayyil's opinion, socialism is an intrinsic part of all reformist thought, it will undoubtedly triumph in the end and the real power will belong to the people, while the power of kings will be abolished forever.[104] Antun, although not preaching outright revolution, does not seem to exclude the need for violence, for as a rider to his abovementioned novel he writes the following epigraph: 'Let the world beware of the day when the weak will be strong and the strong weak,'[105] in which it can be seen that he shares al-Shummayyil's confidence in the eventual triumph of socialism. Elaborating on these principles, Antun insists that it is the right of the government to expropriate factories, shops and farms, which will then become the property of the people. The proceeds are to be distributed among them, but the government should manage these assets, with the people reaping the rewards. This is the only way to enforce justice and assure a better life for everyone.[106] In a list of the great events of the nineteenth century in his article on the New Year of 1900, Antun includes socialism and thanks it for having served real democracy and the weak.[107] Commenting on the thoughts of both these writers, Sharabi says, that:

... in al-Shummayyil and Antun there emerges for the first time in Arab thought an awareness of the common man, of the vast impoverished strata of Arab society. And for the first time the masses are not looked down upon, they are the centre of concern.[108]

Neither al-Shummayyil nor Antun lived to see the collapse of socialism and its failure to make their lofty dreams come true.

Azoury was another writer who seemed to endorse the socio-economic basis of socialism without actually mentioning it by name. This can be deduced from his statement that, 'Fraternity between the states and social equality between the people cannot be achieved until all nations reach the same level of civilization and prosperity'.[109] Thus he sees that economic prosperity and civilization are the basis of all equality, whether between people or among nations, and because of his political awareness he realizes the constant danger of the stronger, more prosperous nations encroaching on the rights and wealth of the weaker ones, with the result that those weaker, poorer nations will not only suffer underdevelopment and inequality vis-à-vis the stronger ones, but among their own population as well.

The Muslim secular writers of this same generation were in this respect closer to their Christian contemporaries than those of the previous generation. Like Zaydan and in harmony with the worldview of Islam, Kurd 'Ali sees it as a normal state of affairs to have rich, poor and a middle-class, due to the difference between people in intellect, diligence and effort, but he believes that it is necessary to limit wealth and improve the standard of living of the poor.[110] That is why he sees that the socialists were right in asking Western governments for a fair distribution of wealth and land, since vast sums are being spent on private grounds and palaces while many people remain poor and hungry.[111] That same social injustice, he says, exists in Syria and Egypt, for example, where landlords own whole villages and vast plots of land that they are incapable of cultivating, while thousands of people can barely eke out a living. As a response to his being attacked for being influenced by communism, he states that he is clearly against communism since many of its doctrines contradict those of Islam, but that the only way to fight communism is by applying what that which is useful in its ideology, such as social justice.[112] Without expounding the various socialist theories, as did Zaydan, he, too, does not believe that socialism is the way to improve his country and bring about its economic progress, and he criticizes socialism for 'promising the people to be able to live without working.'[113] This indicates that he had a very superficial knowledge of its principles. Like Zaydan, he believed in controlled capitalism which would protect the rights of the workers and peasants,[114] but which at the same time would create a strong bourgeoisie that would come into power and be the basis for democratic rule, the way it had happened in Great Britain.[115] This was the sort of attitude that could be expected from someone such as Kurd 'Ali who was himself a bourgeois. Therefore, when seeking economic reform, unlike al-Kawakibi and Amin, he did not believe in applying charity, penitence and the alms tax ordained by Islam, but considered that social evils could only be reformed by applying Western economic principles,[116] even though they contain elements that were inherently contradictory to those of Islam, such as applying interest to loans. Again, feeling the need to defend his position, he asserts that 'times differ today from those of early Islam, for today, unlike early Islam, the nation's life depends on wealth, and real faith is not contradictory to the acquisition of wealth and improving the temporal.'[117] His belief that early Islam was not in need of wealth is beside the point, what is relevant here is his secular attitude towards economic change and progress and, in this respect, his separating the religious from the historical and social in Islam. This is why he insists that the great success of modern economics is due to the diffusion of natural sciences, for the new inventions and discoveries they have brought are what promoted and developed Western economy.[118]

However, Kurd 'Ali's later works sometimes show a few contradictions. For after having encouraged adopting Western economic systems, he strongly defends Islam's prohibition on taking interest and backs up his assertion by describing many economic disasters that resulted from charging interest.[119] In order to reconcile both attitudes, he criticizes those who refuse to charge interest on their savings, asking them not to leave them to the bankers, but to use them for charity.[120]

It was the Muslims of the next generation who took an unmitigated secularist stand towards economic reform and progress, although they were more preoccupied with education than with financial matters.. Hussein was naturally very critical of the feudal system in his country with all the poverty that it entailed.[121] Contrary to the dictates of Islam he did not believe in charity, seeing it a sign of contempt for the poor and considering that it should be replaced by justice and equality, for the masses did not need the pity of the rich and their charity, since they had a sacred right to justice and equality. In that same secular vein, realizing the sociological and historical circumstances that influenced religion and that contradicted the tenets of classical Muslim thought, he shows that there were historical reasons for the division of society into classes and although nature differentiated between people in intelligence and capability, all were human beings and had the same rights.[122] Unlike Zaydan and Kurd Ali, he rejected the division of society into classes, and sought ways to help the poor gain access to higher education in order to improve their social status.[123] Again in a completely secular vein, he rejected the static structure of society, replacing classical Islamic thought with secular principles of equality and a belief in the mobility of society and the possibility of changing its economic structure through education.

Again learning from Western secular systems, he points to the necessity of increasing the taxes imposed on the middle and upper classes, so that the government could spend more on education, and demands that the government learn from the European taxation laws,[124] with absolutely no reference to the Islamic laws of taxation. In this, he was obviously influenced by the Western capitalist system which both Zaydan and Kurd 'Ali also admired and, like them, he linked economics to education – his primary concern – again seeking inspiration in Western secular systems when he wrote:

> If we want to protect our national wealth and be economically independent, we have to apply what the Europeans and Americans do to safeguard their economic wealth and independence, and train our youth the way their youth are trained to do this.[125]

It can thus be seen that whatever Hussein wrote about the means to socio-economic change and progress, he wrote from a completely secular standpoint, with no trace of any religious influence.

This same, purely secular, attitude is also to be found in al-Sayyid's writing on the subject. Unlike Hussein, he belonged to the rich landed gentry, so it was not the plight of the poor masses that occupied him as much as the necessity for economic and mainly political progress (which will be detailed in the next chapter). He starts by stating that the first duty of any society that hopes to develop and become independent is to organize all aspects of its economy.[126] Thus, he rightly sees that the economy of a country is at the basis of its development and independence, although he, like Hussein, stressed the importance of knowledge and education, above all. Al-Sayyid was, however, a firm believer in the capitalist system which is why he urges his countrymen, and mainly the rich among them, to form companies and banks, develop local industry and buy shares in Egypt's debt, so that Egypt's economic dependence would disappear with time and it would also be able to gain political independence.[127] He repeatedly insists that a country's glory and independence are due to its industry and agriculture, and constantly urges the Egyptians to encourage and develop them,[128] for this was the only way to improve Egypt's economy and the plight of her poor peasants.[129]

Whether these writers criticized the feudal system in their countries, as did Kurd 'Ali and Hussein, and/or whether they believed that economic reform could be achieved through socialism or capitalism, regulated and restricted or otherwise, most of them realized that only by industrialization and the development of a modern economy could their countries attain the level of development found in the West.

Since the Arab countries of that period were under foreign occupation, either Ottoman and/or Western, one of the primary means of change and progress they saw was also political, although some rightly considered that economic progress was a necessary condition for political change.

CHAPTER EIGHT

Government and Law

A. *Government*

The Lebanese and Syrians had been ruled first by the Ottoman Turks and then by the French. In the case of the Egyptians, Ottoman rule was succeeded by British occupation. Writers from all these countries, whether Christian or Muslim, had thus lived constantly under foreign domination and bitterly attacked the tyranny and injustice that accompanied it. Dallal, Ishaq, al-Kawakibi and Kurd 'Ali, had themselves suffered its injustices at first hand. Some writers attacked foreign domination directly, others indirectly, by expounding the necessity and advantages of democracy. The very idea of democracy had been imported from the West, whether these writers were conscious of the secular principles underlying it or not.

Among the writers of the first generation, al-Shidyaq for example criticizes the absolute power of the rulers, and the fact that they believed that they ruled by divine right. He gives examples of their merciless tyranny.[1] He asserts that a country under harsh, dictatorial rule that depends solely on the power of the sword, such as the Ottoman Empire, could never create an advanced civilization,[2] and the French revolted in 1789 because their kings believed in the divine right instead of seeing that it was the will of the people that gave them the right to rule.[3]

Dallal attacked tyranny even more fiercely. Like his contemporaries, Marrash and Ishaq, he was influenced by the philosophers of the French Revolution. In his long poem, *al-'Arsh wa al-Haykal* (The Throne and the Temple), Dallal not only dwells on the cruelty and injustice of the tyrannical rulers of his country, but also shows that they hindered progress since they neglected the education of the people, ruined their country's economy, commerce and agriculture, and had they not stolen and exploited the people, they would have been so weak and powerless that they would have died of hunger.[4] Since people are born free according to Marrash, the Romantic, he believed that man should reject any authority that restricts his freedom.⁵ In the introduction to his *Rihla ila Paris* (A Voyage to Paris) he describes the endless deprivations, torture, humiliation, terror and tyranny that the weak suffer at the hands of the powerful, after which he demonstrates his immense admiration for the perfect freedom the French had enjoyed since they were never afraid that they might be crushed by a barbaric, despotic, savage authority.⁶ This is more than an indirect criticism of the rule under which his own country suffered. Likewise, Ishaq repeatedly attacks despotism and criticizes the Egyptians for having put up with the tyranny of their rulers, whether Egyptian or foreign, since the days of the Pharaohs, which caused them to become submissive, accepting without complaint the slavery, injustice, hypocrisy, lies and heavy taxation that accompanied this despotism.⁷ Undoubtedly it was their secular attitudes that drove these Christian writers to strongly oppose every form of tyranny, for before democracy saw the light in Europe, its rulers were believed to have absolute authority and to rule by divine right, to say nothing of the fact that Christianity preaches turning the left cheek if smitten on the right.⁸

Although Islam does not preach that same submission, the history of Islam is replete with absolute rulers, and traditional Muslim political thought, as explained by al-Mawardi, for example, preached submission to the ruler based on the Qur'anic verse 'Obey Allah, and obey the messenger and those of you who are in authority.'⁹ This is why Muslim writers of the next generation, such as al-Kawakibi and Amin, who attacked absolute rule, were undoubtedly influenced by Western secular political thought. Al-Kawakibi sees that the autocratic, absolute and unjust rule in their countries is the cause of Muslim backwardness, and he criticizes the Muslims for accepting humiliation and injustice because they believe this to be a sign of obedience.¹⁰ He also blames the non-Arabs who embraced Islam for this autocratic absolute rule because, influenced by their pagan origins, they gave different interpretation of the *shari'a*.¹¹ His book, *Taba'i' al-Istibdad,* is a fierce attack on despotism in all its aspects. He indicates its causes and effects, and the means of combating and eliminating it. In this book, al-Kwakibi shows, for example, that despotic governments exist due to two formidable and fearsome factors, the ignorance of the masses and an organized standing army, and he encourages people never to accept a despotic ruler, for glory is gained through fighting injustice and despotism as far as possible.¹² Contrary to the Qur'anic verse which promises the pious 'if they be poor, Allah will enrich them with His bounty',¹³ al-Kawakibi says that poor people under despotic rule spend their life between one ailment and another until they die, having thus wasted their life on earth and lost everlasting life to boot,[14] meaning that their poverty would lead them to commit crimes for which they would have to pay in the hereafter.

Amin is no less a severe critic of absolute rule. He stresses that it always becomes tyrannical and misinterprets religion itself to suit its interests.[15] It has already been pointed out that he blamed woman's sorry plight on the despotic rule to which men were subjugated and who, as a result, subjugated their womenfolk in turn.

Although the Christian and Muslim writers of the following generation expounded their thoughts on democracy more than they wrote about tyranny, they strongly criticized tyrannical rule, not only for intellectual and socio-political reasons but for private ones as well, since minorities such as the Christians were usually the first victims of autocratic, despotic rule, as were Muslim liberals such as al-Kawakibi, Kurd 'Ali, 'Abd al-Raziq and Hussein. Zaydan insisted that a tyrannical, absolute ruler had only his personal interests at heart, rather than those of his subjects.[16] al-Shumayyil not only attacks despotic, unjust rulers but, in accordance with his socialist ideas, he foresees a day when the people will revolt and overthrow these tyrants once they become aware of their plight and unite,[17] for despotism is bound to come to an end since it is against the nature of society which is based on cooperation.[18] In an open letter to Sultan 'Abdülhamid, written in 1896, he says that his reason for writing was the deplorable state of social, economic and political affairs in the Empire, injustice and tyranny being the cause of its backwardness and weakness. He then goes on to describe the tyranny of the various government employees and their spies, whose activities caused people to live in constant terror, and become hypocrites and liars.[19] Seeing that his advice produced no result, in 1908 and 1909 he wrote two very bitter and virulent criticisms of 'Abdülhamid's tyranny and that of his cohorts, stating that if the Sultan had granted the country a constitution it was only because he had been forced to do so.[20]

Likewise Kurd 'Ali also severely attacked the tyranny of 'Abdülhamid as well as that of the Young Turks who succeeded him in power,[21] while Azoury strongly criticized the autocratic, tyrannical rule of both the Turkish sultan and the Russian tsar.[22] By publishing a translation into Arabic of the Human Rights Declaration the French had produced in 1789, Antun was obviously attacking tyranny,[23] yet he claimed that tyranny was sometimes necessary, as in the Ottoman Empire:

This is because the different Eastern nations and numerous races would need a power over them all so long as each race is not independent and under self-rule. This is a result of the existence of various races, especially since the race of the majority does not want to introduce any new laws that would give the other races a share in all its rights.[24]

In the absence of democracy, Antun realises that tyrannical rule is the only guarantee of stability and peace. This might be the reason for his having backed the Ottoman Empire in an open letter to Rashid Bey, the former *wali* (governor) of Beirut, because 'the welfare of the Ottoman Empire and all the races of which it consists is based upon agreement, unity and keeping peace'.[25]

A completely different stand is taken by Samné, who was writing more than a decade later. One of the reasons for his opposition to Feisal as king of a united Arab kingdom after World War I was the fact that the Sharifian rule was theocratic and absolute, and was likely to favour the Sunni Muslims to the detriment of Christians, Jews and non-Sunni Muslims.[26] This, of course, was in addition to the fact that Samné did not want to have his civilized Syria attached to the 'uncivilized nomadic Bedouins of the Hijaz' and to change from Turkish rule to the even worse hegemony of Feisal's bedouins.[27]

The Muslims of Samné's generation were just as critical of their traditional despotic rulers. 'Abd al-Raziq also sees the connection between theocratic, absolute rule, despotism and tyranny when he states that the caliphate in Islam was based solely on terrifying armed might, for the caliphs had seized power by the force of arms and by killing people and retained their power and dignity only by depriving the people of theirs. Without this armed power, the caliphate would have disappeared. Elaborating on the subject, he gives examples from ancient Arabic as well as from contemporary Ottoman history.[28] As late as 1935, Hussein was still criticizing the Egyptian government for being despotic, not applying justice and the law and depriving people of their rights.[29]

Nazira Zayn al-Din is the only woman writer of those we are dealing with who tackled the subject of government. She considered that a tyrannical government that prevented freedom of thought, speech and writing was devoid of justice and integrity. It was a government in which evil overcomes good and tyranny, ignorance, slavery and backwardness overcame justice, knowledge, freedom and progress, since it was a government that knew no restraint, opposition or sanction, and there was no power to deter it.[30]

Al-Sayyid repeatedly attacked tyranny in all its aspects, whether as absolute rule, which he saw as the worst form of government[31] or as the traditional belief that the ruler is God's representative on earth.[32] He insists that there is no such thing as 'a just dictatorial regime' or ruler. Disagreeing with 'Abd al-Raziq who considered that all the caliphs were tyrannical rulers with absolute power, al-Sayyid claims that the only exceptions were the Orthodox Caliphs who were absolute rulers but they were just because they applied the teachings of the Qur'an and the Sunna. All the other absolute rulers had been tyrannical and unjust. He saw the detrimental effect that tyranny had on the nation's economy and civilization because it restricted the education of the masses, freedom of thought and the ability to invent, discover and progress intellectually,[33] but insisted much more on the moral damage it did since it corrupts people's morals, makes them hypocrites and liars, and causes them to distrust each other and loose all honour, self-esteem and self-respect, turning people into slaves.[34] Striving to end the tyranny in his country, he did not return to Islam or its political thought but translated Aristotle's *De Re Publica* so that the Arab readers could benefit from it.[35] Under the influence of Western liberalism, he writes:

> Our long history of tyranny made us lose all sense of personal liberty, and this is the cause of our moral, economic and political ills. That is why we are in dire need of expanding the scope of personal liberty so that people can regain the qualities necessary for progress and competition in life's battle. We must completely rid ourselves of dependence on the government, of that feeling which is common in the East that the people in a nation are a flock (*ra'iyya*) and the ruler their guardian shepherd (*ra'i*) who can deal with his flock as he pleases. This is what stopped us from adopting the principles of modern civilization, and discouraged us from depending upon ourselves, which is the basis of an individual's and a nation's success.[36]

It is this same liberalism that set al-Sayyid against socialism, seeing in it another form of tyranny, since he believed that it made people loose their individual freedom and depend upon the state in everything concerning their private and public life, whereas what the Egyptians needed, in his opinion, was how to rely on themselves.[37] Therefore he believed in restricting the power of government to that of maintaining security and justice and defending the country. In all else, he insists that individuals should be completely free, for any extra right the government takes for itself will be automatically detracted from the people's rights.[38]

Few of the writers believed that revolution was the best means of abolishing tyranny. Al-Shidyaq visited Paris in 1848 just after King Louis-Philippe was ousted from the throne, and all he could say about this revolution was that it involved a lot of rioting and bloodshed.[39] A possible reason for his attitude is that he had been influenced by the Christian Socialists who opposed revolution and believed Christian love and cooperation to be the solution for society's ills. In a subsequent article, he calls the revolutionaries of the French Commune mutineers, describing the rape, murders, thefts and destruction they caused.[40] By now, he was writing in Constantinople, under the strict surveillance of the Sultan, and thus could do little else but condemn revolution.

This same anti-revolutionary spirit is found, however, in the writings of al-Kawakibi and Zaydan. Al-Kawakibi says that revolutions cause many innocent victims and might replace a despotic rule by one which is worse.[41] Zaydan sees that the change from absolute to constitutional rule must be gradual, otherwise constitutional rule will fail, so people must be given only as much liberty as they are prepared for. This is why he believed that the Ottoman Constitution of 1876 should include a measure of tyranny for it to suit the Ottoman nation because of the people's ignorance and their having been for centuries under despotic rule, besides the fact that the nation comprises many different races, languages and religions that could be kept more easily united if ruled by a despot,[42] as Antun had also insisted.

Ishaq's attitude towards revolution was different. Although he criticizes nihilist terrorism in Russia and the socialist uprisings in Germany, he insists that revolution will alert a negligent or heedless governor and instigate him to do good, although it could also have a negative effect and leave people worse off than they had been before. He displays great admiration for the French Revolution of 1789 because it abolished tyranny and slavery and established liberty, equality and fraternity.[43] Yet he agrees with Zaydan that freedom should be won gradually, depending on the political and civil awareness of the people.[44] Without actually advocating revolution, al-Sayyid believes that if a government is unjust, the people are bound to revolt against it.[45]

Marrash, Dallal and al-Shumayyil were unequivocal in their support for revolution. Marrash insists that only revolution can abolish tyranny and slavery.[46] In his long poem al-'Arsh wa al-Haykal (The Throne and the Temple), Dallal incites the people to revolt against the Turkish oppressor and drive him out,[47] while al-Shumayyil's socialism made him believe in the inevitability of revolution, as has been shown above.

Whether or not they believed in the effectiveness of revolution, all the writers insisted that positive change could only be brought about by educating the people so as to make them aware of their rights. Influenced by Comte, they asserted that intellectual reform was the way to social and even political reform. Consequently, for all these writers, one of the main aims of education was to create political awareness among the people. Ishaq claims that people must be educated in order to ensure that they elect the right representatives;[48] and al-Kawakibi writes that the only effective way to overcome despotism is by educating the masses so as make them politically aware[49] and this is why, he says, despots fear philosophy, political science, history and similar branches of knowledge that enlighten the people and make them realize what human beings are, what their rights are, whether they have been wronged and how they can go about claiming and winning these rights.[50] Thus, although al-Kawakibi insisted on religious reform, as has been pointed out, he felt that tyranny could not be overcome by religious reform but by purely secular means, such as educating the people so as to make them strive for freedom, but to try and win it gradually so as to ensure that the tyranny that they were overthrowing was not replaced by something worse.

Zaydan also insists that unless there is a proper system of education to develop the intellect and teach people their duties and rights, no real political progress can be made towards democracy and independence.[51] Much as he admires freedom of the press and sees it as a requirement for helping to improve both government policy and society, he admits that it can only be obtained if the public is aware of its importance and enforces it, for it is not in the interest of government to have a free press.[52] Even al-Shumayyil considered education to be a basic condition for obtaining genuinely democratic rule,[53] and therefore realized that the new Ottoman government of 1908 which was supposed to be representative was only a camouflage for the autocratic government that it concealed, since the majority of the subjects of the Ottoman Empire were still ignorant, fanatically religious and had no notion of real civilization based on liberty and cooperation for the general good. Even some members of the *Majlis al-Mab'uthan* (Assembly of Delegates) were ignorant, religious fanatics, he writes, and thus provided no guarantee of real freedom and progressive reform.[54] Azoury also saw that tyrannical rule like that of the Ottoman Empire or Tsarist Russia could only persist if the people were kept ignorant, poor and stultified,[55] and Kurd 'Ali agreed that only knowledge creates awareness in the people and makes them reject the tyranny that deprives them of their rights,[56] and this was why the Ottomans had kept the Arabs in ignorance.[57] Education and a high percentage of literacy were, for him, the only guarantee of obtaining a really representative government, since ignorant people might sell their votes, and those in power forge the results of a general election, thus bringing back tyranny in the guise of liberty.[58] If the West had managed to obtain better governance, he states, it was thanks to an enlightened population that had forced its governments to be better.[59]

Al-Sayyid, too, felt the importance of increasing general education in order to have a public that was aware of its rights and duties and thus use moderation and peaceful methods in order to gradually achieve democracy.[60] Since he was a member of the upper middle class and opposed any form of revolution as a means of change he also saw democracy as a means to enable his social class to participate in government. Similarly, Taha Hussein advocated complete and true democracy; he firmly believed that it could only be achieved if the whole spirit and mentality of the people changed to enable them to understand the moral and intellectual principles without which democracy could not succeed.[61] He attempted to instill such principles by imposing the study of Greek and Latin literature and philosophy which, to him, were the source of democracy's philosophical principles, just as al-Sayyid had translated Aristotle's *De re Publica* with the same aim in mind.

Democracy was the ultimate goal of all these writers, yet in examining their work the question arises as to how deeply they had thought about democracy and to what extent they were really convinced by the liberty and equality it stood for. Was their faith in democratic rule based on an absolutely secular world view? In this respect, there is a significant difference of approach between the writers, whether Christian or Muslim.

Undoubtedly the concept of democracy was one that these writers had learned from the West. Even conservative Muslims such as Muhammad Rashid Rida admitted this influence,[62] as did the Muslim writers under review, Amin, Kurd 'Ali, 'Abd al-Raziq, Hussein and al-Sayyid.[63] Yet apparently for some of these writers it was not quite clear what democracy really meant, since they tried to show that the Muslims had understood and practiced democracy in their early history. This was to completely overlook the historical, economic and social events in Europe that gave rise to democracy and its purely secular principles. On the one hand, al-Kawakibi writes that freedom of speech and of the press are the means to guarantee wise rule, which is why the free nations have parliaments which obligate the ruler and call him to account. On the other hand, he insists that this is exactly what is meant by the Qur'anic verse 'And there may spring from you a nation that invites to goodness, enjoins correct behaviour and forbids indecency. Such as they who are successful'.[64] This is to completely disregard the fact that this verse could not possibly have alluded to any of the principles of democracy such as universal suffrage, the equality of citizens, separation of powers, accountability of the government and the like. Yet al-Kawakibi was aware that these principles were the basis of democracy for he also says that any government that is not accountable for its actions is tyrannical and that political power should be in the hands of the people. He goes on, however, to quote stories and several verses from the Qur'an to prove that:

Islam is based on the principles of democratic rule... principles that were applied in the days of the Prophet and the Orthodox caliphs, before the rulers misused Islam and misinterpreted it to suit their own interests. Thus they convinced the people that they cannot judge their rulers or superiors and hold them accountable, all of which led to the despotism of the Muslim rulers.[65]

When Syria became a French mandate, Kurd 'Ali also tried to show, in contradiction to his earlier convictions, that Islam contained the principles of democratic rule, justice and equality.[66] Even a liberal writer like al-Sayyid claimed that taking counsel, which is one of the principles of democratic rule, was the Prophet Muhammad's policy in the battle of Uhud, for example, when he followed the opinion of the majority.[67] Naturally al-Sayyid does not show that this was not always the Prophet's policy, nor that he was accountable to any one else for his actions.

However, when a Christian such as Ishaq claimed that the *shura* (consultation) the first Orthodox caliphs resorted to was a form of democracy,[68] he completely ignores the fact that this *shura* implied none of the elementary principles of democracy. It could be surmised that his reasons for making such a statement could have been his journalistic interests and/or his precarious position as a Christian Lebanese immigrant in Egypt. A different explanation could be attributed to the examples quoted by al-Shidyaq from Arab history to prove that the early Muslim rulers were not autocratic since they were judged by the people and took their advice.[69] He quotes from the Qur'an to assure his readers that this was a religious commandment.[70] Since al-Shidyaq wrote these articles after he had embraced Islam and was issuing his periodical *al-Jawa'ib* in Constantinople, he might have been insinuating to the autocratic Ottoman Sultan that these principles of democracy were part of the Islam in which the Sultan claimed to believe and which he should be practising. Another reason to believe this is that during this same period, al-Shidyaq wrote about the necessity for democracy and the need for an elected chamber as a means of preventing foreign interference in Ottoman affairs, for to the foreigners whatever the chamber of deputies legislated would be lawful, could not be overruled and had to be accepted by them.[71] Yet while still in Europe al-Shidyaq evaluated the role of the British parliament from a moral rather than a political point of view, stating that parliament only implemented a measure after having fully discussed it, since the British never break their word and always perform what they have promised to do.[72] Here, too, he might have been influenced by the Christian Socialist John Ludlow (d.1911) who also evaluated democracy from a moral point of view.[73]

These are not the only indications that the secular notion of democracy was not always clear to some of our writers, no matter what the reason. Bustani, for example, writes in 1860 that if the people were allowed to participate in government, it would make them feel politically responsible and consequently more patriotic, caring more for the welfare and progress of their country.[74] Yet, at the same time, he believed that the Ottoman sultan's power had been granted to him by God,[75] not appearing to realize the contradiction between these points of view.

Al-Shidyaq was fully aware that in the West government was successful simply because it was democratic, based on the separation of powers,[76] elected by the people, and bound by law and constitution.[77] Two basic principles of democracy were equality before the law and a person's right to complete freedom within the confines of such law. Here, too, al-Shidyaq did not seem to grasp the secular, political connotation of such concepts since – again influenced by the Christian Socialists – he measures liberty and equality with a moral rather than a political yardstick. When writing about freedom, for instance, the only example he gives is that the freedom of trade permits the sale of poisons that cause the death of innocent people.[78] Furthermore, he considers that the reason for England's strong government is the fact that the English do not question their rulers but merely obey them blindly, unlike the French who interfere with what the rulers do and say, and therefore uprisings are very rare in England.[79] Although he admires the fact that all the English are equal before the law,[80] he asks 'how could we ask for equality when God Himself has not created people equal, but has preferred some to others,' adding that the principle of equality judges the virtuous and the immoral by the same yardstick, for a ruler should not judge a complainant and a defendant equally, but should consider the character of each.[81]

In that same generation, Marash, Dallal and Ishaq took a completely secular stand vis-à-vis the principles of democracy. All three were strongly influenced by the slogans of the French Revolution. Marrash believed in political equality and freedom, and thus insisted on the right of the people to participate in government, realizing that a regime cannot be stable unless it is based on the full participation of the majority of the people, on whom the power of the country and its armies are dependent, and who are therefore a crucial factor in politics.[82] The king himself, he says, is no more than a servant to his people.[83] Together with the philosophers of the French Revolution, Marrash insists that man is born free, for God Himself gave man this freedom when He gave him freedom of choice. That is why he attacks slavery and refuses to accept the Bible's acceptance of it,[84] constantly repeating that there can be no civilization without freedom.[85] His whole imaginary story, *Ghabat al-Haq*, is a vision of a kingdom in which freedom reigns.

In his poem *al-'Arsh wa al-Haykal* (The Throne and the Temple), Dallal insists that rulers are ordinary people, and that it is through the masses and because of them that they have conquered, their armies consisting of the people's children, and the money they spend coming from the people. Consequently, when the people have revolted and driven out their oppressors he asks for wise and judicious governance so that justice, equality and peace will prevail.[86]

Like Marrash, Ishaq also insisted that freedom and equality pertain to human existence,[87] that they are inseparable therefrom and the basis of all civilization.[88] He therefore believed that a country can never improve unless it had a democratic government, with a parliament elected by the people.[89] Perhaps because of the application of the Muslim *shari'a* which discriminated against him as it did against all the other non-Muslims, mainly affecting their civil rights, he insisted most strongly on the equality of all citizens before the law, insisting that all should have equal civil and political rights.[90] His struggle was not limited to equality in this domain, however, for he also attacked the social injustice which differentiated between rich and poor and applied a dual standard in judging them.[91] He severely criticizing the Ottoman rulers who completely disregarded the laws or interpreted them to suit their own ends, with the result that injustice and evil prevailed.[92]

Among the Muslim writers of the next generation Zaynab Fawwaz also believed that freedom and equality were the hallmark of civilization,[93] but she avoided going into details as this might have led to her being forced to contradict the teachings of Islam that do not believe in human freedom, in the civil and political equality between free men and slaves, Muslims and non-Muslims, men and women. Instead she dealt with man's existential freedom, denying that it existed since man was fettered by his bodily needs, ill health, his superiors and all the restrictive laws that are necessary to every society.[94]

Influenced by Western secular political thought, al-Kawakibi also insisted that man was born free,[95] and that people should be equal before the law, no matter who they were and what their social position, for not even rulers are above the law.[96] Instead of avoiding the religious consequences of such theories, as Fawwaz did, he claimed that the Qur'an is full of verses calling for justice and equality,[97] ignoring all those that state the opposite. Without realizing the contradiction in his thought, he stipulates in *Um al-Qura* that the society he wished to create must be Muslim, with its official headquarters in Mecca,[98] thus obviously excluding non-Muslims whom he did not consider to be the equal of Muslims. Even so, he deviates from traditional Muslim political thought, in that he considers that one of the reasons for the backwardness of the Muslim countries is that Muslims are deprived of many freedoms, such as freedom of learning, of speech, of the press and of scientific research.[99] Yet again he avoids discussing the possible clash between unrestricted scientific research, for example, and the restraints that could be imposed on it by religion, when he wrote:

... that reason says that foreign kings could better rule the Muslims, because they are more just [than the Muslim rulers], care more for the welfare of the people and are more capable of developing the country and its citizens.[100]

This contradicts traditional Muslim political thought which enjoins Muslims not to accept the rule of a non-Muslim. Influenced by Western secular political thought and Montesquieu's *Esprit des Lois* (which had been translated into Arabic), he insists on a government elected by the people, representing them and accountable to them, and the separation of the judicial, executive and legislative powers.[101] He insists that the people should have the freedom to call the rulers to account and hold them responsible for their actions, and that rulers should always consult the people and never act purely on their own initiative.[102]

In his early writings, Amin did not differ from al-Kawakibi since he, too, claimed that Islam required rulers to be accountable for their actions to the people.[103] In response to the Duke of Harcourt, he claimed that a Muslim society is built on a the concept of equality and fraternity.[104] In his later work, however, he admitted that Muslims had never experienced a democratic government, and were always subject to absolute, autocratic rule in which they had absolutely no say and in which the ruler was accountable to no one.[105] Influenced by secular Western political thought, he began speaking of freedom being at the root of all advancement and the most precious of *human rights*, clarifying that what is meant by freedom is man's freedom of speech and writing,[106] as well as his independence of thought, will and deed, providing the law was not broken and morality safeguarded.[107] Although he agrees with al-Shidyaq in admitting that freedom might have its disadvantages if it were to lead to moral license, he sees that the advantages of freedom are greater than its disadvantages.[108] Although freedom and independence of will are not in opposition to liberal Muslim thought, they do not agree with traditional Muslim political thought, and to consider them a human *right* is undoubtedly the influence of Western secularism. Yet Amin only speaks of freedom without elaborating on equality, another human right and a principle of democracy, thus avoiding what might directly conflict with some of the principles of Islam.

It is only to be expected that Christian writers of this generation should unanimously advocate the adoption of Western democracy, since their intellectual training was Western, influenced by the writers of the Enlightenment as well as by Comte, Mill, Locke, Spencer and Huxley, among others, while nothing in their religion contradicts either freedom or equality. Unlike a Christian of the previous generation such as Ishaq who claimed that the *shura* of the Orthodox caliphs was a form of democracy, Zaydan clearly pointed out the enormous difference between their *shura* and modern constitutional rule.[109] He therefore insists on the importance of a completely democratic government, bound by a constitution, elected by the people and accountable to them,[110] and shows nothing but admiration for the spirit of liberty, equality and fraternity which the French had disseminated throughout the world.[111] In spite of his great admiration for the political freedom the French had enjoyed since their Revolution, which granted the people their political rights, he says that in reality it is not the people who have the real power, but the élite who are more intelligent and have more resources, whereas the common people in France, like everywhere else, were short-sighted, driven by emotion and reacted without foresight or thought.[112] This élitist spirit is not unusual in a self-made man like Zaydan. He had nothing to rely on but his own intelligence, perseverance, hard work and willpower and these enabled him to publish a large number of books, besides editing a leading periodical and establishing a large publishing house.

Neither al-Shumayyil, Azoury nor Antun demonstrated any of this élitist spirit, although the latter was also a self-made man. They adopted all the principles of Western democracy, such as a constitutional government elected by the people and accountable to them, the separation of powers and the guarantee of rights, justice, freedom and equality.[113] Yet unlike the Muslims, al-Kawakibi and Amin, they placed the greatest emphasis on equality. This was probably the influence of their socialist beliefs and the fact that, as a minority, they were not considered equal to their Muslim compatriots and, as a result, played no active role in the government's policy. That is why Azoury demanded a constitutional government based on the freedom of all faiths and the equality of all citizens before the law.[114] When al-Shumayyil advised 'Abdülhamid to form a constitutional government and treat the people equally, regardless of their ethnicity or religion, he enumerated the benefits the European countries reaped from such a rule and says that, if applied in the Ottoman Empire, he and every other citizen would be proud of their Ottoman nationality.[115] At a later stage, again influenced by his socialist ideals, al-Shumayyil says that he does not strive for the usual type of democratic government, but for a true democracy in which work is shared out in a manner that benefits the whole of society, and through which all would profit equally with absolutely no discrimination between individuals.[116]

The secular principles of democracy were also completely acceptable to the writers of subsequent generations, whether Christian like Samné or Muslim like Kurd 'Ali, Hussein, al-Sayyid or even, to a certain extent, an Azharite sheikh like 'Abd al-Raziq. Writing in 1920, Samné opposed the Sharifian theocratic, absolute rule of King Feisal because he hoped that Syria would evolve into a democracy in which the majority would no longer oppress the minorities. He even proposed a detailed draft constitution[117] for the new state. This included two central statements, firstly that it should be a purely secular, civic state and that it be absolutely neutral regarding the different religions and faiths.[118] Equal civic rights and equality before the law were what the minorities lacked and desired most during the last phase of the Ottoman Empire, and that is why Samné hoped for a radical change after the Ottomans had lost the war and were driven out of the Arab Middle East.

However, it was not only the Christians who desired a democracy that would ensure the freedom and equality of all citizens, a democracy 'which copied from the West some of its political principles, such as parliament and constitutional government,'[119] as Kurd 'Ali clearly stated. Writing about his first trip to Europe, he expressed his great admiration for 'French thought that has laid down the everlasting principles in the constitutions of all the civilized nations' and taught all of them freedom.'[120] He thus realized the great difference between a Western democratic government and Ottoman rule which claimed to be representative after 1908 but was in reality hardly different from the despotic, tyrannical rule of 'Abdülhamid, since it was a democracy in name and external appearance only, and lacked its basic principles such as freedom and equality.[121] Therefore, while Syria was still under Ottoman rule, Kurd 'Ali believed in having a constitution that treated all its Ottoman subjects equally, no matter what their religion or ethnic group,[122] taking a lesson from European countries with similar diversity of religion and ethnicity, in which real democracy had solved their problems.[123] The fact that this equality might run counter to many of the Qur'anic laws did not seem to affect his opinion. As a result, he insisted that constitutional, representative government, no matter how corrupt, was always more rational and just than absolute rule.[124]

Neither the Azharite sheikh 'Abd al-Raziq nor the devout Muslim woman Nazira Zayn al-Din could openly endorse completely secular political principles. Yet when writing about the ancient Muslim caliphate, 'Abd al-Raziq insists that it was not elected, representative or democratic since no free thought or formal opposition existed.[125] He considered that contemporary Muslims were now free to choose whatever form of government that suited their desires and interests.[126] From this and from his criticism of the ancient caliphate, it can be inferred that what he had in mind was modern, democratic, elected and representative government, based on freedom and equality such as that which Europe enjoyed and which had been such a powerful factor in European progress and civilization. Nazira also endorsed democracy because it guaranteed freedom of thought, speech and writing,[127] but since she was more concerned about women's rights she also insisted on democracy because it offered women's suffrage. However, instead of seeking her inspiration in the

West, she sought it in Islam, for 'just as the Prophet sought to have the women also acknowledge his leadership,' women had as much right to vote as the men.[128] Like 'Abd al-Raziq, she avoided any of the secular principles of democracy that conflicted with Islam.

In Hussein's and al-Sayyid's thought, there is no such ambiguity. They both clearly state that constitutional government, parliament, the ministries and the separation of powers were European concepts, the like of which Muslims knew nothing about before modern times, and that this form of government had come about as a result of the political thought of philosophers such as Rousseau (d.1778), Locke and Montesquieu.[129] They both insisted that their adoption was the only way to progress.[130] Naturally they also fully realized that this democracy was based on completely secular principles that contradicted Islam. Al-Sayyid translated Aristotle's *De Re Publica* in order to enlighten his compatriots as to Aristotle's political principles and the meaning of words such as autocracy, dictatorship and democracy, which are all Aristotelian terms. Hussein states that the development of reason and free thought in ancient Greece resulted in its becoming a democracy as early as the sixth century b.c.e., and that it was thanks to this democracy that people understood that they were all equal before the law, no individual or class being superior to another, all being born to have equal rights and duties.[131] In his great admiration for Greek thought, Hussein completely overlooked the fact that Greek democracy was different from that which he advocated and which European thought had developed only after the seventeenth century.

Democracy was also based on the concentration of political power in the hands of the people, and thus Hussein sees 'that the people are their own master and the source of all power,'[132] rather than being subject to the divine will, as Islam decrees. However, still thinking within the framework of Islam, Hussein claimed that Islam itself teaches a break from the political past in order to progress, as can be seen in the second chapter of this book. Like 'Abd al-Raziq, he insisted that Islam contained no political system, and only established general rules that enjoined the Muslims to work for a common good and refrain from evil, leaving them free to administer their worldly affairs as they saw fit, so long as they did not transgress these general rules.[133] He was more explicit than 'Abd al-Raziq, however, when he deduced from this that Islam encouraged the adoption of whatever political system suited the Muslims' changing economic, social and political conditions, which, under the prevailing circumstances, meant Western democracy. He realized, however, that democracy could not work unless the people themselves fully assimilated its principles, as has been seen.

Al-Sayyid also believed that the basis of every government, no matter what its doctrines or policy, was the common good (*manfa'a*), and that all these policies have the common good of the nation in mind.[134] The only acceptable rule to him in that sense was that of a constitutional and democratic government,[135] founded on secular, political freedoms which permitted every individual to participate freely and completely in the governance of the country. He considered that political freedom such as this would guarantee freedom of the individual and freedom of speech and deed.[136] Completely echoing Western political democratic and secular thought, he wrote:

> A constitution is the nation's right, just as freedom is the right of the individual, for since every individual is born free, it must follow that the nation was also established freely since man is by nature a social animal. This right means the nation's right to govern itself in the way it sees fit, and this is a right which no one may impair.[137]

For al-Sayyid, therefore, freedom represented not only political freedom, but all aspects of the personal freedom which the nineteenth century philosophers defended. The rights and freedoms of which he writes here are clearly the secular ones of the West. That is why conservative circles attacked him and his ilk, claiming 'they were imitating their European masters' and repeating the lessons these masters had taught them and for which the Egyptian people had no use.[138] But for all his belief in the people, al-Sayyid, like Hussein, realized that they had to be educated and made aware of the principles of democracy before they could really acquire it, and this was why democracy could only be won gradually.[139]

B. *The Law*

The Qur'an contains many laws regulating various aspects of people's political, social and private lives, and since the Islamic state derived its laws from the Qur'an, law-making was outside the prerogative of the ruler. Yet over time, the Ottoman and the Egyptian government passed secular laws inspired by French law, mainly governing trade and the economy, in order to suit changing political and economic circumstances. New interpretations of the *shari'a* (Qur'anic law) were also developed by jurists and the *'ulama* to suit the changing circumstances of the time.[140] These new laws were still based on the *shari'a* and could still be considered to be of divine origin and not completely man-made, so when the Ottoman Empire issued the *Tanzimat* and especially the largely secular *Hatti-Hümayun* in 1856, guaranteeing religious liberty and equal rights and treatment for all Ottoman subjects, regardless of their religion or race, these *Tanzimat* were opposed by the powerful Muslim leaders and the Muslim population in general who viewed such attempts to legislate equality between Muslims and non-Muslims as being sacrilegious and contrary to Islam. These *Tanzimat* were never really applied, however.

In the second half of the nineteenth century, the power of the *shari'a* courts in Egypt was limited by the state, and between 1876 and 1883

> ... new civil courts, the Mixed Tribunals and the National (Native) Courts were charged with the administration of most civil law, the *shari'a* system was expressly limited to questions of personal status: marriage, divorce, inheritance, partnership, guardianship and *awqaf* (religious endowments).[141]

Thus it is mainly with regard to the *shari'a* laws of personal status that the writers' secular stance lies, since the other courts applied man-made laws which were largely inspired by European law.

Although the Christian writers had no problem with man-made laws, under the Ottoman Empire they were subject to the *shari'a* laws just like the Muslims. That is why al-Shidyaq strongly defended the *Tanzimat* in the periodical he produced in Constantinople, assuring that they were necessary in order to enforce justice and the country's rights in the face of the growing power and influence of foreign countries. As if to assuage the fears of the Muslims, he adds that these *Tanzimat* contain nothing contradictory to the Muslim *shari'a*,[142] although he knew perfectly well that they did. Still writing with a Christian mentality, he points out that Europe was better off than the Muslim countries because its laws were created by men for the benefit of the people, separating religious from civil matters, and they were more effective in reforming society than all the sermons the clergy preached in the East.[143] In the same vein, Marrash insists that to a just government all citizens are equal before the law, without distinction of race, religion or class, one law being applicable to all.[144] Naturally to Marrash all laws were man-made, and like Montesquieu and other European philosophers, he saw that one of the basic principles of civilization was for laws to conform to current requirements. He therefore rejected general and immutable laws, such as those of the *shari'a*, believing that all laws should evolve and change according to changing times and circumstances.[145]

This was also the attitude of the later Christian writers. Ishaq, Zaydan and al-Shumayyil, all of whom stressed the need to change laws that were no longer appropriate and replace them with laws created to suit changing situations.[146] However, only al-Shumayyil stated overtly, 'there are no God-given laws. It is man's ignorance and illusion that has made him imagine this. Man's laws are man-made and correspond to his backwardness or progress'. [147] This is consistent with his belief that all religions are man-made, and although Zaydan shared this belief with Antun, they avoided the subject. Al-Shumayyil's claim that laws were passed to serve the interests of those in power and to oppress the weak were consistent with his socialist attitudes. He claimed that although rulers assert that through these laws they enforce justice, in reality they are tyrants.[148] As for the laws themselves, they are despotic because they do not correspond to the laws of nature, and discriminate between people in relation to their rights and duties. Theocratic laws raise the clergy above the people and give them privileges which burden the people with many duties and very few rights; and through autocratic, despotic laws the rulers terrorize the people until they kill their spirit and they become ignorant, with the result that the rulers are easily able to deprive them of all their rights. Thus the interest of the powerful individual takes precedence over that of society. And what is worse in al-Shumayyil's eyes is that, unlike the laws of nature that change constantly, all these laws are stagnant, either because they are theocratic and believed to be God-given, or because those in power refuse to change them to suit changing circumstances. Laws, however, are neither infallible nor immutable, and are required to change, he insists. Only revolutions managed to change them, but these produce much bloodshed. Therefore consistent with his firm belief in natural science he says, very idealistically, that knowing the laws of nature will make people apply them to society. Thus each individual will know his rights and duties and how to lead a healthy life, with the result that their morals will improve, and with them society as well, for people will no longer lie out of fear or self-interest, and both poverty and theft will diminish.[149] Thus, according to al-Shumayyil, society can only improve by knowing true science and by studying the laws of nature and applying them to society, for all the other existing laws, whether believed to be God-given or man-made, are unjust.

Muslim writers had a more serious problem to contend with since the Muslim *shari'a* was believed to be divinely inspired. In spite of this, a fervent Muslim such as al-Kawakibi insisted that those elected by the people should legislate because they know people's needs and interests best,[150] and that the most useful thing that advanced nations obtained was having their laws made by the people, for a people cannot unanimously agree on anything that is wrong.[151] Although this belief in the infallibility of a unanimous opinion complies with the Muslim belief in consensus (*ijma'*), al-Kawakibi was talking about human, rather than divine, legislation. Even with regard to personal status law such as the laws of marriage, he writes that a good government is that which establishes its laws.[152] Amin also criticized the Muslim rulers and jurists for not passing new law designed to regulate matters of personal status such as marriage and divorce, and thus avoid the chaos which prevailed in these matters. 'Just compare them with the European laws that regulate marriage and all family affairs,'[153] he writes, clearly insinuating that Western, man-made laws, even in matters of civil status, were superior to those of the *shari'a* as it was then constituted, and the hidebound interpretations applied by the *shari'a* courts. He also criticizes the Muslim ban on any new and/or independent opinion on legal issues which might be better suited to changing circumstances, even though this opinion would not contradict the general principle laid down by the Qur'an and the Sunna.[154] Thus, without actually breaking away from the *shari'a* laws, both writers urged people to make their own laws to suit changing circumstances, while avoiding possible contradictions between these laws and the *shari'a*.

The same applies to Muslim authors of the following generation. Nazira Zayn al-Din repeatedly insisted that there is a right to make laws that match the changing times and people's general welfare, for what people find is good or bad, useful or harmful, is relative and changes over time. That is why she criticizes sticking to the old interpretations of the *shari'a*, clarifying that what the intellect is capable of understanding today from what the Prophet had said differs from the intellect of the ancients and what they understood by his sayings. Since she wanted to avoid giving the impression that changing the laws is foreign to the essence of Islam, she adds here that even God changed some of the verses He revealed to His Prophet, in order to teach mankind the necessity for change and progress to suit changing circumstances.[155] The Prophet had even said: 'God Himself has authorized what He had previously forbidden because necessity demanded it.'[156] Here Nazira makes it clear that in this she is following the Hanafi school of thought.[157] The Hanafis depended on the legal scholars' interpretations of the Sunna that involved the 'spirit and relevance of a tradition within the context of the *shari'a as a whole*,'[158] rather than on a literal interpretation of each tradition as a separate entity, which would reveal contradictions with other traditions, as well as with the whole spirit of Islam. This is the method Nazira applied when discussing the problem of the veil, as has been shown.

Kurd 'Ali's attitude was ambivalent. Not wanting to break away from his Islamic heritage, he asserted that Western-made laws are no worse than God's laws, and that applying Western taxation laws helps to redress social injustices just as much as does the application of the Muslim alms tax.[159] If new laws had replaced the old *shari'a* laws this was because of the ignorance and stagnation of the jurists who had no real knowledge of the *shari'a* and of that which in its laws was suited to all times and places. He therefore begged the Muslim governments to eliminate many of the books of jurisprudence and the *fatwas* (legal opinions) written by recent jurists that were no longer appropriate.[160] However, at other times, he shows a clear preference for the secular, man-made laws of the West. For example, he asks the Arabs to adopt French law,[161] insists that the people should write their own constitution,[162] and severely criticizes the Saudi kings, demanding that they change their obsolete methods and replace them with new ones, derived from the spirit of Western law which is the result of profound study and wise experience.[163] One of the reasons why he was in favor of a republic was that he considered that it brought in new laws that were the result of experience and the progress of knowledge.[164] When criticizing the law that had been introduced by Atatürk in Turkey after World War I, he rightly saw the difficulty of applying Swiss law in a backward country like Turkey. 'Laws do not make the nations, it is the nations who make the laws,' he wrote,[165] thus clearly indicating his belief in the people's prerogative to set the laws to suit them.

This same secular attitude is also taken by Hussein and al-Sayyid. Writing about the law, the latter never mentions the *shari'a* laws, only considering the manmade laws which he deals with from a purely secular, Western point of view. He regards law-making as one of the most complicated tasks, since lawmakers need an extensive knowledge of law, society and philosophy, besides long experience and a good knowledge of people.[166] On the basis of the secular Western pattern, he says that passing these laws is one of the duties of a parliament, and these laws should guarantee the individual's freedom of thought, belief, speech, expression and education, and ensure that all the people are equal under the law. There should be no difference between them regarding their creed or race, unlike what is practiced in the army which differentiates between races when it comes to promotions.[167] Undoubtedly this complete equality between citizens is derived from secular law, although the examples al-Sayyid gives avoid mentioning the inequality among citizens with regard to the civil status laws that were based on the *shari'a*, thus avoiding any comparison or conflict that might have arisen between his belief in man-made laws and his belief in those imposed by God.

Taha Hussein also managed to avoid this problem. Without discussing the Qur'an itself and whether its laws were God-given, he only mentions Islamic *jurisprudence*, and says that Muslim jurisprudence was more or less influenced by that of the Romans, whether the Muslim jurists realized it or not. The reason he gives is that the Romans had governed the countries the Muslims later conquered, that Roman law had been carefully studied in these countries and had greatly influenced their peoples, as a result of which many Roman laws were absorbed into Muslim jurisprudence, and what are believed to be purely Islamic laws are in reality Islamo-Roman.[168] He thus insinuates that these laws are in reality of man-made origin. Hussein again avoids the problem by only mentioning the civil laws that are applied in the law courts, showing that they are taken from European law, and that even the *shari'a* courts have become more like the European law courts than like the traditional Islamic courts.[169] He becomes more explicit when he writes that by signing the Treaty of Independence with Europe in 1936 and the agreement annulling the Capitulations in 1937, Egypt had taken upon itself the duty of following in Europe's footsteps in passing its laws.[170] This clearly shows that Hussein was totally in favour not only of having man-made laws but even of laws that were influenced and/or inspired by European law.

CHAPTER NINE

Nationalism

The desire of these writers for social, educational and political reform was entirely motivated by their love for their country and its people.

The first evidence of purely secular nationalism among the writers under review is to be found among the Lebanese and Syrian Christians of the first generation. The fact that nationalism had a secular connotation is clear from the way in which they define it. Bustani writes: 'Our compatriots are all those living in [greater] Syria, no matter what their religion, class, race or tribe'.[1] Addressing the Christians and Druzes in Lebanon in the wake of the bitter confessional wars between them in 1860 he tells them: 'You drink from the same water, breathe the same air, speak the same language, and your land, interests and customs are the same'.[2] This is a clearly secular definition of nationalism based on commonly owned land and interests, civilization and language, regardless of any difference in religion. In fact, Bustani believes that the various sects and religions in his country could be beneficial as an enriching element and a means of competition for the improvement of all.[3] This same attempt to remove the religious element from nationalism is also evident when al-Shidyaq analyses the difference between the Muslims of Egypt and those of Damascus, for although their religion is the same, he indicates that each of the two nations has its own distinct characteristics.[4] When writing about the Franco-Prussian war (1870–1871) he assures his readers that the national spirit is stronger than religious ties, for although Bavaria was Roman Catholic like the French, it fought on the side of the Protestant Prussians against them.[5] He also insists that unity of language, ethnicity and land are the basic condition for people to feel that they belong to one nation, and even different religions should not affect this unity.[6] However, writing in Constantinople, and probably to curry favor with the sultan, he sometimes renounces this secular nationalism for one tinged with religion when he writes, in an article, that he strongly desires the unity of all Muslims.[7]

Marrash, too, saw that shared interests, not religion, are what bind people into one nation, with no difference between them. He greatly praised patriotism which he believed to be the cause of Europe's progress, believing that it was through patriotism that the individual sacrificed his personal interest for the general good. This was Montesquieu's definition of political virtue[9] in *L'Esprit des Lois*. Ishaq provides this same secular definition when he says that what binds people into a nation is their common interest in cultivating the land and cooperating to procure their needs and ward off danger.[10] He adds:

> The fatherland (*watan*) is the place to which one relates, that which guarantees one's rights and acknowledges one's duties towards it, in which you and your family and money are secure... But there is no fatherland without freedom.[11]

This definition is clearly influenced by Western secular political thought in which freedom and the equal rights of citizens are basic elements. That is why, to him, a nation could consist of different ethnic groups, religions and even languages, for the land on which they lived was their fatherland and it need not have fixed boundaries because countries that were not originally one country could become united. The only important thing in his eyes was that people should *agree* to be one nation, just like the Americans who were originally English, French, Spanish or Native Americans, or the Ottomans who were Turks, Arabs or Tartars. Ishaq criticizes the Greeks, Serbs, Romanians and Bulgarians for seeking to break away from the Ottoman Empire.[12] Unlike Bustani and al-Shidyaq, who insisted that a single language is a unifying factor in a nation, and not wanting their country to turn into a Babel of languages as it was one of religions,[13] Ishaq rejected the idea that a single language could be a condition for the unity of a nation.[14] However, he contradicts himself when he writes that the Ottoman parliament did not fail only because it was not created by the will of the people, but also because it comprised people of different ethnic groups, various languages and opinions, thus representing the old Tower of Babel of the Ottoman Empire.[15] Here he obviously felt that belonging to one ethnic group and speaking one language does not play a role in the unity of a nation.

These Christian writers' secular nationalism can be traced back to several factors. As has been pointed out in previous chapters, they all had strong anticlerical feelings, and in the Ottoman Empire political differentiation was based on religious grounds. As a minority, the Christians were not really part of the specifically Muslim political administration. As a minority in the mainly Muslim Ottoman Empire, and having suffered from the wars of religion in

1860, it was normal for Christians to feel that only a secular nationalist spirit could unite them with their Muslim compatriots. In 1860, Bustani started a number of periodicals to combat his compatriots' religious fervour and replace it with a spirit of nationalism.[16] One of them, *Nafir Suriyya*, bore the slogan 'Love of the fatherland is part of faith'. To counteract the sectarian spirit, Bustani also founded *al-Madrasa al-Wataniyya*, the first purely national school in Lebanon, expressly stating that it was open to pupils of all faiths. The strong effect the religious wars had on these writers is clearly shown in several articles they wrote. In *Nafir Suriyya*, for example, Bustani severely criticized this 'barbaric' war, expressing deep pain and anger when describing the loss of life, besides the material and non-material damage.[17] Likewise, Marrash wishes that the Arabs had schools like the Europeans that would propagate knowledge and patriotism that were devoid of religious bias.[18]

These writers were also enraged by the foreign interference in Syria and Lebanon, especially during and after the religious conflicts. The relationship of Europe to themselves and their countries could have been another factor that encouraged their secular nationalism, European interference being another wedge driven between them and their Muslim fellow countrymen. Bustani believed that the Europeans had taken advantage of the Lebanese internecine struggle to further their economic, political and religious interests there, and although their interference helped to stop the bloodshed, he realized that it would be detrimental to the country in the long run.[19] Thus, although he admitted the positive role the West and its missionaries had played in 'bringing back to the Arabs the learning they had taken from them,' and helping them to emerge from their Dark Ages, he was enraged by 'the insolence and arrogance of some Westerners towards our Eastern people'.[20] al-Shidyaq, too, criticizes the Lebanese faith in the French, and the way in which they had 'welded their honour to that of the French'.[21] He wrote pages full of scathing irony and sarcasm attacking the foreigners who, having come to Lebanon, nevertheless remain ignorant of everything about the country, distrusting its inhabitants and criticizing everything and everyone, while exploiting the land and its people, just like the haughty foreigners in Egypt who exploited and despised the Egyptians.[22]

Foreign interference in the Ottoman Empire and British hegemony in Egypt were also criticized by Ishaq. In several articles, he attacked the Egyptian rulers who were under the British thumb, and who granted these foreigners every possible social, economic and political privilege, while the Egyptians were deprived of high office and of the wealth of their own country.[23] Although he admitted that the foreigners brought knowledge and education to Egypt, he strongly attacked them for despising the Egyptians, humiliating them and treating them unjustly, and praised the Egyptian National Party (*al-Hizb al-Watani*) for striving to liberate Egypt from foreign domination and ensure freedom, independence and the full rights of the people.[24]

These writers' strong criticism of Western interference in their countries might not be due solely to their nationalism, but also, as has been pointed out, to their desire to distance themselves from a Christian West whose religion they shared, while stressing that it was foreign to them in everything else. This is another proof of their secular nationalism.

Yet a certain ambivalence can be detected in Ishaq's attitude towards France. Although he criticizes its occupation of Tunisia,[25] his great admiration for France led him to claim that it was the only European state that defended the weaker countries. He asserted that if independence were detrimental to them, France helped to strengthen them by occupying them, and thus earned their respect.[26] This not only contradicts the national feeling he had expressed, but also his very claim that national freedom and independence were a people's right.

In their nationalism, the secularism of the writers under review took on different aspects. In accordance with his belief that nationalism is not necessarily based on unity of language and ethnicity, Ishaq often expressed an *Oriental* nationalism which defended the whole of the Orient against European colonization. In this, he was influenced by al-Afghani whose disciple he had been when the latter was in Egypt. Ishaq wrote a long article in praise of al-Afghani.[27] What, in Ishaq's opinion, led to the East's being colonized, especially by the Russians and the British who surpassed all others in their tyranny and cruelty, was the ignorance of the masses, the tyranny of the rulers and the treachery and/or fanaticism of the leaders.[28] He defined the Orient as Asia, minus the Russian part, Egypt and Africa, and the European countries whose predominant religion was Greek Orthodoxy (*Bilad al-Rum*). Consequently, in 1878, he sprang to the defence of Afghanistan when Britain attacked it,[29] and called upon the Eastern countries to unite against the colonizing and exploiting Europeans, whether these Eastern countries be Muslim, Christian, Buddhist or anything else.[30] In this, he differed from his mentor, Afghani, who had mainly Muslim unity in mind. In accordance with his belief that differences of religion, ethnicity and language play no role in nationalist feeling, Ishaq demanded that Orientals eliminate all religious and ethnic fanaticism and unite against the European colonizer.[31] He never took into consideration a possible conflict of interest between the various Eastern countries themselves.

Ottomanism was another aspect of nationalism, but one which naturally disappeared once the Ottoman Empire was defeated during World War I and subsequently disbanded. As Sharabi points out:

> The aspect of Otomanism that was most meaningful from all standpoints was its supra-national, supra-religious, supra-ethnic character. It embraced within its political framework all the different nationalities, religions and ethnic elements in the Empire and provided them with a basis for a workable political and social system... At the same time, the Ottoman framework did not negate national or sectarian interests. Indeed... this framework provided the best conditions for the fulfillment of these interests, at least as far as the upper social and religious strata were concerned.[32]

That is why, for many intellectuals, both Christian and Muslim, there was no contradiction between their nationalism and Ottomanism. Bustani's nationalism was Syrian, as has been pointed out, yet this did not prevent him from supporting the Ottoman Empire and praising the Sultan when he gave him permission to start his national school, for 'in those days all the regions of the Empire enjoyed civilization, freedom and equality,'[33] he writes. The *Hatti Hümayun* of 1856 which guaranteed equal rights to all Ottoman subjects regardless of their religion or race, was never really applied. The new Ottoman Constitution of 1876 reasserted absolute equality between Muslims and non-Muslims and gave the minorities hope of attaining equality, although it, too, was never applied and was opposed by the Muslims.

Ishaq's nationalism was also much more Ottoman than 'oriental'. Influenced by Afghani's political ideas, he repeatedly voiced his support for the Ottoman Empire. Although he demanded reforms within the Empire, he endorsed its remaining united, reiterating that the variety of religions and ethnic groups it encompassed was not an important factor and believing that the unity of the variety of nations within it was a guarantee of its independence and helped it to combat Western power and interference.[34] This made him believe that what rallied the Armenians, Greeks and Arabs to fight for the cause of the Ottoman Empire against the Russians was their patriotism and the good intentions of their government.[35]

At the same time, a secular *Arab* nationalism was also evident in the writings of these Lebanese and Syrian Christians. This did not cause them to demand separation from the Ottoman Empire; Arab nationalism with such political aims did not emerge before the beginning of the twentieth century. These writers probably felt that a secular Arabism was a bond that united them with their Muslim Arab compatriots in a Muslim empire that differentiated between them and the Muslims and, in spite of the *Tanzimat* treated them as *dhimmis*, leaving them to feel like strangers in their own country. Bustani, al-Shidyaq, Marrash and Ishaq were all revolted by the European contempt for the Arabs. Bustani and Shidyaq strongly attacked anyone who criticized the Arabs. If anyone claimed that all Arabs were liars and cheats, Bustani 'felt his Arab blood boil in his veins,' and he staunchly defended the Arabs, saying that only individuals, whether Arab or non-Arab, could be liars and cheats, but never a whole nation. Shidyaq was just as enraged by Europeans who said that the Arabs were dirty, without ever having entered an Arab home or garden.[36] His criticism of the Turks is just as severe because he believed that they humiliated the Arabs, although 'the Prophet was an Arab and the Qur'an was revealed in the Arabic language'.[37] Marrash, too, is revolted by the Europeans' contempt for the Arabs.[38]

Thanks to them, Arabism had a purely secular connotation. Al-Shidyaq criticizes the Maltese who equate Arabism with Islam, and Marrash insists that the fact that he is a Christian does not make him less of an Arab than the Muslim.[39] Proof of this secular Arab nationalism is Marrash's pride in Saladdin having vanquished the Crusaders.[40] He is among the very few Arabs of his day to hint at a desire to break free from the Ottoman Empire. When he stayed in Paris, he greatly admired the freedom, peace and security enjoyed by the French who were unafraid that a 'foreigner would attack them... a wild animal devour them, or a neighbor rob them... Or [that they would] bear the thorns of a barbaric rule or a savage power'.[41] The 'barbaric rule and savage power' of which he writes are undoubtedly those of the Ottoman Turks in his country and he would clearly like to rid his country of them of in order to enjoy the liberty and freedom of the French. Bustani and al-Shidyaq never advocated independence from the Ottoman Empire, probably because they, too, felt that its unity was the only guarantee of strength in the face of Western threats. Because of his official relation to the Sublime Porte while in Constantinople, al-Shidyaq endorsed the Ottoman sultan's Pan-Islamism and his desire to reestablish the caliphate,[42] but he was not sincere in this for, while still in Constantinople, he wrote in a letter to a relative in Lebanon that he did not like the Ottoman rule nor was he attached to it.[43]

A strong element in these writers' Arab nationalism was their love for and pride in their Arabic language and heritage, and their desire to preserve and develop them,[44] for to them these were the basis of their national identity. Bustani, al-Shidyaq and Marrash strongly criticized those of their compatriots who did not know Arabic, or used foreign words in their speech, or, worse still, spoke a foreign language in preference to Arabic.[45] Marrash has an Arab in Bombay ask his daughter's nanny to speak to her only in Arabic 'because I want my language to be that of my children as well, so that through it they will preserve their nationality and origin'.[46] Because their language was so important to them Bustani and al-Shidyaq taught Arabic and wrote books on the language and its literature. Bustani compiled an important Arabic dictionary, *Muhit al-Muhit*, and started the first encyclopaedia in Arabic. One of the aims of his National School was to enable its students master Arabic because he believed that *language* is the basis for the progress of a nation,[47] thus showing once again how far he believed language to be a basic element in nationality. He criticized those who claimed that learning Arabic could never lead to civilization. On the contrary, he claimed that the Arabs could develop much more strongly if they were taught in their own tongue and not in foreign languages.[48] al-Shidyaq strongly criticized the orientalists who claimed to know Arabic and even taught it, although they were ignorant of the language. He attacked those of them who neglected Arabic in favor of Hebrew or Syriac,[49] believing Arabic to be a noble language, superior to any other and distinguished by its eloquence and conciseness.[50]

A factor in their pride in the language was their pride in their Arab heritage. Bustani refutes the claims of those who say that the Arabs only copied and did not invent. He lists everything the Arabs had invented in the fields of medicine, chemistry and mathematics, among others, and this despite the limited resources they had at their disposal, showing the debt the world owed the Arabs in all these fields.[51] Marrash, too, boasts of the Arab civilization and blamed their present backwardness on the wars and the ignorance that spread thereafter, through which reason was destroyed.[52] Ishaq also demonstrates his pride in the heritage and culture of the Arabs, and calls on the Arabs of the Hijaz (now Saudi-Arabia), Syria, Egypt, Iraq, Yemen, Tunisia and Morocco to unite, since they are all Arabs, speaking one language, regardless of any religious differences between them. He believed that such unity would help them regain their rights and their past glory.[53] His Arab nationalism is based here on the unity of language between the Arab countries, and clearly contradicts his having said that language is of no importance for the unity of a country. Thus, his pride in his language and past heritage made even Ishaq revert to the secular Arab nationalism which was so obvious in all the writings of his Christian contemporaries. This is despite the fact that their nationalism remained a cultural, and not a political one claiming Arab independence, or defining an Arab territory and what its borders would be.

This secular nationalism was also endorsed by the Muslim writers of the following generation, with the exception of the women writers Zaynab Fawwaz and Bahithat al-Badiya. Fawwaz's nationalism was not secular but religious and negative, for she did not express pride in Ottomanism, Egyptianism or

Arabism, but solely hatred of the West. She strongly attacks Europe for hating the Muslims and exploiting their countries. When she repeatedly blames the West for having divided the Muslims,[54] it can be deduced that for her, Islam was a sufficient bond to unite people of different ethnicities and languages. Unlike Bustani, al-Shidyaq and Marrash who feared for their Arabic language and heritage if overwhelmed by Western civilization, Fawwaz feared for Islam and that the Muslims would abandon the teachings of their religion under the influence of European civilization and the debauchery it caused.[55] Her nationalism was thus purely religious.

Without expressing that same hatred of the West, Bahithat al-Badiya does not fear for Islam, but for her Oriental/Egyptian identity of which for her Islam constitutes an integral part, as she was a deeply religious woman. She urged her countrymen to adopt only what is laudable in European culture, that is 'the fruits of modern civilization', because adopting European ways of life that do not suit the spirit of the East could cause it to lose its identity.[56] The worst thing that can befall a nation, in her opinion, is for it 'to merge with another one and lose its customs and culture by introducing mores that clash with its own religion and culture'.[57] Among the customs that clash with her religion and one which she strongly criticizes is marriage between a Muslim girl and a Christian.[58] However, her faith in her Egyptian nationality is just as strong as her faith in Islam, and both are intertwined as far as she is concerned. She objects to Egyptian men marrying European women, but she also objects to Egyptian men marrying other Muslim women, such as Turkish, Sudanese, Moroccan or Arab women because they might bring up their children to prefer their mothers' country to Egypt.[59]

It is interesting to note that in spite of both these women having endorsed the liberation of their sex, although to a limited degree, their religious nationalism prevented them from considering women's liberation as part of the liberation of the whole nation, and their nationalism remained Islamic and patriarchal, constantly taking a stand against Western aggression.

The nationalism of their two male Muslim contemporaries, al-Kawakibi and Amin manifested itself slightly differently. Al-Kawakibi's idea of nationalism is ambivalent. On the one hand, he states that what binds a nation are race, language, fatherland and shared rights,[60] with no mention whatsoever of religion. As a result, he expresses a secular Arab nationalism when he urges the Arabs, Muslims and non-Muslims alike to unite as one nation, just as the Americans had done, and to ignore any religious differences between them, 'leaving religion to judge us in the hereafter,' their only motto being: 'Long live the nation, long live the fatherland, may we live free and respected'.[61] This pan-Arabism drove him to boast unrealistically that the Arabs were pioneers in applying equal rights to all citizens, and in understanding the principles of socialism,[62] thus completely ignoring both history and the principles of his own religion.

Besides his having been persecuted by the Ottoman administration, his Arab nationalist feeling also led him criticize the Ottoman Turks for hating the Arabs and despising them, and caused him to attack their government for depriving the Arabs of their right to hold administrative posts relative to their numbers, since two-thirds of the subjects of the Ottoman Empire were Arabs.[63] It is the Ottoman Turks, he writes, who ruined the civilization the Arabs had built. The Arabs had nothing to do with the Armenian genocide perpetrated at the hands of the Turks.[64] Another, and perhaps the main, reason for his opposing the Turks was their claim to the caliphate, which in Islamic tradition and doctrine ought to be Arab. That is why he believed that the Arabs were the only people capable of defending Islam and rejuvenating it since they were free of other people's vices, such as self-abasement, homosexuality, vanity and lust.[65] This was probably a reference to the Turks. Such a statement leads to the deduction that al-Kawakibi's Arabism was religious and not purely secular, incapable of a real separation between Arabism and Islam. What corroborates this deduction is his stipulation in *Um al-Qura* that the members of the ideal society he wishes to create must be Muslims and their official headquarters must be in Mecca,[66] thus expressly excluding all non-Muslim Arabs. It is thus doubtful whether al-Kawakibi's Arab nationalism was purely secular, since, like so many other Muslims, he equated Arabism with Islam.

Unlike the nationalism of the Lebanese and Syrian writers, Amin's nationalism was not Arab but purely Egyptian and secular, a trend that was also noticeable in Bahithat al-Badiya, and emerged again later with the other Egyptians, as a result of Egypt's political circumstances. In fact, Amin insisted that the Egyptian Muslims were *not* of Arab descent, and were only Arab by religion and language, whereas they and the Copts formed one nation. They belonged to the same ethnic group, had similar features and in spite of the divergence in religion:

the Muslims and Copts form a well-coordinated whole, speak the same language, wear the same clothes, have the same customs... Common tragedies united them in patriotic feeling which has made them overlook the difference in religion between them for the sake of the common good.[67]

Thus, for Amin, what forged a nation were a common language and customs and a shared past and destiny, despite any difference in faith among its nationals. The above quotation is taken from Amin's answer to the Duke of Harcourt, written in 1894. In the previous year, the duke had written *L'Egypte et les Egyptiens* in which he attacked Islam and the Egyptians. For Amin, as for other Egyptians, a determining factor in developing the spirit of nationalism was resistance to the European occupation and all that it entailed, resulting in a specifically Egyptian nationalism. Since the Egyptians had their own peculiar problems to contend with, they did not feel they were part of a wider nation to which they were bound by the Arabic language and heritage, as did the Lebanese and Syrian subjects of the Ottoman Empire. Most of the Arabic-speaking countries were provinces of the Empire and, as has been pointed out, it was the Christian Arabs who played a major role in reviving the Arabic language and its heritage, thus helping to develop Arab nationalism in their countries.

This same secular nationalism is found in the Christian Lebanese writers of the following generation – Zaydan, al-Shumayyil, Antun and Azoury. When defining a nation, Zaydan says it is formed by the people of one country who share customs, traditions, moral values and interests, cooperating to gain a livelihood.[68] Neither religion nor even a common language are a basis for a nation according to this definition. In fact, Zaydan seems to consider that common interests are the primary motive for forming a nation. The influence of Jeremy Bentham (d.1832) and John Stuart Mill may be found in Zaydan's argument that people join each other in a group, society or nation out of pure self-interest, even though they may claim that they do so for religious, linguistic, or national reasons.[69] Elaborating on this belief, he goes on to explain that these selfish motives have their origin in man's natural egoism which makes him desire what he thinks is for his own good, and avoid that which might harm him. This egoism and self-interest might be used for material or spiritual profit,[70] and is the cause of all the wars waged throughout history, although the aggressor may claim that his motives are patriotic and nationalistic.[71] Therefore, according to Zaydan's definition, nationalism boils down to a matter of common interests that bring people together, regardless of their ethnic, linguistic or religious affiliations. This might be one of the reasons for his having supported the Ottoman Empire for so long.

Al-Shumayyil, too, insisted that common interests were the basis for national unity,[72] while Antun believed that Pan-Islamism was a useless endeavour if it attempted to unify people of such different nationalities as Persians, Turks, Afghans, Indians, Moroccans and Arabs, for religion alone is not a cohesive force.[73] Thus, Antun not only believed that secular national ties superseded religious ones, but also felt, like his predecessors, that nationalism was a weapon to be used against inter-faith strife from which greater Syria, his country of origin, suffered. That is why he writes that when he started his periodical *al-Jami'a* his aim had been to cleanse the hearts of the Eastern people from their religious fanaticism 'which belongs to the past, to the Middle Ages, the age of ignorance'. They had to unite in order to make progress but this could only be done if each religious group respected the other's beliefs and opinions, for truth and virtue do not are not the sole prerogative of a single group and 'God is everybody's God'.[74] Here, Antun was not only insisting on the importance of religious tolerance, but also insinuating that to 'unite their word' people must believe in something that had nothing to do with their various religious faiths and only secular nationalism was capable of embracing them all. This is corroborated by his great admiration for the American educational system that had succeeded in uniting peoples of different races and faiths into one strong and powerful nation of which each child was proud to say; 'I am an American'.[75]

Similarly, when Azoury says that the Egyptian Muslims and Copts do not hate each other whereas they both hate the Syrians, whether Muslim or Christian,[76] or when he says that the Muslims, Christian Orthodox and Roman Catholics form one and the same nation in Albania,[77] he expresses a belief in a secular nationalist sentiment in which religion plays no part.

The belief of these writers in secular nationalism is the reason why, with the exception of Azoury, they supported the Ottoman Empire after its promised reforms, just as their predecessors had done, and for the same reasons. Zaydan, al-Shumayyil and Antun all felt they were Ottoman subjects and clearly opposed the disintegration of the Empire, not wanting the Arabs to break away and form an independent state.[78] It is clear from the proceedings of the First Arab Congress in Paris, held as late as 1913, that in those days, many Arabs did not seek their independence from the Empire. Zaydan criticized those who did, and welcomed the revolution of the Young Turks, seeing it as the means to implement a democratic constitution under which all citizens, Muslims, Chrstians and Jews, Turks and non-Turks, would all be equal. The break up of the Ottoman Empire would lead, in his view, to foreign (meaning European) occupation and not to Arab independence. That is why in a letter to his son, written in 1908, he expresses joy at his son's decision to learn Turkish, showing the great hopes he pins on the success of the Union and Progress Party and its constitution.[79] In another letter, he condemns the demand for autonomy by the *Comité Central pour la Syrie* based in Paris and adds:

> It is my opinion that the Syrians and the other Ottoman subjects ought to think only in terms of Ottoman unity. As for administrative independence... it will become a necessity at the propitious time, i.e. after the Ottoman people have progressed and have learned their rights and duties.[80]

It was not only just his loyalty to the Ottoman Empire that caused him to view the Turks in a different way to the 'foreign' Europeans, but his desire, like that of his Christian contemporaries and predecessors, to distance themselves from a West their Muslim countrymen tended to associate them with, and to accentuate the fact that they were Christian Easterners and not Westerners.

Al-Shumayyil expresses that same Ottomanism when he does not dispute the legitimacy of the Empire or feel that he does not belong to it. He merely expresses pain and anger at its tyranny, backwardness and weakness.[81] He believes that these were the reasons why various European powers considered they had the right to interfere in its affairs, with the result that it began loosing its colonies.[82] Like Zaydan, he built great hopes on the new representative government of 1908, going as far as to ask it to make Turkish the only language of the country and compulsory in all schools. He saw this as a means of uniting the provinces of the Empire.[83] Yet by 1909, he had already become disenchanted with the new government and aired his views in a long article in which he says that it seems to be a 'leftover from the old, shabby heritage, the constitutional system was merely a camouflage for the autocratic government behind it, and not a parliament elected by the people in order to safeguard their rights'.[84] As late as 1912 he, like Zaydan, opposed the creation of an independent Arab state, and was upset by the Ottoman Empire's loss of some of its provinces. He believed that the best solution to prevent the Empire from breaking up completely lay in decentralization, whereby the Empire would become a union of small states, similar to the United States of America, each province having its own administration, while remaining united to the central core of the Empire for the general welfare of the whole, just like a body in which each organ does its work for the good of the whole.[85] Zaydan forecast to his son that this decentralization would take place at a later date. In 1912, a group of Arabs living in Cairo, both Muslim and Christian, but mainly Lebanese and Syrian had formed the Ottoman Party of Administrative Decentralization as an expression of their desire for decentralization; al-Shumayyil was one of its founding members.[86] In his view, one of the disadvantages of a centralized government, was the way that the schools in the different provinces were forced to teach in a language that was not the native tongue of the pupils.[87] This was a far cry from his plea in 1908 for Turkish to become the compulsory language of instruction in all the schools of the Empire. Most probably the reason for his change of heart was his disappointment with the new government of 1908 which proved not to be as democratic as he had hoped..

Even though Zaydan and al-Shumayyil supported the Ottoman Empire, at the same time they both expressed a feeling of alienation with it, due to the fact that they were Lebanese Christians (though at the time, Lebanon was a province of Syria) who believed in a secularism the Ottomans had never applied. In defence of Christian emigrants like himself, Zaydan points out that the Lebanese emigrants would remain in their country of emigration, mix with its people and become part of them, speaking their language and adopting their customs. If this were defined as treason to one's country and being unpatriotic, what was a fatherland? A fatherland is the country whose people have shared interests and establish laws that apply to all. It is not a person's duty, however, to stay in the fatherland if his livelihood lies elsewhere. Naturally, he will go on loving it, missing it and helping it in time of need, but it is not his duty to remain there or even to return to it.[88] He then defines what patriotism means to him:

> Patriotism is meaningless unless supported by a state that employs its citizens to serve it, or to carry arms in order to defend its independence; that gives its citizens their rights and shares their language. The Christian Syrians have nothing to do with this, for they are part of the Ottoman entity but are not part of its army, do not defend it in times of war and do not speak its language. Therefore the Ottoman Empire is no concern of theirs, and the Syrian fatherland has no need of them in this respect, so to leave it is neither treason nor negligence. The more so, because those who have left were obliged to do so in search of a livelihood after they had uselessly tried to make it here... It is as if their fatherland had abandoned them and evicted them against their will.[89]

This definition is that of a non-religious individual who believes that all the citizens of a country should have equal rights and obligations, and be subject to the same laws. These lines thus express all the pain and bitterness that the alienated minorities felt in an Empire that neither treated its citizens equally nor defended their rights. As if to show what their country of origin was deprived of as a result of its sectarianism, Zaydan repeatedly indicates his pride in what the Christian emigrants had achieved all over the world, whether in literature, science, commerce, industry and the various professions.[90] His own achievements in the world of literature, journalism and publishing were living proof of his claims, as were those of al-Shumayyil, Antun and Sarruf, to mention only those of his contemporaries with which this book is concerned.

The same sentiment is expressed by al-Shumayyil when in 1909 he wrote to the Syrian and Lebanese emigrants in New York that it is the tyranny, fanaticism and poverty of the Ottoman Empire that drove the Christian Syrians to emigrate. Although their love for their fatherland made them long to return, as long as their homeland deprived them of all the *rights and duties* that the other citizens enjoyed, they were better off in their country of emigration where they had all the advantages of the local residents.[91] Like Zaydan, he expresses pride in all that the Christian Syrians had done to revive and promote Arabic culture and journalism not only in Syria, but in Egypt and even in the New World.[92]

Zaydan's and al-Shumayyil's defence of the Lebanese emigrants contains a subtext of Lebanese nationalism they were driven to feel in spite of their Ottoman affiliation. As a result, al-Shumayyil demonstrates an overtly secular Lebanese nationalism when in 1912 he defends Lebanon's rights to the Beka'a and the coastal lands which Lebanon was then demanding, in addition to its autonomy as a province within the Ottoman Empire.[93] The fact that the majority of the population of the Beka'a and the coastal plain were Muslims did not affect his secular thinking. His Lebanese patriotism came to the fore again during the 1916 famine in Lebanon when he cried out in anguish: 'My country! My country... is perishing with no help!... Let all Europe and America die as long as all my country is dying'.[94]

Azoury was the only strongly anti-Ottoman writer among the secular writers of this period but this was not for religious reasons. In a whole chapter of his book *Le Réveil de la nation Arabe* (The Reawakening of the Arab Nation) which was published in 1905 he describes in great detail the different aspects of the injustice, tyranny, debauchery, exploitation and corruption of the Turks and the Ottoman civil servants whom he calls 'bandits.' He condemns the bloodthirsty, barbaric intrigues of Abdülhamid and his savagery in the Armenian genocide, showing how these conditions caused Arabs to emigrate.[95] In a completely secular national spirit, without differentiating between Muslims and Christians, he asks the Kurds, Armenians, Albanians and Arabs to demand their independence from such an empire.[96]

The main reason for this demand was his *secular political Arab nationalism*. Zaydan, al-Shumayyil, Sarruf and Antun all felt they were Arabs, but their Arabism, like that of their Christian forebears, was still *linguistic and cultural* rather than political, and it was the Arabic language and its heritage that were the cornerstones of their Arab nationalism. In his novel *Urushalim al-Jadida* (The New Jerusalem) Antun has his Arab Christian protagonists insisting that the Arab Muslims who were conquering Jerusalem at the time the story takes place entered the land in order to bring peace and reform, and to respect and protect all those who, like the Christians and Muslims themselves, worshipped one God.[97] Antun's Arabism is thus obviously secular.

Zaydan was the first of the writers under review to clearly defined Arabism. For him, the Syrians Christians (meaning Syrians, Lebanese and Palestinians) were Arabs because they spoke Arabic, were born in Arab countries and had

Arab customs and moral values, although ethnically they are not all of Arab origin. Therefore he considered the Christians who lived in Anatolia to be Turks because they spoke Turkish, although most of them were of Greek origin.[98] This definition excluded all differences in ethnic origin or religion, and accentuated the importance Zaydan attributed to *language and heritage* as a unifying force. His Arabism, like that of Bustani and al-Shidyaq before him, was still literary and cultural, and like them, it was to the Arabic language and its heritage that he devoted his life. Zaydan was particularly proud of this heritage and insisted that modern Arab writers should study it and use a pure Arabic style in their writing, not one influenced by European styles and idioms.[99] Staunchly defending the use of literary Arabic and refusing categorically to replace it with the colloquial form, he claims that it is thanks to the Qur'an that the Arabic language remained a unifying force among the Arab peoples.[100] Although he admitted that foreign science text books were more advanced than those in Arabic, Zaydan says that 'the aim of teaching is to develop the nation and unite it... and this cannot be achieved without developing its language and reviving its culture by writing scientific and literary books, journals and magazines in Arabic'.[101] This is what Antun took upon himself to do in his *Jami'a*. Sarruf did the same in his *Muqtataf*, al-Shumayyil in the numerous scientific articles he contributed to this and other periodicals and so did Zaydan in his *Hilal* and his life's work. The dozens of Arabic historical novels and books on classical Arabic literature and civilization that he wrote are proof of his concern with the Arabic language and its heritage, as well as proof of his secular Arabic nationalism. When he names one of his books *Tarikh al-Tamaddun al-Islami* (The History of Islamic Civilization) he is not writing about Islamic but about Arabic civilization, of which Islam forms a natural part. Thanks to his love and interest in Arabic, on a secular basis, he was criticized by some Christians for praising the Muslims, while being attacked by some Muslims for having criticized Arab civilization in his *Tarikh al-Tamaddun al-Islami* and elsewhere,[102] and by other Arabs for having opposed Arab independence from the Ottoman Empire.[103] In spite of this, his works, mainly his novels, were widely read and made the Arab reader aware and proud of his cultural heritage. As Philipp rightly puts it:

> With his definition of the Arab identity by a common language and a common history... Zaydan laid the secular foundation for a specific brand of Arab nationalism, that Pan-Arabism which would reach its full development one generation after his death.[104]

The secular *political* Arabism was left to Azoury to define and fight for.

Depuis le Tigre jusqu'à l'Isthme de Suez, et depuis la Méditerranée jusqu'à la mer d'Oman, il n'y a *qu'une seule nation, c'est la nation arabe,* qui parle la même langue, possède les mêmes traditions historiques, étudie la même littérature... Les habitants de cet immense pays ne se distingue, les uns des autres, que par les religions, les confessions et les rites... Il y a infiniment moins de dissentiments entre Musulmans et Chrétiens... qu'il n'en existe entre les différents rites catholiques.[105]

[From the Tigris to the Suez isthmus, from the Mediterranean to the Gulf of Oman, there is *but a single nation, the Arab nation,* which speaks the same language, possesses the same historical traditions, studies the same literature... The inhabitants of this vast country only differ from each other in their religions, sects and forms of worship... There is infinitely less dissent between Muslims and Christians... than there is between the various Catholic rites.]

This is a purely secular definition of the Arab nation, and whatever discord might exist between Arab Muslims and Christians, Azoury blames on the Turks, who implemented the 'divide and rule' policy, for he considered that the Arab Muslims had never been religious fanatics.[106] Azoury excludes Egypt from this united Arab nation because he did not consider the Egyptians to be ethnically Arab, but African Berbers. Furthermore, a natural, geographic barrier existed between Egypt and what he considered to be the Arab Empire.[107] Therefore, as early as 1905, he severely attacked the Zionist movement which aimed at implanting a Jewish state in an Arab Palestine their Jewish ancestors had never possessed,[108] and gives details showing the Zionist intrigues and threats and the Western consuls' support of their movement.[109] Like all the other Arab nationalists, Azoury, too, expressed his pride in his Arab heritage, showing how the Arabs had developed literature and science and, in the space of a few years, had given the world numerous poets, historians, philosophers and scientists. The obscurity into which Europe had been plunged during the Middle Ages came to an end thanks to Arab science and culture, but the Turkish occupation of the Arabs had caused them to regress into the Dark Ages,[110] he insisted.

It is not surprising that with his hatred of the Turks and his strong political Arab nationalism, Azoury urged Arab independence, 'for we Christians and Muslims in Syria are so oppressed, that we would welcome with joy the first power that would come to rescue us from servitude'.[111] Accordingly, he praises the Americans for having intervened with Sultan 'Abdülhamid to persuade him to adopt a more liberal, humane and just rule, and felt that the Arabs could depend on America for moral and diplomatic support from the day they gained their independence.[112] It is not only America that Azoury admires, but also France for being the standard-bearer of civilization and liberty, protecting the oppressed and spreading education in the Arab East.[113] He also admired Great Britain, for refraining from the use of force to impose its language and civilization on its colonies, trying to do so by peaceful means. He then compares Egypt under British occupation with the countries under Ottoman rule.[114] Perhaps the difference between these forces of occupation made his admiration of the West become exaggerated at times, for instance, when he claims that the subjects of the British Empire enjoy complete freedom and tolerance;[115] or that the Crusades were beneficial for the whole world, and that the French occupied Algiers mainly in order to rid the Mediterranean of the barbaric piracy that ruined international commerce.[116] Yet in spite of this great admiration for the West, and mainly for its having spread education and humanitarian institutions through the Arab countries, Azoury insists that the Arabs *do not want* the military aid of Europe and America in their struggle for independence. All the Arabs want of the West is its sympathy, moral support and encouragement.[117]

Yet even those writers who did not advocate separation from the Ottoman Empire had reason to admire the cultural influence of the West on their countries. It was mainly the British, not the French, whom Zaydan, al-Shumayyil and Sarruf admired. One of the reasons might be that, unlike the French-educated Azoury, they were products of the Syrian Protestant College in Beirut, that is of the Anglo-Saxon culture. Another reason was that in their days Britain ruled over a large part of the Orient, and they, like Azoury, compared its colonies with those of the Ottoman Empire, whose subjects they were. Seeing the backwardness of the Ottoman provinces, Zaydan, Sarruf and al-Shumayyil demonstrate the advantages Egypt, Syria and Lebanon gained because foreigners were allowed to establish schools and teach the inhabitants foreign languages and cultures and improve their economy.[118] They also realized the difference between the two colonial systems. Zaydan overlooked the injustice and economic drive behind colonization when he wrote that it was the morality of the English that made them rule the world, and that the administration of their colonies made these colonies virtually independent.[119] When describing the statues and artifacts from Egypt and the Middle East in the Louvre and the British Museum, all he says is that their like cannot be found in their countries of origin,[120] without once commenting as to why this is the case or on the fact that they had been smuggled, stolen or taken by force from these countries.

Although al-Shumayyil was fully aware that the European powers interfered in the Ottoman or Lebanese affairs in order to serve their own interests, and that the British, for example, were only interested in improving their trade and thus did not spread or improve education in Egypt,[121] yet he considered that the only hope for reform in the Ottoman Empire or in Lebanon was with the help of European experts who would have to be apolitical. As long as the Eastern nations were in a state of underdevelopment their only hope for progress is to resort to the help of those who are more advanced. What made Egypt more developed than the Ottoman provinces was the fact that it was under British rule, and he believed that as soon as the British left, Egypt would regress immediately.[122] al-Shumayyil not only praised the British for all the economic improvements they had implemented in Egypt, besides the freedom they had granted the people, but also showed great admiration for Cromer and even defended Kitchener's war in the Sudan.[123] His belief in the survival of the fittest made him accept as normal the West's exploitation and colonization of the East.[124]

These ideas did not arise from any pro-imperialist or anti-Egyptian feeling, but from his secular socialist *anti-nationalist* ideas, and his belief that the whole world should be one nation and all its inhabitants one people. In this, he differed from all the others. He criticized all forms of nationalism and saw that real reformers see the world as a whole, and consider the homeland in context wider than that of one nation and its frontiers.[125] Moreover, he believed that nationalism had, until recently, been the cause of many wars in Europe, before the people realized that the only ones to profit from the unrest were a few capitalists. For this reason, nations in the modern world tended to be peace-loving and disregarded their frontiers, working for the common good of all, this being the aim of socialism.[126] This anti-nationalist feeling and the belief that nationalism was one of the root causes of wars might have been the result of the influence of Aldous Huxley who severely criticized nationalism and the evils resulting therefrom, not the least of which were wars and their attendant horrors.[127] al-Shumayyil was writing prior to the outbreak of World War I which crushed these Utopian dreams. He went so far as to believe that even language barriers would one day be eliminated, for the only languages that would survive were those in which sciences are taught and written – English, French and German – while all the others would die out.[128] al-Shumayyil had boundless faith in science and could only see its positive, beneficial effects. He therefore asserted that thanks to the progress of the natural sciences and the scientific discoveries and inventions which were of benefit to all nations, the barriers between them would diminish until all countries finally merged into one nation.[129] This is why he considered in 1909 that the Egyptians should not oppose the extension of the Suez Canal concession for another sixty years, for 'the Canal today is a public facility serving the whole world, and in the near future it will not be considered as belonging to Egypt any more than it would belong to China or America'. The rights of nations are above those of the individual, but the rights of the whole world are above those of each nation,[130] he wrote. Naturally such a statement aroused the Egyptian nationalists against him, and one of them told him 'to keep his science for his own country',[131] i.e. Lebanon, which shows how precarious was the position of Christian Lebanese in a foreign country that was predominantly Muslim.

The Syrian Kurd 'Ali was a Muslim contemporary of Zaydan, al-Shumayyil, Antun and Azoury, but unlike them he did not emigrate, although he spent several years in Egypt. His writings span two generations, and a difference in nationalist feeling is noticeable from one to the other. Having been a fervent admirer and student of Muhammad 'Abdu[132] it is not surprising that Kurd 'Ali's early writings demonstrated that he believed that religion and not nationalism to be the bond between people. He wrote that 'Islam abolished nationalism,'[133] and tried to show by quoting historical examples that Islam had united various peoples under the Abbasids and forged them into one nation.[134] Writing in 1909, he finds no difference between the Syrian and Egyptian Muslims since they shared a religion and language, whereas he shows animosity towards the Syrian and Lebanese Christians in Egypt.[135] Even as late as 1934, while insisting on democratic rule by the majority, he considered the majority as being either Christian or Muslim. Therefore he writes that just as the Christian majority in Romania and Yugoslavia had the full right to rule the Muslim minority, the Muslim majority in the Middle East had the full right to rule the Christian minority.[136] He did not realize that the majority and minority in any European democratic régime represented political parties whose members could belong to any faith or even be atheists. What irked him during the French and British mandates over Syria, Lebanon and Palestine was the fact that the Christian minority monopolized the best civil service posts, although the Muslims formed the majority of the population in these countries.[137] He also claimed that the Muslims were less fanatical than the Christians.[138]

Like his Lebanese Christian contemporaries, before the end of World War I he strongly supported the unity of the Ottoman Empire as a power against the West, since unity was the only guarantee of strength.[139] Due to his strong religious feelings it might well be asked whether, unlike them, he supported it mainly because it was an Islamic empire. Although he claimed to know how tyrannical and cruel Jamal Pasha was, he did not feel him to be an enemy and even befriended him.[140] During the battle of Gallipoli in 1915 he expressed an Ottoman pride in 'his' soldiers, captains and leaders, boasting of their victory and addressing the Ottoman sultan as 'caliph'. He asserts that the Muslims were waging a Holy War (*jihad*), defending their holy cities and the last independent Muslim state which had united the Muslims, with no difference between Arab, Turk and Kurd.[141] Such assertions illustrate the big difference between his Ottomanism and that of his Christian contemporaries, although, like them, he criticized the tyranny and corruption of the Ottomans even when they were still in power, and realized that the Constitution of 1908 had not changed anything, since the Turks were still living parasitically off their provinces.[142]

Yet despite the religious bond that he felt united him to the Turkish Ottomans, Kurd 'Ali could not but express a certain Arab nationalism even when the Ottomans were still in power. Like the nationalism of his Christian contemporaries, his was linguistic and cultural, rather than political. He strongly criticized the Turks for trying to eradicate the use of Arabic, neglecting to teach it in the Arab countries they occupied and replacing it with Turkish, and blamed them for the decline of Arabic culture and civilization during their long rule.[143] In his *Memoirs* he claims that the Young Turks tried to bribe him and even threatened to kill him because of his Arab nationalist articles,[144] yet he also blames the Arabs themselves for neglecting their language while foreign orientalists perfect it.[145]

After the Turks were defeated in World War I, Kurd 'Ali's Ottomanism disappeared, to be replaced by Arab secular nationalism. Now he writes: 'I look at Ottoman history through Arab, not Turkish, eyes'.[146] He candidly admits that 'the West taught us the meaning of fatherland and patriotism, love of nation and of language, all of which were new to the Arabs who had suffered for centuries from the despotism of their rulers'. That this feeling was secular to a large extent is demonstrated by the fact that he adds that, thanks to the West, the Arabs 'learned that nationalism was their only route to progress, that religion alone could not save them from their plight, and that neglecting the temporal will destroy both the religious and the temporal'.[147] When attacking those who advocated the use of colloquial Arabic instead of the literary classical language, he writes that by doing so 'the Arabs will become divided as they have become politically divided, for it was the language of the Qur'an that protected them all these years in spite of the adversities they faced at the hands of Eastern Muslim or Western Christian states'.[148] For him, the Eastern Muslims became just as much of an enemy as the Western Christians were, and he no longer felt that the Turkish Ottoman soldiers were 'on his side', but states clearly that the Arabs are not Turks, that they are more advanced than the Turks and have a great and ancient civilization.[149] To him, an Arab is not an Arab by race, but by his culture and education. Thus Ibn Sina, al-Biruni, and al-Razi, for example, might not be Arab by birth, but are Arabs by education and culture, and those who, like Jahez, Ibn Rushd or Ibn Khaldun are Arab by birth are of no greater importance than them.'[50] So it is not religion or race but culture and education that play a role in his definition of an Arab. Like the Christian writers before him, Kurd 'Ali shows pride in Arab history and civilization, alluding to them as being Arab rather than Muslim,'[51] and he devoted several books to Arab inventions and discoveries in all fields of learning,'[52] often boasting of all that Western civilization owed to the Arabs. Elsewhere, he says that 'we are bound to the Maronite, Catholic, Orthodox, Anglican, Alawite, Ismaili, Jew and others by a bond that is stronger than any other, that of the same interests, a common fatherland, language and related ethnicity'.'[53] He thus tried to reconcile the various religious sects and propagate Arab nationalism, urging the various political parties in the country to have one thing in common, namely, patriotism, and to emulate each other only in their striving for the common good.'[54] This Arab nationalism made him attack Zionism and the British for having misled the Arabs in 1916, and helping the Jews in Palestine against the Arabs.'[55] Since his country, Syria, was ruled by the French under a mandate, he severely criticized French colonialism, especially when the French bombed Syrian cities in 1925–1926, destroying them and killing innocent civilians.'[56]

Here his nationalism became ambivalent. Sometimes he appeared to advocate Arab unity, for he says that he does not differentiate between a Syrian, Egyptian or Moroccan, for example, because there is no real difference between them,'[57] and he strongly attacks those Egyptians who advocated Pharaonic nationalism.'[58] On the other hand, he often insisted on the need to unite Syria and Lebanon because he believed that they were one country geographically and that most of the Lebanese would want to become part of Syria again.'[59] Yet he never advocated that such a union should be based on secular principles, as Samné did. The above quoted passages concerning his attitude towards the favouritism shown to the Christians by the mandatory authorities show that it still was religion and not secularism that had the upper hand in his thoughts.

The Lebanese Christians Julia Tohmi Dimashqiyya and Georges Samné were contemporaries of Kurd 'Ali in this second phase. Dimashqiyya's nationalism was a secular Arab nationalism that made her feel a bond with other Arab nations and a belief that she shared their problems. That is why she urged the Palestinians to form national, rather than sectarian, associations, begging them all, Muslims and Christians alike, to *unite as Arabs*, and to take positive action to counteract Zionist activity and activism, instead of just passively hating the Zionists.'[160]

Samné agreed with his Syrian Muslim contemporary and even with al-Kawakibi on some points, but disagreed on many others. Writing in 1919, Samné affirms that the Syrians were never hostile to the Ottoman Empire, and that all they desired were peace and freedom. They would voluntarily have accepted Constantinople's tutelage had the Ottomans not been so hatefully brutal. As proof, he cites the Syrians' enthusiasm for the Young Turks' revolution in 1908, and their hope for a liberal régime before they awoke to the cruel realization that nothing had changed.[161] What Zaydan and al-Shumayyil had written at the time shows that he was right. He then goes on, however, to assert his belief in secular nationalism. The first chapter of this book discussed Samné's belief that Islam had never formed more than a religious bond between the Muslims who belonged to separate and autonomous states. He now asserts that when the Ottoman Sultan Salim I (d.1520) conquered Egypt in 1517 and declared himself caliph, he was usurping the title which, by Islamic law, belonged to Quraish, and therefore several Islamic states broke even the nominal ties they still had with the caliphate.[162] Here Samné agrees with al-Kawakibi in attacking the Ottoman sultan for usurping a title that rightfully belonged to an Arab, although as a Christian he had a secular understanding of history, whereas the Muslim was writing from an Arab Muslim point of view. Thus Samné goes on to insist that with the Ottoman sultans the caliphate became, first and foremost, a political, temporal power.[163] He believed that Sultan 'Abdülhamid had used pan-Islamism merely to frighten the Western powers, and that the Muslim Syrians in general did not subscribe to it. All they wanted was peace and security, the enjoyment of progress and prosperity, and the opportunity to live in perfect harmony with their Christian and Jewish compatriots. Besides, he realized that the Islamic world was split into separate countries, each with its own traditions and interests which sometimes caused friction between Muslim countries, any of whom might be on the side of the 'infidel'. 'With time and by force of circumstance and local interests... the idea of national patriotism replaced the original idea of religious solidarity,'[164] as in the case of Kurd 'Ali after World War I. All this proves Samné's belief that people were united by secular nationalism and not by a common faith.

Samné's secular nationalism was not pan-Arab as Kurd 'Ali's was on occasion, but Syrian, resembling Kurd 'Ali's in this respect. What he wanted was an independent and united greater Syria, though Samné was more explicit and purely secular, unlike Kurd 'Ali, when he demanded a federal organization based on *democratic and secular* principles.[165] This Syrian confederation would include the land from the Taurus Mountains to Sinai, in which Lebanon and other areas would be distinct regions enjoying their own rights and privileges.[166] The first step towards this secular confederation would come through the formation of an autonomous Greater Lebanon 'which would be for the whole of Syria the pledge of her complete development'.[167] He realized that the rivalry between the different religions and sects and this greater Syria was detrimental to nationalism which faced three main dangers – Christian conservatism, pan-

Islamism and Jewish Zionism. He therefore begged his compatriots to abandon these disastrous attitudes and to subscribe to nationalism.[168] Kurd 'Ali opposed Zionism for Arab nationalist reasons, whereas Samné was against it for Syrian national and secular reasons. He devotes a whole chapter of his book to a severe criticism of the Zionist aim to found an independent Jewish state in Palestine, reiterating his idea of a secular federal Syria in which the Jews would have their members of parliament, and in a federal state like Switzerland in which they would have their own religious and racial canton.[169] Another reason for his opposition to Zionism was his belief in the danger of a Jewish state quickly turning into a theocracy in which nationality will be based on religion and governed by religious clerics.[170] He also realized that in the new secular Syria, the Christian patriarchs would also be confined exclusively to spiritual matters,[171] as would a Muslim caliph in each Muslim country. It would not be the first time in the history of Islam that more than one caliph ruled at the same time, he claimed. Besides, no Muslim text or doctrine ever maintained that it was mandatory to have only one universal caliph.[172] From this secular point of view, he wanted the Muslims, Christians and Jews of Greater Syria to consider themselves brothers, all alike in the same fatherland, with no trace of any religious division between them.[173]

This demonstrates that he did not believe in an Arab but in a Syrian nationalism. In fact, he realized that it was wrong to claim that the Syrians were Arabs, for they are a mixture of all the races that conquered them, Persians, Romans, Phoenicians, Aramaeans, Greeks and Arabs. The Syrians absorbed the Arab conquerors and their language, and 'through their own particular qualities the brilliant Arab civilization was founded'.[174] Thus Samné, like the other Christian writers before him, felt that he was culturally an Arab, displaying great anger at the Turkish persecution of the Arabs, especially between 1908 and 1914, by depriving them of their share in government and responsible positions.[175] Yet he denies any racial or political affiliation with the Arabs. This could be related to the political events of the time.

Feisal, son of the Sharif of Mecca aspired to be king of a united Arab kingdom, based on promises made to his father by the British, and had therefore triumphantly entered Damascus in 1918. In 1919, Syria's National Party demanded Syrian independence within the country's natural boundaries, i.e. Syria, Lebanon and Palestine, under a constitutional monarchy headed by Feisal. Samné vehemently rejected unification of Syria with the kingdom of the Hijaz (now Saudi-Arabia), on the grounds that the social, economic and religious differences between both countries were enormous, for the Syrians were not Arabs, and could not form one nation with the Arab inhabitants of the Arabian peninsula.[176] This was besides the fact that the Sharifian government was theocratic, Sharif Hussein having called for a revival of pure Islamic life and institutions,[177] which meant that the secular state that Samné hoped for was out of the question. That is why he supported the temporary French mandate over Syria, since France was a democratic, secular country and its secular régime was the only one capable of uniting the numerous religious groups in Syria, as well as ensuring the democracy and secularism which he believed to be the only possible foundations for a Syrian constitution.[178] He very soon expressed his disillusionment with the French occupying forces, however. He wrote bitterly that the French companies would not employ Syrians, and worse, that the Syrians were even kept out of the High Commission's administration, under the pretext that they were incompetent. To top it all, there were no signs that the French were preparing to enable Syria to become united and independent.[179] Whereas Kurd 'Ali had deplored the French favoritism of the Syrian Christians at the expense of the Muslims, Samné deplores their favoritism of *foreigners* at the expense of the Syrians, be they Muslims, Christians or Jews. Thus Samné comes to the sad conclusion that all President Wilson's and the Allies' declarations that the end of World War I would ensure a peace based on respect for the rights and independence of all the nations had never been implemented in the Middle East.[180]

Syrian and Lebanese writers of the following generation still lived under French rule, and like Kurd 'Ali and Samné, Nazira Zayn al-Din also believed in a secular nationalism, devout Muslim though she was. She declared that the Christians and Muslims were one nation, and that both their religions instruct them to be good, charitable and just, and to desire liberty, fraternity and peace, as well as to respect each other.[181] But unlike Samné's hers is not a Syrian but an Arab nationalism, for she declares: 'We have only one nationalism which is neither Christian nor Muslim, it is an Arab nationalism free of all traces of fanaticism'.[182] However, what is new in her secular national feeling is that she is among the rare writers to *unite nationalism with women's liberation*. Defending woman's right to freedom and independence both Qasim Amin and al-Sayyid said that 'a slave does not raise free men'. But Nazira was more explicit when she clearly stated that:

> The spirit of nationalism cannot be separated from that of liberty, equality and fraternity, and one cannot live without the other. Therefore, if we want to obtain independence and freedom, and abolish the French mandate, we have to give women their freedom and equal rights. If the mother is freed, the country will be likewise.[183]

All the writers realized that nationalism involved fighting for freedom and independence and that secular nationalism meant equality between all citizens. This woman alone, however, took into consideration the fact that citizens are both men and women, and realized that a nation cannot be free so long as half its citizens live in servitude, and that this half cannot bring up and educate the other half to be free and independent. How could a woman who does not know the meaning of freedom and independence instill these qualities in her progeny? Thus, for Nazira, nationalism and women's rights were inseparable, and the right to self-determination could not be achieved without women's rights.

The Egyptians of this period had to deal with problems that were different from those faced by the Syrians and Lebanese, so their nationalism took on a different aspect. In spite of Ottoman suzerainty over Egypt, the country had enjoyed virtual autonomy from the Ottoman Empire since the rule of Muhammad Ali, until it was occupied by the British in 1882. As a result, the nationalism expressed by both al-Sayyid and Taha Hussein, like that of Amin and Bahithat al-Badiya before them, is typically Egyptian, being not only free of any Ottoman or Arab nationalism but clearly antagonistic towards both, which shows how secular and local their nationalism was. The pharaonic allegiance that Kurd 'Ali so severely criticized are present in both, especially in al-Sayyid. When defining Egypt, he writes:

> Mondern Egypt does not exist independently of its pharaonic past, for a nation is one continuous whole that cannot be divided or separated into parts. The nation was born the day it took possession of this land and had a known and distinctive social order... The knowledge of the ancient Pharaonic and Arabic heritage is important not only as a source of pride in our past, but, more significantly, as a source of knowledge of our past so that we can reform the present and replace it with a bright future.[184]

Al-Sayyid even boasts of the colonization of parts of Africa by the ancient Egyptians, stating that the pharaohs used the same methods as modern European colonizers, although they were 'the most tolerant' colonizers. In this, he saw a means of convincing his countrymen 'not to despair of Egypt's progress... and her natural inclination to independence'.[185] Taha Hussein only cites pharaonism as part of Egypt's civilization. When writing about Egypt's culture he says that it is 'the heritage of ancient pharaonic art, the Arab-Islamic heritage and what Egypt has acquired and is still acquiring from modern Europe'.[186] Neither writer shows a preference for the Arab-Islamic element over the pharaonic element in Egyptian history and culture.

In defining the Egyptians, al-Sayyid writes:

> None of us doubts that we are a nation with specific characteristics that distinguish us from all other nations. We have a particular colour, particular tastes and one common language. The majority have one religion, similar ways of going about their work, and almost the same blood runs in our veins. Our country has clearly defined the natural borders that separate us from the others... We have a long and ancient history of varying fates in a chain of solidly welded links, the first link lies in pre-history and the last being ours... Thus we are the pharaohs of Egypt, the Arabs of Egypt, the Mamelukes and the Turks of Egypt. We are the Egyptians.[187]

Clarifying this definition, he adds that local factors such as climate, proximity as well as relationships and shared interests moulded the Egyptians into one nation, and that only the ignorant would want to relate solely to the Arabs or pharaohs or Turks or Circassians.[188] Thus, religion is completely absent from his definition of Egyptian nationalism. Without ignoring the different faiths of the Egyptians, he insists that the Muslims and Copts are one nation, and severely criticizes those who provoke religious fanaticism in either group and thus seek to destroy national unity. 'Judaism, Christianity and Islam are all monotheistic religions, and if fanaticism is eliminated and the people have true faith, we need not fear for a nation that believes in all three of them'.[189] Furthermore, he declares that the old belief that the Muslim countries are a fatherland to all Muslims is no longer valid, and has been replaced by the desire to have a clearly defined country and the feeling of patriotism.[190]

Thus, too, Hussein insists that unity of religion and language are no basis for political unity and the formation of a state. What unites people into one nation are the *practical economic benefits and a geographic unity* in which al-Sayyid also believed. He is influenced by Bentham and Mill, as Zaydan had been before him. 'The Copts are Egyptians who have perfectly fulfilled their national duties, exactly like the Muslims, and they should enjoy their national rights just like the Muslims,'[191] writes Hussein. Instead of considering the different religions in Egypt to be a factor of division he sees them as enriching to the country and an element of strength: 'The difference between Christians and Muslims does not endanger the unity of the nation, on the contrary, it is enriching and strengthening'.[192] Unlike the Christian Lebanese and Syrian minorities who saw how the unity of their nation was endangered by the difference between Muslims and Christians, Hussein who belonged to the vast Muslim majority in Egypt felt at ease and only saw the enriching aspect of this difference. Therefore, when addressing himself to the Azharites whose belief in

Muslim unity was strongest, he tells them that they need to know that, besides Islam, it was the geographic boundaries of Egypt that constituted a nation.[193] He then refers back to history to prove that religion was never a unifying factor in the Muslim world. Before the end of the ninth century, he asserts, the Muslims themselves based their politics on practical benefits, renouncing unity of religion, language and race when the Ummayads of Andalusia fought with the 'Abbasids of Iraq. Since the tenth century, the Muslim world had been divided into many different states, based on economic advantage and geographical unity, or any other advantage, and Egypt was one of the first Muslim countries to regain its own ancient personality. It had opposed the Persians, Macedonians, Romans and eventually the Arabs as well, and only stopped revolting against the Arabs after it had regained a measure of independence under the rule of Ibn Tulun and the various dynasties that succeeded him.[194] Hussein is referring here to the Tulunids(868–905) and the Ishkhids (935–969) who established quasi-independent dynasties in Egypt, followed by the Fatimid state (969–1171), the Ayyubids (1171–1252) and the Mameluke dynasties (1252–1517) that were completely independent of the Abbasid caliphate before Egypt became part of the Ottoman Empire.

Thanks to their strong Egyptian national feeling, both al-Sayyid and Hussein were anti-Ottoman and anti-Turk, as well as anti-Arab. This is further proof of their secular nationalism. Thus, al-Sayyid did not appear to identify more closely with the Muslim Ottomans than he did with the Greek Christians when, in a completely secular and Westernized nationalist spirit, he defends the Greek nationalists who had fought the Ottoman empire and succeeded in breaking away from it in 1829.[195] When he and his friends formed their *Hizb al-Umma* (People's Party) in 1907, one of their demands was complete independence. They were strongly criticized by those who wanted to remain part of the Ottoman Empire which still held suzerainty over Egypt before the British abolished it at the outbreak of World War I. Al-Sayyid admits that they paid no attention to those critics.[196] As a result, he refused to permit Egyptians to send representatives to the Ottoman Assembly of Delegates when the Ottomans declared their Constitution, insisting on Egypt's right to complete independence.[197] It was not at all in Egypt's interest, he believed, to have the Egyptian consider himself Ottoman, nor does it show Egypt to be an independent country like Bulgaria.[198] In 1912, he demanded that the Ottoman flag be replaced by an Egyptian flag,[199] and points out that Egypt's humiliation under Turkish (Muslim) rule was no less than its mortification under the (Christian) British.[200] Likewise, Hussein said that when the Turks occupied the Muslim countries around the Mediterranean they caused their decline into ignorance and weakness, eliminating the progress, learning and power they had

had.[201] By calling the Ottomans Turks, Hussein demonstrates that in his opinion the differences between one country and the next were nationalistic, even though they might share the same religion.

From this purely Egyptian secular nationalist stand, al-Sayyid strongly criticizes all those who live in Egypt and profit by its riches, while secretly professing allegiance to another country, be it Arabia, Syria or Turkey, but never Egypt.[202] In this, he is primarily and indirectly criticizing those of Lebanese or Syrian origin who lived in Egypt and still felt themselves to be Ottoman, Syrian or Lebanese, as well as those who professed any pan-Arab feeling. Taha Hussein was no less anti-Arab, though not for cultural or linguistic reasons but on political grounds. In an interview conducted in 1923, he declared that a political union between Egypt and Greater Syria could only be detrimental to both, for it would arouse Europe's resentment and hostility.[203] He strongly believed that unity of religion and language do not create a nation, nor can they be a basis for political unity. Thus he declares: 'It is true that we share our language with the other Arab countries, yet Egypt has its own peculiar speech and thought'.[204]Hussein even refused to consider Egypt as an oriental country and insists that it is part of the European West: 'Although Europe embraced Christianity, its countries are not considered Eastern, so why should we consider Egypt an Eastern country just because it embraced Islam, when it is well-known that the Qur'an merely corroborates and completes the New Testament'.[205] Thus he not only accentuates the fact that there is no essential difference between Christianity and Islam when considering whether Egypt is non-European, but also points out that neither a shared religion nor a shared culture were enough to link Egypt to the rest of the Arab-Islamic world. The feeling that Egypt was not part of the Arab world was not unnatural or unusual there at the time; it was only after the mid-1950s that the Egyptians started to identify with the Arab world.

No matter what the reason, al-Sayyid's and Hussein's attitude here is the diametrical opposite of that of Kurd Ali, Samné, Dimashqiyya and Nazira, who were Syrian or Arab nationalists. In fact, in 1911 al-Sayyid criticized the Arabs' desire for independence from the Ottoman Empire.[206] Was he so immersed in his local Egyptian problems that he did not realize that his burning desire for his country's independence could be shared by nationals of other countries, and that his definition of nationalism could also be applied to the Syrians and/or Arabs? Whatever the reason, al-Sayyid's nationalism gravitated around Egypt alone, 'Egypt for the Egyptians' was his motto. He clarified that by 'Egyptians' he meant all those who felt they had no other homeland than Egypt, and therefore asks those of Syrian origin to register themselves in their province (*muhafaza*) so as to become Egyptians.[207] He believed that it was in

Egypt's interest to have all those living in Egypt, whether Ottomans or foreigners, *regardless of their ethnicity or creed*, to become Egyptians with the rights and obligations of an Egyptian. For those who had emigrated to Egypt and chosen is as their homeland, had proved to be useful to the country by their intelligence and ability. Therefore 'we, the majority, should make use of those who consider themselves foreigners, and especially the Syrians, and make into them real Egyptians with political and civil rights, so that they will be able to truly serve Egypt, their homeland'.[208] Based on his belief that common interests and advantages are what make people unite into a nation, those al-Sayyid considered to be Egyptians were primarily all those who served Egypt's interests, regardless of religion or race. Commenting on al-Sayyid's nationalism in this respect, Wendell writes:

> The homogeneity and solidarity that Lutfi spoke of in innumerable essays were based finally on neither genetic nor religious factors, but were rather the inevitable product of universal secular education, a complete reevaluation of the national history and recognition by all of an all-embracing sphere of common interests. John Stuart Mill, whose thought exerted a powerful influence on Lutfi, expressed something close to the Lutfian definition of 'nationality'.[209]

Naturally, al-Sayyid's strong Egyptian nationalism made him oppose the cosmopolitanism that al-Shumayyil so strongly advocated. He claimed that it was not in Egypt's interest at the time to strive for internationalism:

> The only one who profits from the idea of internationalism... is the strong country, for this idea helps it to colonize and exploit the orientals.
> We may admire these ideas and those who believe in them, but for us what we must do is develop our Egyptian patriotism'.[210]

The colonization from which Egypt suffered at that time was probably the main reason for his fervent Egyptian nationalism and his indifference to the other Arab countries' plight. For example, neither he nor Hussein referred to or commented upon the British treachery towards the Arabs in the Sykes-Picot and Balfour agreements which so infuriated Kurd 'Ali and Samné. Al-Sayyid's only concern was Egypt's complete independence since 'liberty is the necessary nourishment of our life'.[211] He was one of the founding members of the Wafd party which in 1918 started negotiating for Egypt's independence from Britain.[212] True, he assessed Cromer's role in Egypt in an objective spirit, pointing out his country's economic progress thanks to Cromer's rule, and praising Cromer for having encouraged individual freedom and the respect of rights and equality between the classes in Egypt.[213] Yet, at the same time, his desire for Egypt's independence made him criticize the injustice of British rule in Egypt, Britain's colonial spirit,[214] and Cromer's giving the real power in the country to British or pro-British officials while neglecting the education of the masses.[215]

In spite of their desire for Egyptian independence, neither writer believed it could be obtained by revolutionary methods which, according to al-Sayyid, only result in bloodshed and destruction, and replaced the old regime by one that could prove to be even worse.[216] It has been pointed out in a previous chapter that these writers had enormous faith in education as a means of creating political awareness. Al-Sayyid reiterates that the nation's independence can only be achieved through undisrupted work and peaceful means and the education of several generations.[217] al-Sayyid and Hussein both criticize the schools for not instilling a national, patriotic spirit in their students. Hussein asked for government supervision of all schools in order to guarantee this. He claimed that it was the government's role and duty to safeguard Egypt's independence, this could only be achieved by educating the children to love and defend this independence, and to instill in them a sense of justice, freedom and equality.[218] al-Sayyid criticized the Egyptian schools for having adopted Western subjects, teaching methods, morality and tastes, with no trace of anything Egyptian remaining in them. Even Arabic, he says, had been neglected in favor of foreign languages, and insisted that the educational programmes that suited Europe did not necessarily suit Egypt.[219]

In this lies the difference between Hussein and himself, despite their agreement about secular Egyptian nationalism. Hussein's secularism went as far as to insist that it was the 'Greek civilization that was most strongly influenced by the Egyptian mind, and the Greek mind that later most strongly influenced Egyptian civilization'.[220] Since he felt that the Egyptians were influenced by the Greek mind and civilization more than by anything else (this 'else' including the Islamic-Arabic civilization), he was obviously trying to prove a predominant secularism in Egypt's civilization. Here, he quotes Paul Valéry in stating that the European mind was composed of three elements, namely, Greek civilization with its literature, philosophy and art, Roman politics and law and Christianity. From this Hussein goes on to assert:

> If we look at the Muslim mind in Egypt and the Near East, we find that it, too, is composed of the same elements, and that Islam, like Christianity, exhorts people to be good and charitable, besides the fact the Islam came to corroborate and supplement the Bible.[221]

From this, he deduces that 'there is no difference between us Egyptians and the Europeans, since our essence, character and mind are the same'.[222] Thus Hussein, unlike all the other writers, tries to assert complete identity between Egyptians and Europeans in which even the difference between their religions plays no part. This is consistent with his belief that modern times have brought about the separation between the spiritual and the temporal, as has been shown in a previous chapter. Another reason for Hussein's theory is his nationalism and his strong desire to motivate his countrymen, to give them confidence in themselves and their ability to emulate Europe. His aim was similar to that of al-Sayyid, although it took on a different aspect. 'The European spirit is productive,' he says, 'one that has produced philosophy, science and inventions, and that sacrifices life itself in order to advance science and empower the mind so as to control nature'. He adds: 'I want us to emulate the source of this European civilization'.[223] Thus, with only his country's progress at heart, he transcends all individual, cultural and historical differences between Egypt and Europe, looking to the future and not to the past. In response to those who attacked his attitude, he points out that European civilization is one of the mind, imagination and spirit, and not merely materialistic, as its detractors claim.[224] In answer to those who accused him of wanting to destroy the Egyptians' distinctive characteristics he says that he is not afraid that they would lose them and become europeanized,

> ... for if we seek to preserve our religion but make it suit our present life, and if we seek to preserve our Arabic language and heritage but develop them the way that European languages and heritages developed, this does not mean that we want Egypt to become europeanized.[225]

He seems to have overlooked the fact that, had the European civilization not become a completely secular one in which Christianity no longer played a role, unlike Islam in the Egyptian mind, its science would not have advanced the way it did, nor would it have invented what it did, or become the civilization it had become. His insistence on the Egyptians' preservation of their religion was bound to interfere with the absolute freedom of scientific research and progress, no matter how much religion was re-interpreted to suit modern times, as the development of science in the history of Europe has proved. It can thus be seen that Hussein's nationalism, no matter how secular, was still tinged with religious feeling.

Despite their strong nationalism, both al-Sayyid and Hussein were strongly against chauvinism. On the contrary, both advocated a general love of humanity, peace and understanding. Al-Shumayyil's call for cooperation between peoples was linked to his opposition to nationalism due to his socialist views, whereas al-Sayyid's and Hussein's strong nationalistic feelings did not stop them from advocating cooperation between nations, regardless of religion or ethnicity, in a completely secular spirit. Al-Sayyid asserts that true patriotism is not contradictory to the love of humanity in general,[226] and that the aim of education should be to teach love of peace and human brotherhood, 'not ethnic pride and a belief that one particular ethnic group is superior to another; an education that leads to universal cooperation and respect for all nations, regardless of the level of their civilization'.[227] Likewise, Hussein disregards all differences between religions and the commonly-held belief among Muslims in Islam's superiority, when he writes:

> The ideal for humanity now is for all people to understand each other perfectly well... to have their intellectual and emotional life as closely intertwined as their economic and political life. National and ethnic differences should not stop people from feeling that they all belong to a humanity which is similar in its parts, having the same interests and obliged to cooperate in everything.[228]

Undoubtedly, both were influenced by secular idealism in their belief in the equality and brotherhood of all nations and creeds, since they shared one humanity, had the same interests and, as a result, should have their intellectual and emotional lives closely intertwined.

CHAPTER TEN

Language, Literature, Art

The Arabs have been proud of their language and literature since pre-Islamic times. They continued to be so after the coming of Islam, but the language and all the studies connected therewith then became associated with the Qur'an. With the subsequent political break-up of the Islamic world and its partial occupation by the European powers, the Arabs, and especially the Muslims, felt that it was thanks to the Qur'an that the Arabic language had been preserved from disintegration and even obliteration. This reinforced the religious aura of Arabic. The Muslims categorically refused to have the holy language of the Qur'an translated into the languages of non-Arab Muslims and the teaching of Arabic in most Arab countries became the sole prerogative of the Muslim religious clerics. It has been shown in previous chapters how Hussein severely criticized this phenomenon, and how Zaydan was denied the university post of lecturer in the history of Islam just because he was a Christian. In the nineteenth century, however, mainly thanks to the Lebanese Christians, the language and its literature were revived,[1] and the numerous periodicals they published and the articles and books they wrote, played a major role in secularizing the language and its literature, separating them from Islamic studies. Having been exposed to European literature and thought and influenced by them earlier than their Muslim contemporaries, thanks to the numerous missionary schools, Christian writers published many works about Arabic grammar, simplifying it and making it more accessible to schoolchildren. They wrote articles on various scientific and literary subjects, as well as stories, novels and poems that reflected the society in which they lived and the problems, emotions and thoughts of the individual. Commenting on this change in content of Arabic literature, its genres and its language, al-Sharabi wrote:

> The distinctive Christian contribution lay in a transformation from within, both emotionally and intellectually, the literary sensibility and creation.

This achievement is reflected, above all, in the shift from a transcendentally dominated perspective to one in which man and his condition begin to occupy a central position. Literature acquired the potential to become the medium of social and aesthetic awareness, after having been exclusively the vehicle of ritual and ceremony.[2]

The previous chapter has shown the importance of the role played by the Arabic language in the Arab-nationalist feelings of Bustani, al-Shidyaq, Marrash and Ishaq, and how much the first two contributed to reviving, teaching and developing the language. This, in itself, is proof of the purely secular attitude of all four writers towards Arabic.

As a result of his secular attitude towards the language, Bustani wanted to simplify traditional Arabic style, believing that the complexity of the ancient Arabic texts was what discouraged his contemporaries from reading and studying the language. Arabic, like all languages, must develop, he wrote, otherwise it will become a dead language like Latin, and be replaced by dialects, 'which would be an unparalleled loss.'[3] al-Shidyaq also insisted on the need to develop Arabic, adding new words to suit the changing times,[4] asserting the close relationship between civilization and language, for language does not emerge all at once, but grows and develops with life.[5] Clearly, they both considered Arabic from a socio-historical perspective, as a purely social phenomenon subject to temporal and historical changes like all other social phenomena. This is a very far cry from the traditional Muslim belief in the divine origin of Arabic because it is the language in which God revealed the Qur'an. As a result, Bustani believed much of the Arabic vocabulary to be completely useless in modern times, such as all the synonyms for camel or lion, for example. He never considered that these numerous, apparently useless, synonyms might constitute proof that Arabic was a rich language, especially since it lacked many words in other useful fields.[6]

Al-Shidyaq's attitude towards language was not only secular, but sometimes involved a surprisingly modern, feminist analysis. In his autobiography, *al-Saq 'ala al-Saq* (The Leg over the Leg) his wife claims that Arabic:

... was formed by men whose despotic rule over women is as clear in it as in everything else, although the gender of the word 'language' (*lugha*) in Arabic is feminine. Had women formed the language, and this would have been fairer, its essence would have been feminine, and women would have compounded words that reflect their concept of man's mentality.[7]

Thus, for al-Shidyaq, language was not only an exclusively sociological pheno-menon, closely reflecting the life and civilization of the people speaking it. He was also aware of how it reflected the *patriarchal* mentality of that society. Although he did not go into details, what he wrote in the middle of the nineteenth century was a point not made by the feminist movement until the second half of the twentieth century.

It was not only the attitude towards language of the writers under review that was secular, their attitude towards literature was also secular. Bustani, al-Shidyaq and Ishaq were among the first Arab journalists, a genre to which the Arabs were only introduced in the 1820s. As previous chapters have shown, their articles dealt with contemporary secular social and political issues aimed at raising the consciousness of their readers. Besides these, Bustani wrote poetic articles expressing his pain and anger while describing the results of the 1860 civil war in his country and listing all the material and non-material losses it caused.[8] The articles in his encyclopedia dealt with secular subjects such as history, science, economics and the like.

Al-Shidyaq and Marrash used different genres with which to create social and aesthetic awareness. Al-Shidyaq's medium was autobiography. Previous chapters have shown the numerous aspects of society that he criticized in *al-Saq 'ala al-Saq, Kashf al-Mukhabba 'an Tamaddun Uruppa* (Uncovering the Hidden in Europe's Civilization), and *al-Wasita fi Ma'rifati Ahwal Malta* (The Means of Knowing Malta's Circumstances), such as the religious fanaticism and ignorance of the Maronite clergy, the injustice of the feudal system, the restrictions imposed on women, and the like. He also sought to create aesthetic awareness. He drew attention to purely literary criteria in his literary criticism, focusing on style and authenticity, criticizing his contemporaries' poetry and prose for imitating the style and content of ancient Arabic literature, making it devoid of all emotion, truth or authenticity, and not reflecting real life.[9] To clarify his ideas, he demonstrates the difference between his contemporaries' versifying and what real poetry should be.[10] al-Shidyaq also introduced his readers to European arts that were unknown to them, such as opera, ballet and the theatre,[11] but it was music and theatre that he mainly wanted people to appreciate. He criticized their ignorance in the field of music and their judging music by moral instead of aesthetic standards.[12] The same aesthetic criteria which he applied to literature he also applied to the theatre, describing the art of acting and how plays are directed, analyzing the subject, plot and the value of humour in the plays he attended, as well as the relationship between life and the language of these plays.[13]

Marrash used a different medium to express his ideas and emotions and create both social and aesthetic awareness in his readers. He used the novel, which was another new genre in their time, which the Arabs had adopted from European literature. The most significant of his novels in this respect is probably *Ghabat al-Haq* (The Forest of Truth) which expresses his social and political ideas in a symbolic, poetic style, using religious metaphors as symbols to depict the world in a new personal way, his poetic visions often expressing an interior terror. He might have been influenced by European Romantic literature in his use of symbols and visions, but for the first time in Arabic literature we find a writer using a *biblical style, religious metaphors and Qur'anic expressions* in a purely socio-political novel, thus even secularizing the style of religious books.[14]

Naturally, it was only later that a Muslim writer would take that same secular attitude towards the Arabic language. Qasim Amin refused to consider it a 'holy' one that should not be changed.

> For this belief to be true, we have to assume that this language is the result of a miracle, and that it was perfect ever since its existence in the world. This is contradicted by the fact that all languages are subject to the laws of change and general progress, their different phases complying with the course humanity takes.[15]

Therefore he believed, as did the other secular writers before him, that if Arabic were to remain a living language it should be developed to suit the changing times. But whereas the Christians, Bustani and al-Shidyaq, insisted on developing it from within its own structure and not resorting either to foreign words or the vernacular,[16] Amin realized that the means for developing it were innovation, borrowing from other languages and from the colloquial, both of which his Christian forerunners had categorically refused to do. In order to simplify the language, Amin went as far as to suggest eliminating the inflections (*harakat al-i'rab*) on the last letter of each word and keeping it vowelless (*sakin*), thus simplifying Arabic grammar and avoiding all the mistakes people make when reading.[17] With the same aim of simplifying the language Bustani had written books simplifying the grammar without changing the spirit or beauty of the words. It is true that both he and al-Shidyaq, unlike Amin, were linguists and could deal with the language in a way that Amin could not, yet it is significant that the earlier Christians cared more to preserve the spirit of Arabic than did the Muslim. Another reason could be that Amin felt completely secure in his Muslim environment, with no fear of anyone doubting his allegiance to Islam and its language, and could therefore suggest radical secular measures that would separate the language from its past. The Christians refused to take similar measures, not because they had no such feeling of security, but because of their strong attachment to and pride in their language and the feeling that it was the only bond between them and their Muslim brethren, as well as that which separated them from the Christian West to which they were bound by religion but to which *they could not and would not* be bound politically and culturally.

This trend is more obvious in the Christian writers of the next generation. Zaydan, like Bustani and al-Shidyaq, dedicated his life to writing about the Arabic language, civilization and history. Like al-Shumayyil, Sarruf, Kurd 'Ali and all their predecessors, he felt that Arabic was inadequate to express the aspects of a modern civilization which was changing fast. They all insisted that language is a living being which, like everything else, develops and changes, Zaydan and al-Shumayyil explained this according to the law of evolution in which they believed.[18] As a result, they both called for the eliminiation of those obsolete, unnecessary words to which Bustani had alluded and demanded that they be replaced by new words and scientific and technical terms which the Arabic language lacked.[19] Kurd 'Ali, on the other hand, asserted that no language could be considered a living one unless it was above all, a language of science.[20] He defended the lack of modern scientific terms in Arabic by saying that, for all the ancient Arabs' scientific achievements, they did not know what modern science had discovered and invented.[21] Because of their firm belief that Arabic was a living language, Zaydan and Sarruf, like Bustani half a century earlier, insisted on its being the language of instruction in schools and universities, the former criticizing its replacement by English or French in Egypt and Lebanon, while Sarruf attacked the Syrian Protestant College in Beirut for having replaced Arabic with English in teaching medicine and the other branches of science.[22] Their primary aim was the progress of their society, and they saw that the only way to make knowledge accessible to all students was to convey it in their own language.

These writers also wanted to demonstrate that the change and development of the language was not something foreign to Arabic. From a completely secular point of view, Sarruf points out that in the past Greek, Coptic, Persian and Assyrian words had infiltrated Arabic, and 'to which until now foreign words have been added and will continue to be added so long as Arabic is a living language and the Arabs mix with people of other tongues. This did not diminish its prestige in the past, nor will it diminish it now.'[23] Zaydan, who was more of an historian and linguist, wrote a book entitled *al-Lugha al-'Arabiyya Ka'inun Hayy* (The Arabic Language is a Living Being), in which he deals with Arabic in a purely secular fashion. He shows that even in pre-Islamic Arabic, which some scholars consider to be the purest language, hundreds of words which were regarded as Arabic were, in fact, of foreign origin. He proves this through comparative linguistics with other Semitic and non-Semitic languages, showing how these words became Arabized and replaced the original Arabic words which became obsolete.[24] He pursues this same secular method in tracing the development of Arabic after Islam to elucidate how original Arabic words acquired new connotations, while new words were introduced into the language and thousands of others became obsolete, even as early as the first century after the Hegira [25] (the Prophet's migration from Mecca to Medina in 622 AD). Kurd 'Ali showed how many foreign words had infiltrated the Arabic language since the past in order to express new political, economic and scientific changes in the lives of the Arabs.[26]

Although all agreed that Arabic should be allowed to develop as a living language, a process which they ought to help along, they did not agree as to the method by which to achieve their aim. There was a significant difference between the Muslim Kurd 'Ali and his Christian contemporaries. Kurd 'Ali established an Arabic language academy in Damascus, al- Majma' al-'Ilmi al-'Arabi, in order to develop the language and revive its literature, but he insisted on using only literary (classical) Arabic words, categorically rejecting colloquialisms or foreign words, such as 'telephone' or automobile', even if they were in current use.[27] He believed that all the difficulties of learning Arabic would disappear if the language were taught using modern methods, and abolishing unnecessary rules of grammar and rhetoric, but using only the literary language in the classroom, the theatre, cinema, radio and the like.[28] In spite of his admission that Arabic had changed with the times, which simply proves its adaptability, he contradicted himself when he insisted that the *language of the Qur'an is suited to civilization, regardless of time and place*.[29] Thus it can be seen that he could not completely secularize Arabic, divorcing it from the Qur'an, so that for him still retained the sacred religious aura, by virtue of which it is deemed to transcend all time and place.

Naturally, the Christians felt no such constraints. For them, Arabic was part of their heritage, not part of their religion. Sarruf corroborated what Amin had written earlier. Like him, he demanded the elimination of the dissential inflections at the end of words, except in poetry and reading the Qur'an, for eliminating them would make it easier to read and write Arabic, without changing anything in the meaning.[30] al-Shumayyil believed that the vernacular which expresses society's needs is just as valid as the literary language,[31] and advocated the use of the technical terms employed by craftsmen and mechanics in their everyday life and work.[32] Without actually favouring the use of the vernacular, Zaydan indirectly defends it. He shows that the compilers of the Arabic dictionaries had failed to include many words that they deemed to be colloquial despite the fact that they were used by some of the greatest Arabic writers.[33] He thus defends the use of words that are not necessarily found in dictionaries, (or in the Qur'an for that matter), and begs linguists not to be afraid of employing a new word not previously used in Arabic.[34] Even so, he is more of a purist than his two Christian contemporaries. He explains that although one should not disdain every word that had not been used by the Bedouin, this does not mean that the language should be corrupted by the introduction of colloquial words and structures and many foreign words. Foreign words should only be used where absolutely necessary, for that was part of the evolution of language, not a sign of its regression.[35] Here, Zaydan might be thinking of classical Arabic, that had borrowed Persian and Greek words, or the European languages which borrowed from each other without this corrupting any of them. However, Zaydan did not stop there. He suggested the positive, constructive steps to be taken if the Arabs did not want their language to decline and finally disappear. He proposed forming a specialist academy of writers, journalists, linguists, scientists, doctors, historians and poets, as well as specialists in other Eastern languages and Greek and Latin (note that he mentions only secular occupations). This academy would then produce a modern dictionary, discarding the old and obsolete words and adding new ones which would be either translated, borrowed, coined or developed from the roots of Arabic words. In accordance with his belief in cultural and linguistic Arab unity, he recommended making scientific terms uniform throughout the Arab countries,[36] a uniformity which even today has still not been implemented..

This secular outlook was not restricted to the Arabic language alone. When writing his books and novels on Arab history and literature, Zaydan wrote about Arabic, not Islamic culture, although Islam, naturally, formed part of it. Thus in his book *Tarikh Adaab al-Lugha al-'Arabiyya* (The History of Arabic Literatures) he writes about the cultural, secular aspect of Arab history, tracing the history and development of Arabic prose, poetry, mathematics, sciences, astronomy and all the other branches of Arab culture. When Kurd 'Ali reviewed Arab history, it was often from the perspective of a modern, secular scholar. Of the four Orthodox Caliphs, the second, 'Umar ibn al-Khattab (d. 644), is considered by Muslims to be a paradigm of righteousness and justice, worthy of emulation. Kurd 'Ali criticizes him, however, for having started the custom of distributing part of the treasury to the Prophet's extended family, who, with time, began leading a lazy, dissolute life, receiving money for which they did not work, and spending it on their pleasures and debauchery. This money, Kurd 'Ali says, rightly belonged to the people and should have been spent for the public good.[37] Here he is no longer judging Arab history by religious and traditional standards, but by the modern secular principles of a ruler's duties and the people's rights.

The writers of this generation naturally continued the new aesthetic awareness which their predecessors had started to create, with the criteria they used to judge literature. Kurd 'Ali saw that literature which was merely an imitation of the ancients had no value,[38] that literature is what expresses truly and honestly the writer's life and spirit.[39] Zaydan attached the value of literature to its didactic and moral message,[40] criteria he clearly applied in his historical novels, in which he very often sacrificed the art of the novel for the sake of his primary aim, teaching the Arabs their history.

Using those same secular standards, Kurd 'Ali judged art, even that which was forbidden or discouraged by traditional Islam. 'There was a time,' he writes, 'when our religious clerics considered anyone who sang for money to be a criminal'.[41] He had only praise and admiration for the places of entertainment he visited in Europe.[42] When commenting on the *Moulin Rouge* show in Paris where the dancers were semi-nude, he says that Arab Muslims who are not used to such things might consider them immoral, but every nation has its own customs and morals which it considers right and decent.[43] The fact that he himself did not consider the show to be indecent indicates that he was not judging it by moral, religious standards. What corroborates this is his adding that dancing was a necessary relaxation for Westerners, just like music, and when Arab civilization was at its zenith music and singing were also greatly appreciated. It was only when Arab civilization deteriorated that the fine arts similarly declined, for song and music are proof of a nation's development.[44] Likewise, he believed that had the Arabs loved theatre the way the Europeans do, their society would have been more advanced than it was in his day.[45] Thus he considered the arts to be an aspect of society's progress, and did not judge them either by religious or by traditional moral standards.

With this same secular attitude, he appreciated the other fine arts that Islam had forbidden. He expressed nothing but admiration for the paintings and sculptures he saw in the Louvre and the palaces of France and Italy.[46] Yet he insists that these arts were forbidden by Islam only when the Arabs were still idolators, for as soon as paganism was eradicated the Muslims had beautiful paintings in their palaces, and even in their mosques. He then adds that if these paintings had not attained the level of Western painting, the reason was that in the West, painting only reached its present level after four centuries of progress, whereas the paintings in the Islamic world were hundreds of years old at the most and art, like everything else, takes time to develop.[47] In all this, there is no trace of religious bias against sculpture and painting, no moral judgment passed on the nudity of many of these Western works of art, but a modern secular appreciation of art as one of the important aspects of civilization.

True to his secular, political Arab nationalism, Azoury considered Arabic solely from this point of view. He wanted the various Christian sects to use nothing but Arabic in their services, for this would unite them

> ... in a national Arab religion in which all the prayers would be said in Arabic, not Greek, Latin, Syriac or Chaldean. Arabic is already the language of the Qur'an and Islam all over the world, and what serious inconvenience is there in its becoming that of Catholic worship as well? ...The Orthodox churches will also join because they would be pressed to do so by the general movement of the nation. Even the Muslims will sympathize with the Christians when they see them siding with them coming close to them for the liberation and greatest benefit of their common homeland, the Arab homeland.[48]

Azoury considered Arabic to be the language of all the Arabs, regardless of religion, and thus insists that all religious services should be conducted in Arabic, just like those of the Muslims. This is clearly a secular attitude towards language, completely separating it from Islam, the religion to which it was so closely connected.

Dimashqiyya shares this attitude. Although she sees the importance and necessity of teaching foreign languages to Lebanese children, she insists that 'Arabic is our country's language, the basis of our nationalism, and the cornerstone of our independence.'[49] Her association of language with nationalism proves that for her it has a completely secular connotation, and that is why she encourages her compatriots to speak only Arabic instead of the foreign languages they are in the habit of using, for 'we would be humiliating ourselves and our noble language if we addressed our Arab neighbours in a foreign tongue.'[50] Inseparable from language is its whole heritage, and this, too, Dimashqiyya sees through secular, nationalistic eyes when she insists that children must become thoroughly versed in their own Arab history and the glories of their past Arab civilization.[51]

When Lutfi al-Sayyid and his friends founded the new Egyptian university, one of their aims was to encourage social progress by renewing the language and literature,[52] a renewal upon which Hussein also insisted, just as science and medicine had been renewed. He therefore severely criticized those who studied and taught nothing but ancient Arabic thought and literature.[53] Like their predecessors, the aims of al-Sayyid and Hussein were to enable their country to make progress, and they fully realized the important role language played in this since, as Hussein clearly pointed out, it is the instrument of thought and feeling.[54] Hussein also insisted on mastering Arabic for purely secular, nationalistic reasons, just as the previous writers had done, asserting that it was one of the most important elements in the Egyptian nationality. He therefore asked the government to supervise foreign schools in the country and oblige them to teach Arabic properly,[55] and to permit no language other than Arabic to be taught in the elementary schools, so as to create a strong national feeling in the children.[56]

Without denying that Arabic was also the language of Islam, Hussein was the only Muslim of his day to directly address the religious connotation given to Arabic, *by completely separating it from religion*. He asserts that the national language of many nations differs from that of their religion; for example, Latin and Syriac are used in religious services but are not spoken languages. Besides, there are many Muslims whose mother tongue is not Arabic. Therefore it was wrong to claim that Arabic is only the language of Islam and, as a result, constrict and fossilize it.

> Arabic is not the property of the religious clerics, and they are not the only people to be entrusted with it, to defend and deal conclusively with it. It is the property of all those who speak it, and every one of them is free to deal with it so long as he fulfills the requirements that permit him to do so.[57]

As a result he severely attacks all those who believe that only al-Azhar and its graduates have the right to teach Arabic. Pursuing his secular view of nationalism and language, he points out that there are *Arabs who are not Muslims*, and non-Azharites and non-Muslims who have learned and taught Arabic. Besides, those who, like al-Khalil, Sibawayh, al-Akhfash and al-Mubarrad, laid down the rules for the Arabic language lived long before al-Azhar was founded.[58] He not only denied al-Azhar the right to monopolize Arabic, but also accused it of damaging the language because all its adherents know nothing but their barren, useless books. They have no freedom of thought, no knowledge of modern education and science or other Semitic languages, nor any idea of foreign languages and how they developed and progressed.[59] Thus Hussein not only separated language from religion, but also believed that renewing the language and its literature had nothing to do with religion and its clerics, and should be solely based on the knowledge of secular branches such as science and Semitic and European languages. Again, using secular Europe as an example, he says that in Europe it is *lay people* and not the clergy who teach Greek and Latin, the languages of the Church which are dead languages. So how much more important is it for Arabic, a living language, to be taught by lay specialists, reiterating that Arabic should be considered from a purely *civil perspective*.[60] Therefore it is the duty of the state to reform the Arabic language and simplify it, whether al-Azhar agrees or not.[61]

Al-Sayyid and Hussein disagreed as to how to simplify and develop the language. Although al-Sayyid was not as explicitly secular in dealing with Arabic as was Hussein, his secular attitude can be deduced from his suggestions for reform. If one does not renew the language it will die,[62] he writes, and it is here that we find him agreeing with the radical changes Amin, Sarruf and al-Shumayyil had suggested, sometimes being even more extreme. He concurred with them that the inflections on the last letter of the word were the cause of many mistakes in reading Arabic, and therefore suggested a new form of writing that would indicate these inflections.[63] Reviving the language also means following the law of evolution by dropping the obsolete and bringing in new and useful, necessary words,[64] just as all his predecessors had argued. Taking a more radical step, al-Sayyid proposes using foreign words such as *jaketta* (jacket) and *bantalone* (trousers), instead of wasting time and effort in finding or inventing Arabic words for the thousands of foreign words that have entered Arabic speech with the European inventions that penetrated the Arab world. He even objects to using the Arabic word *sayyara* for 'car', since the word *otomobil* is used by the Egyptians in their everyday speech. Defending his position, he says that just as Arabs in the past had adopted foreign words he saw no reason why the same should not be done now.[65] Besides foreign words, he also advocated a moderate use of some colloquial words and phrases, for this would help keep the Arabic language alive.[66] Separating Arabic from Islam, as did Hussein, he says that he cannot see what harm this would do to the language of the Qur'an[67] which hardly anybody, outside the learned élite, understands in any case.[68] Here, al-Sayyid seems to be dividing Arabic into two languages, that of the religion and the Qur'an, and the secular language of everyday life. He seems to consider the former as being similar to Latin which is used only in the liturgy, while he takes a completely secular stand towards the latter, allowing all kinds of changes, additions and linguistic aberrations, though these would not affect the language of religion since it is a completely different language. Thus al-Sayyid reconciles the religious aspect of Arabic with its secular aspect.

A problem all writers of Arabic faced and still do is the discrepancy between the colloquial (*'ami*) and the literary (*fusha*). Al-Sayyid considered that if writers used colloquial words and expressions they would actually be raising the standard of the colloquial and reducing the difference between it and the literary language. He rejected the use of the purely colloquial, however, in any artistic work.[69] Unlike him, Hussein opposed the use of the colloquial and believed that the literary language and the colloquial could be brought closer together if the literary language were reformed and simplified by people who were better educated and more cultured than the Azharites who monopolized it in his day.[70]

Just as the secularism of earlier writers had not been restricted to the language itself, neither was Hussein's. His book on pre-Islamic poetry represents the first time in modern Islamic thought that a Muslim took a purely secular look at the Arabic literary heritage, separating it completely from religion. He starts by stating:

> When we want to study Arabic literature and history we must... forget our religion and all that is related to it... and all that contradicts it. We should be bound by nothing but the methods of pure scholarly study... otherwise our minds will be fettered by that which suits religion. This is exactly what the ancients did, and it impaired their scholarly research.[71]

He then explains how their religious fervor harmed their research; they studied and retained in literature and art only that which agreed with Islam and endorsed it, discarding everything else. Had they not been influenced by religion, they would have left a literature that was very different from that which came down to succeeding generations

Being more concerned with literature than al-Sayyid, Hussein judged it by a new aesthetic yardstick, thus also creating a purely secular awareness in his contemporaries. He greatly admired ancient Greek literature and art, severely criticizing the Egyptians for their ignorance thereof, and the government for neglecting to teach these subjects in schools,[72] never hesitating because of their paganism and the naked bodies, both of which Islam utterly condemns. This, of course, is consistent with his belief in the separation of literature and art from religion. In an effort to make this pagan Greek literature accessible to Egyptians he translated some of its masterpieces.

On the basis of this new aestheticism, he also judged ancient Arabic literature. Like Kurd 'Ali, he criticized the exaggeration, hypocrisy and lies in the panegyrics, for example, both of them asserting that literature should honestly reflect the writers' feelings, thoughts and life.[73] Thus Hussein completely re-evaluated ancient Arabic literature in such books as *Hadith al-Arbi'a', Min Hadith al-Shi'r wa al-Nathr, Ma' al-Mutanabbi, Tajdid Dhikra Abi al-'Ala', Ma' Abi al-'Ala' fi Sijnih* and *Fi al-Adab al-Jahili*, among others. He himself admitted having been influenced in his literary criticism by the French critics Hyppolite Taine (d.1893), Charles Saint-Beuve (d.1869) and Jules Lemaître (d.1914).[74]

With the new secular aesthetic values they had acquired, both al-Sayyid and Hussein insisted on the importance of teaching the arts, especially music and singing which they believed had a good effect on morals,[75] contrary to what the religious clerics declared, according to Kurd 'Ali. Elaborating on the subject, Hussein writes that enjoyment of theatre, cinema, music, singing and dancing had improved the French people's character and morals, making them tolerant and moderate, unlike the Egyptians who are aggressive, exaggeratedly self-confident and intolerant.[76] This seems to suggest that Hussein believed art to be more influential than religion in improving morality, and sometimes more important. This is manifest in his artistic analyses of the plays he saw in Paris.[77] For example, commenting on a play about adultery, he clearly asserts that he does not care whether it is moral or immoral, what is important in a play is its artistic beauty, its action and plot, or its philosophical meaning.[78] In that same vein, he also showed his great appreciation of the beautiful paintings in Europe's museums, not as manifestations of religious subjects, but as sublime works of art.[79]

Conclusion

It is clear from the preceding chapters that the main concern of all the writers whose work has been discussed here was to overcome the backwardness of the people in their countries of residence once they had discovered the gap between them and the political, economic, social and scientific development of the West. The only way in which to bring this about, in their opinion, was by emulating the West. All of them admired Western civilization and believed that its emulation was the means to progress, although politically both the Christians and the Muslims rejected Western aggression and occupation. All were wise enough to differentiate between Western civilization and Western politics.

Even the most devout believers in Islam among these writers realized that Western civilization had only begun to progress once it had separated the religious from the temporal in every sphere of life, for this is what led to complete freedom of thought and scientific research and to progress in every field. Since Islam, unlike Christianity, mingles the spiritual with the temporal, it was easier for the Christians to visualize this separation. Besides being well versed in Arabic, the Christians had also mastered European languages before the Muslims, and were thus introduced to modern science and secular thought before them. The Christians therefore advocated secularism before the Muslims, and remained much more adamantly secular, for national, personal and intellectual reasons, as has been shown.

Not all the writers in question were equally interested in the various aspects of secularism. Some were more concerned with politics, while others were more interested in its social and educational aspects. All were eager, however, to achieve progress and to develop their respective countries, in whatever sphere – religion, politics, law, learning, social problems, civilization, language, literature and the arts. Most considered economics to be of secondary importance, accentuating the political, scientific and educational factors.

When the Muslim writers of the second and third generations voiced their secularism they agreed with the Christians that the nucleus of all religions was the same, that religion played an important role in public morality, but that its values were relative. Besides, they were unanimously anticlerical, undoubtedly due to the ignorance and fanaticism of the clergy in their time, as well as the political, intellectual and social power that these clerics wielded.

The fact that the Christians were more adamantly secular than the Muslims is shown in their attitude towards their respective religions. None of the Muslim writers considered religion to be useless or even a handicap to civilization, or believed that it could be replaced by a secular humanism or by science, as did some Christian writers. The Christians also criticized certain beliefs of the Catholic Church, such as Transubstantiation, directly attacked the Bible, and rejected the very principles of Christianity, such as Resurrection, divine retribution, heaven and hell, the Ten Commandments and the Trinity, or tried to analyze them philosophically or scientifically as their knowledge of Western science improved towards the end of the nineteenth century. Yet with the exception of al-Shumayyil their secularism did not end in atheism. The Muslims, however, only criticized the *misinterpretations of Islam by the 'ulama*, or the authenticity of some of the Hadith, but never the Qur'an itself or the principles of Islam. Even Hussein restricted his doubts to the veracity of some of the historical facts in the Qur'an, but never doubted or criticized the essential principles of Islam, or even the Qur'anic story of the Creation, as had his Christian predecessors.

And whereas the Christian secularists believed religion to be a social phenomenon, even the most courageous Muslims, such as Hussein and Nazira Zayn al-Din, believed only certain of the social injunctions in Islam to be social phenomena, and did not take the step the Mu'tazilites had taken in the eighth century in saying that the Qur'an was created, and thus showing that it was written by men, influenced by their culture and environment. The nearest Hussein came to this was when he stated that certain socio-political circumstances influenced some of the facts mentioned in the Qur'an, thus agreeing with all the Christians that religion is a social phenomenon, yet nevertheless affirming his belief in the Qur'an's being God's revealed word.

No matter how much the Muslim secular writers still clung to their religion, the influence of Western secularism on their thought is undeniable and it increased over time. When advocating the separation of the spiritual from the temporal, even an Azharite sheikh such as 'Abd al-Raziq referred to Western philosophers. With the increasing influence of Western thought and their deeper and better knowledge of it, a Muslim such as Taha Hussein could tackle even such spiritual themes as determinism and God's omnipotence in the perspective of Western secular philosophy.

Similarly, Muslim and Christian writers were influenced by secular Western, rather than by Arabic and/or Islamic thought, even when dealing with subjects that Islam encouraged, such as responsibility, rationalism and freedom of choice. The influence of the philosophers of the Enlightenment, and later of Comte, Mill, Hobbes, Locke and Huxley, among others, could be felt in their belief in rationalism, as was Renan's influence in their separation of the realms of science and religion to avoid the conflict between them. The philosophers of the Enlightenment and those of the French Revolution had a great impact on all of these writers, hence their emphasis on liberty, equality and freedom of thought, belief and speech, and on the Christian writers' attitude towards religion and the Catholic Church.

Western hegemony and/or occupation played a major role in arousing secular nationalistic feeling in the writers, whether this feeling was Ottoman, Arab or Egyptian. Turkish tyranny later gave way to political Arab nationalism. Social as well as intellectual and political reasons were the root cause of the Christians' purely secular nationalism.

The Christians enjoyed a very marginal status in the Ottoman Empire. They were and remained a minority in a mainly Muslim society, and suffered from the bloody sectarian strife in Lebanon and Syria, the narrowmindedness of the Maronite and Catholic clergy, as well as the fanaticism of Muslims. For all these reasons, Christian Arabs felt that secularism was the only way out of their estrangement from the society in which they lived, and they thus strived for complete separation of the spiritual from the temporal, although, ironically, this would also estrange them from their own sectarian societies. At the same time, they wanted to distance themselves from the Christian West with which their Muslim compatriots often associated them. Therefore, they expressed a purely secular nationalism, be it Ottoman or later Arab or Syrian, one in which not religious, but political, social and/or cultural unity were the basis of the concept of a homeland. As a result, they strongly criticized Europe's political interference in their countries and its exploitation of their resources. Spurred on by their secular, nationalist feelings, they clung to their Arabic heritage, the strong bond between them and their Muslim compatriots. They secularized the language which they no longer considered a vehicle for Islamic studies alone, but as a means of creating political, social and aesthetic awareness, and introduced the Arabs to new literary genres that had been imported from European literature; this same secularism was evident in their studies of Arabic history and literature. It was only later that the Muslim writers adopted this secular attitude towards their language, history and literature.

It was the Muslim writers of the second and third generations who began demanding a separation of the spiritual from the temporal, but at first this was mainly in the political sphere. It is thus among these later writers that one first finds a feeling of secular nationalism, albeit not always devoid of religious feeling. Whereas Lebanese and Syrian nationalism was Arab, that of the Egyptians was always Egyptian, anti-Ottoman and even politically anti-Arab. However, their attitude towards Arabic and its heritage also became secularized. They began adopting secular values in judging literature and the history of Islam, and used these values even to criticize paradigms in that history. Sometimes they were even more liberal than their Christian contemporaries in the linguistic reforms they proposed, probably because they were not afraid of being stigmatized as anti-nationalist, anti-Islamic or pro-Western, as the Christians feared.

Since Islam, as such, had no clear injunctions regarding forms of government and political administration, by separating the spiritual from the political, Muslim writers hoped that political reform would be a means of overcoming the tyranny and injustice of the ruling powers. Traditional, political Muslim thought enjoined Muslims to obey their rulers uncond-itionally, and the history of Islam only knew absolute rule, which more often than not was despotic and tyrannical. Thus, both Christians and Muslims realized that only democracy could accomplish the desired reform, yet by advocating the prevalence of popular will they contradicted the very principles of Muslim political thought. However, in seeking democracy, most of the Muslims only insisted on its principle of freedom, whereas the Christians insisted on equality, which the Muslims, with the exception of Hussein and al-Sayyid, avoided since it contradicted several Qur'anic injunctions. Some Muslim writers even denied the existence of such contradictions, while others overlooked them completely.

With political reform in mind, the Muslims thought that it was essential to link modern legislative and constitutional development to traditional Islamic thought. The earlier writers presented modern democracy as being merely a form of the traditional *shura*, for example, and the *ijma'* (consensus), the public opinion which limits the power of the ruler. That democracy should be inherent in Islam and its history is to overlook the historical and social events that gave rise to it. Therefore they chose from their religion and history whatever happened to suit their modern outlook, or reinterpreted them to show that they contained either the seeds or the manifestations of separation of the spiritual from the temporal. They claimed that democratic principles were, in fact, Muslim, and that Islam represented the whole of history and society.

In believing that the development of knowledge and learning would inevitably lead to democracy and progress, these writers were influenced by the Enlightenment and its authors. In stressing the importance of knowledge and education as an essential condition for progress all these writers stressed that it must be free from any religious influence, some even rejecting the teaching of religion in schools. They also realized that the borrowing of Western thought had to be accompanied by its methods of education, rationalism, criticism and self-criticism, analytical observation and the like. Most of the writers who dealt with the subject separated the realm of religion from that of science in order to avoid conflict between them, thus not fully realizing that only a complete and systematic secularization of all knowledge could be the basis for the scientific thought and the progress they hoped to achieve.

Although both Christians and Muslims realized that educating the people was an important condition for achieving democracy, and that democracy could not be implemented overnight, with the exception of the socialists al-Shumayyil and Antun, none of these writers fully realized that the modern principles of democracy and the secular ideas of equality, freedom and tolerance which accompany it had been less a product of education, of the philosophers and political scientists whose works they read, wrote about or translated in order to create political awareness in the people, as it had been of economics. They also did not seem to fully realize that underdevelopment was due to a combination of various causes, and that the only way to progress was to eliminate all of them. It had taken the West centuries of political, social, industrial as well as economic change to develop their democratic system. Education alone in countries that were still agrarian and feudal could not change the mentality of the people in one generation so democracy could not work. In general, the importance the writers attributed to the development of knowledge, education and science was disproportionately greater than that which they gave to economic and industrial reform.

Later Muslim writers differentiated between spiritual and sociological Islam, probably another example of the influence of Western secular thought. The former, they insisted, was immutable, whereas the latter had to change with the changing times. Again they referred to the tradition whereby the Prophet had asked the people to manage their worldly affairs as best they saw fit. Even the most devout Muslim writers saw the impossibility of sticking to the Qur'anic *shari'a*, and the need to establish new secular laws to suit the changing times if they wanted their society to progress. Some of them did not directly address the consequences of the separation of the spiritual from the temporal in laws pertaining to the social and personal spheres of life, so they refrained from discussing details that might highlight a conflict with Islam. The attitude of others in this respect was ambivalent, and they occasionally contradicted themselves. Yet in spite of everything, it was from Europe, rather than from Islam, that they derived such moral and social values as the need for hard work, ambition, perseverance, self-sacrifice, willpower, free will and the like, as well as the necessity to change the status of women in the Arab world.

The women writers, with the exception of their champion Amin, were more interested in this social aspect than in the political implications of secularism, since they were the victims of the patriarchal, theocratic system. Yet no matter how conservative their views concerning women's liberation, all the writers agreed that the progress of their nation depended to a large extent on improving the condition of women. However, some of the completely secular Christian male writers retained the traditional, conservative, even misogynistic opinion of women, whereas all the women and some Muslim men championed the cause of women's social and economic liberation. A few women showed a surprisingly modern feminist attitude, while a devout Muslim like Nazira Zayn al-Din even challenged some of the Qur'anic verses that were unjust to women.

In the social sphere. the secularism of the later Muslim writers is also evident in their appreciation and praise of arts that were forbidden or discouraged by Islam, such as painting and sculpture. They considered all art – music, dancing, theatre and fine art – to be another aspect of an advanced civilization, judging them by purely aesthetic values, rather than by the moral or by the religious yardstick.

All the writers, whether Christian or Muslim, were inconsistent in their thinking and sometimes contradicted themselves, even without realizing it. This might be partly due to the fact that most of them were journalists, so their articles varied according to the circumstances which gave rise to them. These changing circumstances included political relations with the West. Thus, for example, what Kurd 'Ali wrote while living under French occupation some-times contradicts what he had written when he was a subject of the Ottoman empire. Furthermore, all our writers, even those such as Amin, 'Abd al-Raziq, Nazira and Hussein who were not journalists, were not systematic thinkers who could formulate a comprehensive philosophy comprising a global, consistent worldview. Some of the contradictions in their writings also stemmed from the pressures of the traditional, conservative environment in which they lived, and which forced them to retract some of their more liberal and daring opinions, especially those directly concerning religion.

Although there is a difference in degree between the secularism of the earlier Muslims and that of the Christians, the secularism of the Muslim writers of the later generations very often resembled that of their Christian contemporaries. There remain fundamental differences between them, however. As has been shown, the Muslims never directly attacked religion or engaged in serious criticism of the Qur'an, as the Christians attacked Christianity and the Bible. In their demands for political or social reform the Christians usually believed in radical change and in emulating Europe, whereas the Muslims always referred to Islam and its heritage in order to justify their demands for change, always thinking within the framework of Islam and never accepting change independently of religious considerations. Of course, they chose from their religion and heritage only that which suited their secular ideas, or avoided details that contradicted these ideas, or reinterpreted Islam and its history to show that they contained Western values and the seeds of the political, economic and social principles of secular Western civilization. From this it can be deduced that the Muslim regarded the West as a complete 'other', while rejecting a total break with his/her heritage. The Christian, however, only regarded the West as an 'other' politically and culturally, but since his/her education had been Western as much as it had been Arab, the secular ideas and values were what he/she clung to in the Arab heritage. This is demonstrated by the early, strong secular nationalism of the Christians who felt it to be the only bond between them and their Muslim compatriots, since they sensed their estrangement in a Muslim world, unlike the Muslims who felt they belonged to it completely.

However, no matter what the contradictions and/or shortcomings in the secularism of these writers, what is important is how both Christians and Muslims dealt with their legacies, how they considered them in the light of secular thought and modern life and its necessities, and how they dealt with their religion, traditions and heritage, adapting them to suit the changing times and issues of modern life.

Notes

Introduction

1. Daher, 'Adel, *al-Ussus al-Falsafiya lil 'Ilamaniya*, p. 38.
2. Khater, Khalifa, 'A Rereading of Islamic Texts in the Maghrib in the Nineteenth and Early Twentieth Centuries: Secular Themes or Religious Reformism?' in: Ruedy, John,(ed.), *Islamism and Secularism in North Africa*, p. 49.
3. El-Mansour, Mohamed, 'Salafis and Modernists in the Moroccan National Movement', in: *Islamism and Secularism in North Africa*, p. 66.
4. Ibid., p. 64.
5. Ibid., p. 57.
6. See: Yared, Nazik Saba, *Arab Travellers and Western Civilization*, pp. 24–42.
7. Haddad, al-Taher, *Imra'atuna fil-Shari'a wal-Mujtama'*, p. 22. The translation is by Khater, Khalifa, in 'A Rereading of Islamic Texts in the Maghrib in the Nineteenth and Early Twentieth Centuries: Secular Themes or Religious Reformism?' in: *Islamism and Secularism in North Africa*, pp. 46–47.

   The secular changes that the Tunisian Code of Personal Status introduced during the rule of the Social Constitutional Party headed by Habib Bourguiba only came after the middle of the 20th century.
8. Hermassi, 'Abdelbaki, 'The Political and the Religious in the Modern History of the Maghrib', in: *Islamism and Secularism in North Africa*, p. 95.
9. Al-Rasy, George, *al-Islam al-Jazairi*, pp. 92–111.
10. Ibid., pp. 113–147.
11. Ibid., pp. 149–161.
12. Al-Azawi, Abbas, *Tarikh al-Adab al-Arabi fil-Iraq*, vol.II, pp. 224–237.
13. Simon, *Iraq Between the Two World Wars*, p. 43.
14. Al-Azmeh, *al-'Ilmaniyya min Manzur Mukhtalif*, pp. 177, 208, 223.
15. Simon, *Iraq*, p. 75.
16. Harris, George L., *Iraq its People its Society its Culture*, p. 289.

Chapter 1

1. This chapter draws extensively from the works of Holt, Antonius, Kirk, Ammoun, Longrigg, Salibi,Tignor, Simon, Harris and Makdisi. All of them are listed in the bibliography.
2. Tignor, *Modernisation and British Colonial Rule in Egypt, 1882–1914*, p. 343.
3. For details, see Holt, *Egypt and the Fertile Crescent*, pp. 224–225.

4. Tignor, ibid., *1882–1914*, p. 373.
5. For full details of this revolt see Makdisi, *The Culture of Sectarianism*, pp. 96–117.
6. Ibid. p. 119. For a full account of the 1860 war see pp. 118–145.
7. Khoury, *Urban Notables and Arab Nationalism*, p. 23.
8. For details see Makdisi pp. 146–165.
9. In 1610, a Lebanese monastic press printed Arabic psalms in Syriac characters. The first press that used Arabic letters was established in 1702 in Aleppo, also under Christian auspices.
10. Salibi, *The Modern History of Lebanon*, p. 140.
11. These writers will be discussed in detail in subsequent chapters.
12. For details see Ammoun, *Histoire du Liban Contemporain*, pp. 93–110.
13. For details of these negotiations and agreements and their outcome see Antonius, *The Arab Awakening*, Chapters viii and ix, and Holt, ibid., pp. 262–277.
14. For details of the post-war settlement see Holt, ibid., pp. 278–298, Antonius, ibid., pp. 276–324.
15. Kirk, *A Short History of the Middle East*, p. 164.
16. The greatest of the Common Interests was the important customs administration. The whole financial and administrative operation of the Common Interests was the prerogative of the High Commission and its dependent services.
17. Through which the British administration was gradually transferred to the Iraqis and Iraq admitted to the League of Nations as an independent nation, with Britain still holding special military and diplomatic privileges.

Chapter 2
1. Al-Mawardi (d.1058), for example, defined the caliphate as being 'for the protection of religion and the world.' *al-Ahkam al-Sultaniyya*, p. 3. In this book (Ordinances of Government) he formulated the theoretical principles for Islam as a religion and a state at the same time, thus uniting the spiritual and the temporal.
2. For his biography see: Khalaf Allah, *Ahmad Faris al-Shidyaq*. Mas'ad, *Faris al-Shidyaq*. Shikho, *Tarikh al-Adaab al-'Arabiyya*, II:37,86–88, 98,107. Tarazi, *Tarikh al-Sahafa al-'Arabiyya*, IV:61–64. Zaydan, *Tarajim Mashahir al-Sharq*, II:101. *Tarikh Adaab al-Lugha al-'Arabiyya*, I:261. Sarkis, *Mu'jam al-Matbu'at*, 1104–1107. Al-Zirkili, *al-A'lam*, I:164–184. Al-Sandubi, *A'lam al-Bayan*, pp. 111–170. 'Abbud, *Ruwwad al-Nahda al-Haditha*, pp. 199–203.*Judud wa Qudama'*, pp. 143–161. Daghir, *Masadir al-Dirasa al-Adabiyya*, II:471–478. *Encyclopedie de l'Islam* (1962), II:819. Brockelmann, *Geschichte der Arabischen Literatur (GAL)* SII:867. A.J.Arberry, 'Fresh Lights on Ahmad Faris al-Shidyaq', in: *Islamic Culture* (1952), pp. 155–168.
3. *Al-Saq 'ala al-Saq*, I:133. See also his article: 'Fi Usul al-Siyasa wa Ghayriha' in: *Kanz al-Ragha'ib*, I:109–111.
4. *Kashf al-Mukhabba*, pp. 205, 217, 218, 258–260, 265, 323, 325, 330, 357.
5. Ibid. pp. 238, 240, 243, 245, 257–259, 271.
6. For his biography see: Tarazi, I: 89–92. Shikho, II:126–127. Zaydan, *Tarajim*, II: 35. Sarkis, 557. *GAL*,SII: 767. Bustani,Fuad, *al-Rawa'i'*, vol.22.
7. *Qissat As'ad al-Shidyaq*, p. 63. The translation here and all other quotations are those of the author of this book, unless otherwise stated.

8. *Nafir Suriyya*, pp. 38, 49.

9. Makdisi points out that 'there were several understandings, translations and fragmentations of the imperial discussions of the reform' of the Tanzimat. *The Culture of Sectarianism*, p. 12. For a full discussion of the effect and results of these different interpretations in Lebanon, see pp. 63–95.

10. *Nafir Suriyya*, pp. 57–59.

11. For his biography see: Dahhan, *'Abd al-Rahman al-Kawakibi*. Khalaf Allah, *al-Kawakibi, Hayatuhu wa Ara'uhu*. Tabierot, *AL-Kawakibi*. Kayyali, *al-Adab al-'Arabi fi Suriyya*, pp. 65–73. *Muhadarat 'an al-Haraka al-Adabiyya fi Halab*, pp. 89–112. Tarazi, II:222–223. Zaydan, *Tarajim*, I:437–441. Amin, Ahmad, *Fayd al-Khatir*, VI:179–207. *Zu'ama' al-Islah fi al-'Asr al-Hadith*,pp. 249–279. Daghir, *Masadir*, II:672–675. Al-Zirkili, IV:68. Al-Tabbakh, *A'lam al-Nubala' fi Tarikh Halab al-Shahba'*, VII:507–524. 'Abbud, *Ruwwad*, pp. 201–206.

12. *Um al-Qura*, p. 228.

13. Ibid. p. 229. The Rashidun caliphs' rule lasted from 632 till 660. 'Umar ibn 'Abd al-'Aziz died in 720.

14. Ibid. pp. 229–231.

15. It was first published as a series of articles in the Egyptian periodical *al-Mu'ayyid* and came out in book form in 1900. Ahmad Amin believes Kawakibi's book was taken from that of the Italian Vittorio Alfieri (1749–1803) (*Fayd al-Khatir*, VI:183), and Hourani corroborates this since there was a Turkish translation of the book (*Arabic Thought*, p. 271). Kawakibi knew Turkish, but no European language.

16. *Taba'i' al-Istibdad*, p. 130.

17. *Um al-Qura*, pp. 235–236.

18. Ibid. p. 237.

19. Ibid. p. 70. The next chapter will show the negative influence the 'ulama had on politics.

20. *Um al-Qura*, p. 196.

21. Ibid. pp. 193 & 200.

22. For his biography see: Khaki, *Qasim Amin*. Daghir, *Masadir*, II:138. Zirkili, VI:19. Zaydan, *Tarajim*, I:420. Sarkis, 1482. 'Abbud, *Ruwwad*, pp. 207 &ff.

23. *Al-Mar'a al-Jadida*, p. 8. A later chapter will explain his secular ideas concerning women.

24. *Al-Mar'a*, p. 109.

25. For his biography see: *His autobiography* (translated by T. Philipp). *Al-Hilal, al-Kitab al-Dhahabi* (1892–1942). Zirkili, II:108. Daghir, *Masadir*, II:442. 'Aqqad, *Rijal 'Araftuhum*, pp. 191–198. Nasr, *al-Nubugh al-Lubnani fi al-Qarn al-'Ishrin*, I:244. *GAL*, SIII:186–190.

26. For his biography see: Ishaq, *al-Durar*, introductions by 'Awni Ishaq, pp. 5–15, and Jirjis Nahhas, pp. 16–22.Ishaq, *al-Kitabat al-Siyasiyya wa al-Ijtima'iyya*, introduction by Naji 'Alloush, pp. 5–60. Zirkili, I: 274. Shikho, II:133–134. Tarazi, II: 105. Daghir, *Masadir*, II: 111–114. Sarkis, 418. Zaydan, *Tarajim*, II: 94–100. 'Abboud, *Ruwwad*, pp. 184–195. Kayyali, *al-Adab al- 'Arabi*, pp. 54–57.

27. For his biography see: *Mudhakkirat* Shibli al-Shummayyil. Al-Sa'id, Rif'at, *Thalathatu Lubnaniyyin fi al-Qahira*, pp. 12–68. Hourani, *Arabic Thought*, pp. 248–253. 'Abbud,

Ruwwad, pp. 198&ff. Shikho, II:75. Daghir, *Masadir*, II:497. Tarazi, II:124. Zaydan, *Mukhtarat*, II:176–178.

28. For his biography see: Isma'il, *al-Mujtama' wa al-Din wa al-Ishtirakiyya, Farah Antun*. Al-Khoury, *Fi al-Yaqza al-'Arabiyya*. Al-Mu'min, *Min Tala'i' Yaqzat al-'Umma al-'Arabiyya*. Al-Sa'id, *Thalathatu Lubnaniyyin*, pp. 76&ff. 'Abbud, *Judud*, pp. 17–66. *Ruwwad*, pp. 209 &ff. Shikho, *Tarikh al-Adab fi al-Rub' al-Awwal min al-Qarn al-'Ishrin*, p. 112. Majmu'at al-Mu'allifin, *Adwa' 'ala al-Ta'assub*, pp. 65–66. Daghir, *Masadir*, II:147.

29. Zaydan, *Letters*, in his *Autobiography*, translated by T.Philipp, pp. 80–83.

30. *Al-Durar*, pp. 189–190.

31. Shummayyil, *Kitabat Siyasiyya wa Islahiyya*, pp. 62–63.

32. *Majmu'at al-Doctor Shibli al-Shummayyil*, II: 297.

33. *Kitabat*, p. 161.

34. 'Abdu's comments were published in *al-Manar* and Antun's answers in *al-Jami'a*. 'Akra published them all in his edition of Antun's book *Ibn Rushd wa Falsafatuhu*, pp. 97–198.

35. *Ibn Rushd wa Falsafatuhu*, p. 31. The translation is from Hourani's *Arabic Thought* pp. 254–255.

36. *Ibn Rushd*, p. 185.

37. Ibid. pp. 144–145.

38. 'al-Ijtihad fi al-Nusraniyya wa al-Islam', in: *al-Jami'a*, III, part 8 (June 1902), pp. 538–539.

39. *Ibn Rushd*, p. 144.

40. Ibid. p. 196.

41. Ibid. p. 145–146.

42. Ibid. p. 145.

43. Ibid. p. 154.

44. Ibid. p. 156.

45. Ibid. p. 146.

46. Ibid. p. 157.

47. See Makdisi, *The Culture*, pp. 91–95.

48. Afghani believed that religion was enough to bring different peoples together, although religion combined with Ibn Khaldun's 'asabiyya would also form a strong bond. Yet even his disciple and collaborator 'Abdu saw the impossibility of a political union between all Muslims, and understood Pan-Islamism only to mean Muslims co-operating in the reform of whatever had gone wrong in their beliefs and deeds, and to oppose tyranny and disaster. For details about the ideas of both thinkers, see Hourani, *Arabic Thought*, Chapters V and VI. Ramadan, *Aux sources du Renouveau Musulman*, Chapters II et III.

49. 'Falsafat Jamal al-Din al-Afghani', in *al-Jami'a*, V, part 4 (Sept. 1906), pp. 150–152. Friedrich Nietzche died in 1900.

50. *Ibn Rushd*, p. 163. Mu'awiya was the first Umayyad caliph who ruled from Damascus (660–680 AD) but he had no real power over the far-lying parts of the empire.

51. *Ibn Rushd*, p. 150.

52. Philipp, *Gurgi Zaidan*, p. 85.

53. For his biography see: *Encyclopedia of the Modern Middle East*, I: 272–273.
54. A Lebanese Christian who was the general secretary of the Syrian Central Committee in Paris. See: Hourani, pp. 286 & 289.
55. *Le Réveil de la Nation Arabe*, pp. 245–247.
56. Ibid., Preface, pp. I-II. Azoury was the first writer to openly suggest Arab independence from the Ottoman Empire.
57. *Le Réveil*, pp. 246–248.
58. *La Syrie*, p. 314.
59. *La Syrie*, pp. 599–620.
60. For his biography see: His autobiography *Qissat Hayati*. Najjar, *Ahmad Lutfi al-Sayyid, Ustadh al-Jil. Lutfi al-Sayyid wa al-Shakhsiyya al-Misriyya*. Sharaf, *Lutfi al-Sayyid, Failasuf aiqaza Umma*. Dagher, *Masadir*, II:582. Wendell, *The Evolution of the Egyptian National Image*, pp. 205–221.
61. *Muntakhabat*, I:309.
62. *Safhat Matwiyya*, p. 34.
63. Ibid. pp. 99–101.
64. Ibid. p. 7.
65. For his biography see: His *Memoires* (3vols.). Kurd 'Ali, *Khitat al-Sham*, VI:411–425. Al-Dahhan, *Muhammad Kurd 'Ali*. Jabri, *Muhammad Kurd 'Ali*. Al-Alussi, *Muhammad Kurd Ali*. Zirkili, VII:73. Dagher, *Masadir*, II:655. *GAL*, SIII:430–434. Pérès, *L'Espagne vue par les Voyageurs Arabes*, pp. 122 ff.
66. *Al-Qadim wa al-Hadith*, pp. 20–21, 23.
67. Ibid. pp. 305–306.
68. *Ghra'ib al-Gharb*, I:116.
69. Ibid. I:49.
70. Ibid. II: 222–225.
71. Ibid. I:216–217.
72. *Al-Mudhakkirat*, I:166–168.
73. *Al-Islam wa al-Hadara al-'Arabiyya*, I:41, 178, 335.
74. Ibid. II:46.
75. *Al-Mudhakkirat*, IV: 1020, 1057.
76. Ibid. III:966.
77. For her biography see: Dagher, *Masadir*, II:369. *Qamus al-Sahafa al-Lubnaniyya*, pp. 159,259,287. Zirkili, II: 147. Ibrahim, *al-Haraka al-Nisa'iyya al-Lubnaniyya*, p. 82. Nuwaihid, *Nisa' min Biladi*, pp. 110–114. Kallas, *al-Haraka al-Fikriyya al-Nasawiyya fi 'Asr al-Nahda*, pp. 245–246.
78. *Al-Mar'a al-Jadida*, July 1924 (vol.7), p. 279, & Aug. 1925, (vol.8) pp. 309–310.
79. For his biography see: *GAL*, SIII:329. Hourani, *Arab Thought*, p. 183.
80. The twenty-four leading *'ulama* who judged him, headed by the principal of the Azhar, pointed out seven main ideas in the book which they considered contradictory to Islam and its history. See: *Hukm Hay'at Kibar al-'Ulama*, pp. 8–32.
81. *Al-Islam wa Usul al-Hukm*, pp. 22–25, 27.
82. See D.B.Macdonald, *Development of Muslim Theology, Jurisprudence and Constitutional Theory*, pp. 65–117.
83. *Al-Islam*, pp. 32–33.

84. Ibid. pp. 46–48.
85. Ibid. p. 76.
86. Ibid. pp. 77–78.
87. Ibid. p. 82.
88. Ibid. pp. 84–88.
89. Ibid. p. 92.
90. Ibid. p. 100.
91. Ibid. p. 91.
92. Ibid. pp. 97–100.
93. Ibid. pp. 103, 105.
94. Ibid. pp. 107, 109–111.
95. Ibid. pp. 120–121.
96. *Hukm Hay'at Kibar al-'Ulama'*, pp. 10–13, 20–23.
97. *Al-Islam*, p. 19.
98. Ibid. p. 24.
99. *Hukm*, p. 24.
100. *Al-Islam*, pp. 124–136.
101. Ibid. p. 137.
102. Brown, *Rethinking Tradition*, p. 67.
103. For his biography and autobiography, see *al-Ayyam* (3 vols.). Hussein, *Min laghu al-Saif*. Cachia, *Taha Hussein, His Place in the Egyptian Literary Renaissance.GAL*, SIII:284–302.
104. *Al-Fitna al-Kubra*, in: *Complete Works*, IV: 220.
105. *Fi al-Shi'r al-Jahili*, p. 52.
106. *Mustaqbal al-Thaqafa fi Misr*, p. 30.
107. *Min Ba'id*, p. 230.
108. Ibid. p. 234.
109. *Al-Fitna*, in: *Complete Works*, IV: 219.
110. *Mustaqbal*, p. 71.
111. For her biography see: Nuwaihid, *Nisa' Min Biladi*, pp. 94–98. Zaydan, *Masadir al-Adab al-Nisa'i fi al-'Alam al-'Arabi*, pp. 122 ff. Sha'ban, Introduction to Zayn al-Din's book *al-Sufur wa al-Hijab*, pp. 7–14. *GAL*, SIII:415.
112. *Al-Sufur wa al-Hijab*, p. 54.
113. *Al-Fatat wa al-Shuyukh*, p. 78. This, her second book, was her answer in 1929 to the uproar her first book had caused in conservative and religious circles.
114. *Al-Fatat*. pp. 80, 131.
115. Ibid. p. 78.
116. *Al-Sufur*, p. 269.
117. *Al-Fatat*, p. 132.
118. She is referring here to an Ottoman decree issued on 21 February, 1912,which had given Muslim men and women equal rights in inheriting state-owned (*miri*) and endowment land on the grounds that they were public and not private property.
119. *Al-Fatat*, p. 131.
120. Ibid. p. 81.
121. Ibid. p. 113.

122. Ibid. p. 273.

Chapter 3

1. *Nafir*, p. 20.
2. *Ta'lim al-Nisa'*, pp. 3, 7, 22.
3. *Qissat As'ad*, pp. 18, 23, 27–29, 32–33, 39.
4. Ibid. pp. 42, 46, 54, 57, 58.
5. *Nafir* p. 20.
6. *Al-Saq*, I: 75–76, 135–139.
7. Ibid. II: 218.
8. Ibid. I: 31.
9. *Al-Wasita fi Ma'rifati Ahwal Malta*, p. 27.
10. *Al-Saq*, II: 16.
11. Ibid. I: 128, 321–322.
12. Ibid. I: 155–156.
13. Ibid. I: 92.
14. *Kanz*, II: 212–213.
15. *Kashf*, p. 256.
16. For his biography see: al-Humsi, *al-Sihr al-Halal fi Shi'r al-Dallal*. Shikho, *al-Adaab al-'Arabiyya*, II: 147–149. Kayyali, *al-Adab al-'Arabi al-Mu'asir fi Suriyya*, pp. 58–65. *Muhadarat 'an al-Haraka al-Adabiyya fi Halab*, pp. 55–85. Tarazi, *Tarikh al-Sahafa al-'Arabiyya*, II: 230–234. Daghir, *Masadir al-Dirasa al-Adabiyya*, II: 367–368. Sarkis, *Mu'jam al-Matbu'at*, 878–879.
17. The whole 152–verse poem is printed in: Kayyali, *Muhadarat*, pp. 78–85.
18. Kayyali, *Muhadarat*, pp. 80–82.
19. *Al-Kitabat al-Siyasiyya*, pp. 110–111.
20. *Al-Durar*, p. 72.
21. Ibid. pp. 447–448, 459–460.
22. For his biography see: Shikho, II: 41–42. Tarazi, I: 141. Al-Humsi, *Udaba' Halab*, pp. 20–30. Sarkis, 1730. Zirkili, V: 344. Daghir, II: 693. Zaydan, *Tarajim Mashahir*,II: 337. *Tarikh Adaab al-Lugha al-'Arabiyya*, IV: 236. Abboud, *Ruwwad*, pp. 121–136. *GAL*, SII: 755.
23. *Mashhad al-Ahwal*, pp. 59–65.
24. *Shahadat al-Tabi'a fi Wujud Allah wa al-Shari'a*, p. 62.
25. *Rihlat Paris*, pp. 39–40.
26. *Mashhad*, pp. 2–3.
27. *Shahadat*, p. 12.
28. Ibid. pp. 33–34.
29. Ibid. p. 37.
30. *Um al-Qura*, p. 77.
31. Ibid. pp. 71–72, 95–99, 129–131, 140–141.
32. Ibid. pp. 54–55. *Taba'i'*, pp. 26–28.
33. *Um al-Qura*, p. 86.
34. *Taba'i'*, 30–31.
35. Ibid. p. 86.

36. Amin, *Complete Works*, I: 104 & 154.
37. *Mukhtarat*, II: 44–46. *Ibn Rushd*, pp. 139, 175–178.
38. *Ibn Rushd*, p. 163.
39. *Mukhtarat*, II: 35. *Al-Jami'a*, vol. III, part 8 (June 1902), p. 527.
40. *Mukhtarat*, II: 181. *Ibn Rushd*, p. 64.
41. *'Aja'ib al-Khalq*, pp. 3, 58–63. But he goes back to the Biblical story of the creation in a school book of history and geography he wrote: *al-Tarikh al-'Am*, I: 24–25. This shows how far the conservative environment sometimes forced him to renounce his secularism. *
42. *Al-Jami'a*, vol. V, part 4, (Sept. 1906) p. 155. & vol. III, part 9 (Aug. 1902) p. 633.
43. *Al-Jami'a*, vol. IV, part 2, (March 1903), pp. 67–78.
44. *Mukhtarat*, II: 193–195.
45. Ibid. II: 175–176.
46. Ibid. II: 171.
47. Ibid. II: 181–182.
48. Ibid. II: 163–167.
49. *Ibn Rushd*, pp. 61–62, 71–75.
50. *Rihlat Jurji Zaydan*, pp. 34–35.
51. *Mukhtarat*, II: 21, 34–36.
52. Ibid. III: 21.
53. *Al-Din wa al-'Ilm wa al-Mal*, p. 78.
54. *Ibn Rushd*, pp. 123–124.
55. Ibid. pp. 137–138. *Al-Jami 'a*, vol. V, part 4, (Sept. 1906), p. 149.
56. The article appeared in *al-Jami'a*, June 20, 1902, and Rida asked 'Abdu to answer in *al-Manar*, vol. VI, pp. 361 ff. A long debate followed between them which 'Abdu published in *al-Manar* and Antun in *AL-Jami'a*. The whole debate was published by 'Acra in his edition of *Ibn Rushd wa Falsafatuhu*, pp. 97–198.
57. *Ibn Rushd*, p. 98.
58. Ibid. pp. 51, 74, 138.
59. 'al-'Anasir al-Sharqiyya wa al-Taqrib Baynaha', in: *al-Jami'a*, vol. IV, part 4, (June 1903), p. 245.
60. For his biography see: Daghir, II: 540. Tarazi, II: 124. Sarkis, 126. *Al-Kitab al-Dhahabi li Yubil al-Muqtataf, 1876–1926*. Faraj, Nadia, 'The Lewis affair and the Fortunes of al-Muqtataf' in: *The Middle Eastern Studies*, London, VIII, N°21, (1972), pp. 73–83.
61. *Al-Muqtataf*, vol. 7 (1882), pp. 2–6, 65–72, 121–127; vol. 72 (1928), p. 121; vol. 73 (1928), p. 121.
62. *Al-Muqtataf*, vol. VII (1882), p. 6; vol. VIII (1884), p. 71.
63. 'al-Sahafa al-'Ilmiyya wa al-Nahda al-Sharqiyya' in: *al-Muqtataf*, vol. 72 (1928), p. 484.
64. 'al-Harb wa Tanazu' al-Baqa'' in: al-*Muqtataf*, 72 (1928), p. 361. Shummayyil's opinion was that war is a necessary aspect of the struggle and survival of the fittest.
65. 'Allah wa al-'Alam' in: *al-Muqtataf*, 75 (1929), pp. 126–128.
66. 'al-Madhhab al-Darwini' in: *al-Muqtataf*, 7 (1882), p. 127. 'Gharad al-Hayat' in: *al-Muqtataf*, 74 (1929), p. 482.

67. 'Allah wa al-'Alam' in: *al-Muqtataf*, 75 (1929), p. 123.
68. Quoted in: Mazhar, *Mu'dilat al-Madaniyya al-Haditha*, p. 193.
69. 'Allah wa al-'Alam' in: *al-Muqtataf*, 75 (1929), p. 128.
70. *Majmu'at Shibli al-Shummayyil*, I: 44–48.
71. Ibid. II: 119.
72. Ibid. I: 3.
73. Ibid. I: 14 & 36.
74. *Al-Manar*, vol. 19, p. 625.
75. *Majmu'at*, I: 51 & 238.
76. Ibid. I: 231.
77. Ibid. I: 28.
78. Ibid. I: 284.
79. Ibid. I: 48–49. II: 205–206.
80. Ibid. I: 50.
81. Ibid. I: 328.
82. Ibid. I: 318–320.
83. Ibid. I: 30. The italics are mine.
84. Ibid. I: 240.
85. *Al-Kitabat*, p. 222.
86. *Majmu'at*, I: 31, 51–52.
87. Ibid. I: 318.
88. Ibid. II: 58, 72, 75.
89. Ibid. II: 61–62.
90. Ibid. I: 269.
91. Ibid. II: 285–286.
92. *Arab Intellectuals and the West*, p. 74.
93. *Al-Saq*, I: 62.
94. *Al-Kitabat*, p. 270.
95. *Al-Mar'a al-Jadida*. pp. 61, 97, 117–119, 121. *Mukhtarat*, II: 206.
96. *Mukhtarat*, I: 130–132.
97. *Majmu'at*, II: 7.
98. Ibid. I: 53.
99. *Al-Islam* I: 59.
100. Ibid. I: 71.
101. Al-*Mudhakkirat*, II: 491–492. III: 985.
102. *Al-Islam*, I: 69.
103. Al-*Mudhakkirat*, II: 490; III: 987.
104. *Al-Qadim*, pp. 5–6.
105. *Safahat Matwiyya*, pp. 118–119. Translation from Hourani, p. 172.
106. *Safahat*, p. 102.
107. *Qissat Hayati*, p. 74.
108. Wendell, *The Evolution of the Egyptian National Image*, pp. 239–244.
109. *Safahat*, pp. 34, 107–109.
110. *Min Laghu al-Saif ila Jid al-Shita'*, pp. 45–46.
111. *Rihlat al-Rabi'*, p. 116.

112. *Mustaqbal,* p. 181.
113. Ibid. p. 320.
114. *Fi al-Saif,* pp. 12, 18–19.
115. *Min Ba'id,* pp. 47–52, 204.
116. *Min Ba'id,* pp. 94, 219–220, 227.
117. *Fi al-Shi'r,* pp. 15–23, 88.
118. *Al-Fitna al-Kubra,* in: *Complete Works,* IV: 205–206.
119. Al-Azmeh, *al-'Ilmaniyya,* pp. 226–227.
120. *Fi al-Shi'r,* p. 26.
121. Ibid. pp. 27–28. Quraish was the Prophet's tribe that ruled Mecca. The Ka'ba is a holy shrine in Mecca.
122. *Qadat al-Fikr,* in: *Complete Works,* VIII: 192–193.
123. *Min Ba'id,* pp. 16–17
124. *Al-Manar,* vol. 28, p. 377.
125. *Min Ba'id,* p. 204.
126. *'Ala Hamish al-Sira,* pp. 11–12.
127. *Naqd wa Islah,* pp. 11–12.
128. *Arabic Thought,* p. 334. 'Uthman and 'Ali were the third and fourth Rashidun (Orthodox) Caliphs. 'Uthman was killed in 656. Hussein's Islamic books were writen between 1943 and 1960.
129. *Al-Fatat wa al-Shuyukh,* pp. 27, 113.
130. *Al-Sufur wa al-Hijab,* pp. 252, 256–258.
131. Ibid. pp. 71–73, 76.
132. *Al-Fatat,* pp. 42, 126, 377. Doubting the *Hadith* is nothing new. Muhammad 'Abdu and Rashid Rida had done that before. Brown devotes a whole chapter of his book *Rethinking Tradition in Modern Islamic Thought* to the problem of the authenticity of the *Hadith* (pp. 81–107).
133. *Al-Sufur,* p. 44.
134. *Al-Fatat,* p. 336.
135. 'The Throne and the Temple' in: Kayyali, p. 83. See also: Bustani, *Nafir,* p. 58. Marrash, *Rihla,* p. 35.
136. *Al-Saq,* I: 119–124, 128, 132–140, 150, 155. II: 18–19.
137. *Kashf,* pp. 186–187.
138. *Rihla,* pp. 47–48.
139. 'The Throne and the Temple' in: Kayyali, p. 83.
140. *Le Réveil,* pp. 165, 177.
141. *Al-Din,* pp. 72,79–80.
142. *Al-Mar'a al-Jadida,* p. 108.
143. *Al-Qadim,* pp. 55, 59–60.
144. *Al-Sufur,* pp. 44, 47, 49, 67, 68–70, 72.
145. *Al-Islam,* II: 38–50. *Al-Qadim,* pp. 49–50, 54–55.
146. *Min Ba'id,* pp. 236–244. It was written in 1923.
147. *Al-Saq,* I: 18, 19, 74, 76–77, 82, 94, 213–214. II: 129–130, 133, 146–147.
148. *Um al-Qura,* pp. 56–57. *Tahrir al-Mar'a,* in: *Complete Works,* II: 74. *Min Ba'id,* pp. 119, 123–125, 167–169. *Naqd wa Islah,* pp. 247–249, 254–255. *Al-Fatat,* p. 113.

149. *Fi al-Saif*, pp. 44, 46.
150. *Naqd*, pp. 252–253, 264–266, 276–277. *Mustaqbal*, pp. 338, 340–341.
151. *Um al-Qura*, pp. 39, 46. *Tahrir*, in: *Complete Works*, II: 83, 98–102. *Al-Qadim*, pp. 49, 56–60. *Al-Fatat*, p. 113.
152. *Al-Sufur*, pp. 44, 47, 49, 68–69, 72. *Majmu'at*, II: 63, 71. *Naqd*, pp. 247–249.
153. For her biography see: Zirkili, III: 108. Kahhali, *A'lam al-Nisa'*, pp. 491–500. Daghir, II: 637. *Majallat al-'Irfan*, vol. 2 (1910), pp. 229–221; vol. 13 (1927), p. 609; vol. 18 (1929), p. 229. Najm, *al-Qissa fi al-Adab al-'Arabi al-Hadith*, pp. 159–161. Muhammad, *Balaghat al-Nisa' fi al-Qarn al-'Ishrin*, pp. 116–160. Badran and Cooke, (ed.), *Opening the Gates*, p. 220.
154. 'The Throne and the Temple' in: Kayyali, p. 79. Fawwaz, *al-Rasa'il al-Zaynabiyya*, pp. 47–54, 68–71, 157–168. *Um al-Qura*, pp. 41–44, 93. Antun, *al-Wahsh, al-Wahsh*, pp. 99–101. Kurd 'Ali, *Mudhakkirat*, II: 352.
155. *Al-Saq*, I: 58. 'The Throne and the Temple' in: Kayyali, p. 79. Marrash, *Rihla*, p. 35. *Al-Rasa'il*, pp. 47–54. *Um al-Qura*, pp. 50, 65. *Mukhtarat*, II: 24–25. *Ibn Rushd*, pp. 157–158. *Al-Din*, pp. 73–75, 78–79. *Majmu'at*, II: 243–244. Al-*Qadim*, pp. 49, 56–60.
156. 'The Throne and the Temple', in: Kayyali, p. 80. *Al-Saq*, I: 77–78, 87, 94, 97–99. II: 116, 119, 147. *Um al-Qura*, pp. 48–53, 65.
157. *Al-Saq*, I: 77–78, 87, 94, 97–99. II: 116, 119, 147. *Um al-Qura*, pp. 43–44.
158. *Al-Saq*, I: 76–77, 94, 128–129. *Le Réveil*, p. 27. *Urushalim al-Jadida*, pp. 187–188, 214–215. *Majmu'at*, II: 220–221.
169. *Al-Saq*, I: 155. *Ibn Rushd*, p. 156.
160. *Kanz*, I: 110. II: 141. *Majmu'at*, I: 11.

Chapter 4

1. *Kanz*, I: 191–192. II: 146, 148. *Dalil al-Hurriyya al-Insaniyya*, p. 2.
2. *Rihla*, p. 37.
3. *Ghabat al-Haq*, pp. 15–16, 29, 76–86.
4. *Al-Durar*, pp. 124, 127, 159–161, 164–166, 455, 183–185.
5. *Um al-Qura*, pp. 27, 158. *Taba'i'*, p. 89.
6. *Um al-Qura*, p. 18. *Taba'i'*, p. 51.
7. *Al-Rasa'il*, p. 20. The translation is by Marilyn Booth in *Opening the Gates*, p. 222.
8. *Al-Rasa'il*, p. 91.
9. *Al-Mar'a*, p. 51.
10. Surah VIII, Spoils of War, verse 53.
11. *Al-Islam*, I: 377.
12. *Mukhtarat*, I: 23, 49–55.
13. Ibid. II: 158–162.
14. Ibid. II: 162–163.
15. *Al-Jami'a*, vol. IV, part 1, (Febr. 1903), p. 21.
16. 'Sir al-Najah' in: *al-Muqtataf*, vol. 62 (1923), p. 395.
17. *Majmu'at*, I: 13. II: 291.
18. *Qissat Hayati*, p. 173.
19. *Muntakhabat*, I: 98.
20. *Qissat*, p. 45. *Muntakhabat*, I: 25, 317–318.

21. *Ta'mmulat fi al-Falsafa wa al-Adab wa al-Ijtima'*, pp. 50–54.
22. *Ghara'ib*, I: 236.
23. *Ghara'ib*, I: 300–303, 334–336. *Al-Qadim*, pp. 233, 238–241. *Al-Mudhakkirat*, I: 198.
24. *Al-Mudhakkirat*, III: 1054.
25. *Al-Mar'a al-Jadida*, Jan. 1925 (vol. 1), pp. 2–3.
26. Ibid. Dec. 1923 (vol.12), p. 426.
27. *Al-Sufur*, p. 39 . *Al-Fatat*, p. 102.
28. *Al-Fatat*, p. 146.
29. *Al-Sufur*, p. 44.
30. *Mustaqbal*, pp. 359–360, 362.
31. *Tajdid Dhikra Abi al-'Ala', Complete Works*, X: 24–25.
32. Durkheim, *Règles de la Méthode Sociologique*, pp. 5–15.
33. *Rihla*, pp. 30–32.
34. *Al-Mar'a al-Jadida*, May 1925 (vol. 5), p. 176.
35. *Al-Sufur*, p. 120.
36. *Al-Fatat*, p. 370.
37. *Taba'i*, p. 2. *Al-Mudhakkirat*, II: 619.
38. *Al-Mudhakkirat*, III: 862.
39. *Tahrir al-Mar'a*, in: *Complete Works*, II: 71.
40. For her biography see: Nasif, *Athar Bahithat al-Badiya*, pp. 6–68. *Tahrir al-Mar'a fi-al-Islam*, pp. 41–68. Ziadi, May, *Bahithat al-Badiya, Dirasa Naqdiyya*. Al-Jabri, *al-Muslima al-'Asriyya 'inda Bahithat al-Badiya*, pp. 7–32. Daghir, II: 739. Sarkis, 1788.
41. *Al-Nisa'iyyat*, I: 34–35, 46–48, 52–55, 58–61, 62–68, 90.
42. Ibid. I: 121.
43. *Ta'mmulat*, p. 106.
44. *Muntakhabat*, I: 38–41, 49–50, 175–176, 186–188.
45. *Qissat*, p. 213.
46. *Mustaqbal*, pp. 352, 358–359.
47. *Kashf*, pp. 151–152.48. *Rihlat Paris*, p. 34. *Ghabat al-Haq*, p. 75.
49. *Um al-Qura*, p. 184. *Al-Nisa'iyyat*, I: 146.
50. *Majmu'at*, I: 55. II: 5–6.
51. 'Falsafat Jamal al-Din al-Afghani', in: *al-Jami'a*, V, part 4 (Sept.1906), p. 150.
52. *Ghara'ib*, I: 259. II: 243,265.
53. *Al-Qadim*, pp. 241–242.
54. *Mustaqbal*, pp. 10, 359, 360–362.
55. *Qissat*, pp. 118, 195.
56. Ibid. pp. 168–169.
57. *Qissat As'ad*, pp. 63–64, 66.
58. *Al-Saq*, I: 119–123, 133–135, 140. II: 106.
59. *Al-Wasita*, pp. 45–46.
60. *Al-Kitabat al-Siyasiyya wa al-Ijtima'iyya*, pp. 81, 117. *Kitabat Siyasiyya wa Islahiyya*, pp. 205–206. *Al-Jami'a*, vol.V, part 5 (Sept. 1906), pp. 187–191. *Al-Islam*, I: 17–19, 25–26, 30–34.
61. *Al-Durar*, pp. 52–54, 147–149.
62. *Kitabat Siyasiyya wa Islahiyya*, pp. 11–12, 21.

63. All his novel *Urushalim al-Jadida*.
64. *Al-Jami'a*, vol. III, part 9 (Aug. 1902), p. 632.
65. *Ghara'ib*, II: 133–138, 200–206, 215–217.
66. Letters to his son on October 12, 1910 and March 28, 1912 in: *Autobiography by Gurgi Zaidan*, trans. by T. Philipp, pp. 80–83, 85–86.
67. *Kitabat*, pp. 17–20.
68. *Majmu'at*, I: 354, footnote 2.
69. *Al-Durar*, pp. 56–57. *Urushalim*, p. 235. *Majmu'at*, I: 54.
70. *Al-Sufur*, p. 45.
71. The Cow, verse 256. *Al-Sufur*, pp. 44, 52, 61, 63.
72. Khaki, *Qasim Amin*, p. 48.
73. *Ghara'ib*, I: 93.
74. *Qissat As'ad*, pp. 16–39, 41.
75. Adaab al-'Arab, in: *Rawai'*, XXII: 27.
76. *Kanz*, I: 160.
77. Marrash, *al-Jinan*, vol. II (1871), p. 157. *Kitabat*, p. 35. *Al-Nisa'iyyat*, I: 17.
78. *Al-Durar*, pp. 108–109, 140–142, 418–419. *Mukhtarat*, III: 112–120, 125. *Al-Jami'a*, vol. IV, part 4 (June 1903), p. 231. *Ibn Rushd*, p. 31. *Al-Mudhakkirat*, I: 51–53, 64, 84–86, 89–93. II: 536–538. *Qissat*, pp. 46, 175. *Muntakhabat*, I: 297–301. II: 62.
79. *Kitabat*, pp. 17–20.
80. *Muntakhabat*, II: 83–85.
81. *Al-Mudhakkirat*, IV: 1176–1177.
82. Adaab al-'Arab, in: *Rawai'*, XXII: 27. *Al-Saq*, I: 156–157. II: 15. *Dalil al-Hurriyya*, p. 2. *Al-Durar*, pp. 45, 337–338. *Um al-Qura*, pp. 14–15, 120–125. *Al-Nisa'iyyat*, I: 24, 76.
83. *Al-Durar*, p. 45.
84. *Ghara'ib*, II: 219, 258, 260. *Al-Qadim*, pp. 54–60.
85. *Al-Islam*, I: 1.
86. *Khitat al-Sham*, IV: 6.
87. *Um al-Qura*, p. 32.
88. *Mudhakkirat Jurji Zaidan*, p. 68. *Mukhtarat*, I: 26–33, 38–39, 44–45, 46, 47.
89. *Al-Muqtataf*, vol. 24 (1881), p. 299; vol. 72 (1928), p. 484.
90. *Majmu'at*, I: 343–344.
91. *Ibn Rushd*, p. 144.
92. *Al-Jami'a*, vol. III, part 4 (Nov. 1901), p. 253; vol. IV, part 4 (June 1903), p. 231.
93. *Ibn Rushd*, p. 31.
94. *Le Réveil*, pp. 105–106.
95. *La Syrie*, pp. 389, 412.
96. *Al-Islam*, p. 40.
97. Ibid. pp. 120, 123.
98. *Ara' Hurra*, p. 132.
99. *Rihlat al-Rabi'*, p. 9.
100. *Ara' Hurra*, pp. 142, 149, 152–153.
101. Ibid. p. 137.
102. *Fi al-Shi'r*, p. 11.

103. Ibid. p. 6.
104. *Mustaqbal*, pp. 365–366.
105. Ibid. p. 473.
106. *Muntakhabat*, I: 184. II: 86–87, 93–94.
107. *Al-Sufur*, p. 56.
108. *Al-Fatat*, pp. 39–40.
109. Ibid. p. 111.
110. *Um al-Qura*, pp. 14, 145–147.
111. Ibid. pp. 145–147.
112. *Al-Islam*, p. 59. *Naqd wa Islah*, pp. 234, 237. *Al-Sufur*, p. 49.
113. Al-Islam, p. 120.
114. Ibid. p. 59.
115. *Min Ba'id*, pp. 204–206.
116. *Naqd*, p. 229.
117. Ibid. pp. 237, 240.
118. *Mustaqbal*, p. 339.
119. *Al-Sufur*, pp. 47–49, 57, 71.
120. Ibid. p. 61.

Chapter 5

1. Khoury, *Urban Notables*, pp. 56–57.
2. *Al-Saq*, II: 88–91, 112–114, 134, 135–136, 138. *Mukhtarat*, I: 143–144.
3. *Al-Rasa'il*, I: 110–111, 190.
4. *Tahrir al-Mar'a*, in: *Complete Works*, II: 16–17.
5. *Al-Mar'a*, p. 32.
6. *Al-Sufur*, pp. 83–84.
7. *Al-Nisa'iyyat*, I: 22, 66–68, 70–71, 73–74, 81–82, 84–85.
8. Ibid. II: 9.
9. *Al-Rasa'il*, I: 168–172. *Al-Fatat*, p. 71.
10. For example: The Cow, verses 231, 232. Women, verse 19.
11. Women, verses 3, 11. The Cow, verse 282.
12. Women, verse 34.
13. *Ta'lim al-Nisa'*, pp. 2 & 10. *Al-Saq*, II: 206.
14. *Ghabat al-Haq*, pp. 18–19.
15. *Al-Mar'a al-Jadida*, June 1923 (vol. 6), pp. 186–187. Oct. 1924 (vol. 10), pp. 426–427.
16. *Al-Rasa'il*, I: 15, 21, 30, 46, 168–172. *Tahrir*, in: *Complete Works*, II: 22–23. *Al-Mar'a*, pp. 26, 38–39. *Al-Nisa'iyyat*, I: 72. *Qissat*, p. 191. *Al-Sufur*, pp. 77–81, 83–84, 86, 88, 134–135.
17. *Al-Rasa'il*, I: 110–123.
18. *Al-Sufur*, pp. 96–104.
19. *Al-Fatat*, p. 112.
20. *Fusul fi al-Adab wa al-Naqd*, in: *Complete Works*, V: 392.
21. *Majmu'at*, II: 92–104, 106, 107, 108–117.
22. *Al-Jami 'a*, vol. II, part 5 (Aug. 1900), pp. 288–291. *Rihla*, p. 46.

23. *Al-Muqtataf*, 8 (1884), pp. 473–474.

24. *Ghara'ib*, I: 185–186.

25. *Al-Jami'a*, vol. II, part 8 (Nov. 1900), pp. 470–480, & vol. VI, part 6 (July 1908), p. 155. *Mukhtarat*, I: 134–135.

26. *Al-Nisa'iyyat*, I: 173–174.

27. *Al-Mar'a*, p. 9.

28. *Tahrir*, in: *Complete Works*, II: 15, 82.

29. *Al-Fatat*, pp. 56, 81. See also: *al-Nisa'iyyat*, I: 75, 85.

30. *Al-Sufur*, pp. 78–81.

31. Tucker, *Women in Nineteenth Century Egypt*, pp. 127, 129, 131.

32. *Ta'lim al-Nisa'*, pp. 10–21.

33. *Al-Saq*, I: 63. II: 56. 'Fi Tarbiyat al-Nisa" in: *al-Jami'a*, vol. III (1872), pp. 769–770. *Um al-Qura*, pp. 174, 179.

34. *Al-Durar*, pp. 301–302. *Al-Rasa'il*, I: 10, 15, 193–195. *Al-Nisa'iyyat*, I: 34–36, 72–73. *Al-Mar'a*, pp. 99–103. *Mukhtarat*, I: 125–129. II: 32–33, 133–135. *Al-Mar'a al-Jadida*, June 1921 (vol. 3), p. 69. *Al-Sufur*, pp. 228–236. *Al-Fatat*, p. 112.

35. *Qissat*, p. 191.

36. *Ta'lim al-Nisa'*, pp. 17, 22.

37. *Al-Nisa'iyyat*, I: 32.

38. *Al-Mar'a al-Jadida*, Aug. 1921 (vol.5) p. 136. Dec. 1921 (vol. 9) p. 265.

39. *Muntakhabat*, I: 33–35, 126–131, 226–228.

40. *Al-Nisa'iyyat*, I: 72–73, 125–146. In his sister's biography, her brother Majd al-Din writes that all the different books she read made her 'combine the Arabic and European mentality, creating for herself from them both a moderate, intermediate policy'. Nasif, *Tahrir al-Mar'a fi al-Islam*, p. 46.

41. *Al-Mar'a*, p. 95.

42. *Al-Mar'a al-Jadida*, June 1922 (vol. 6), pp. 170–171. Oct. 1924 (vol 10), p. 426.

43. *Al-Sufur*, p. 51. See also: pp. 63–64.

44. Ibid. pp. 65–66, 68, 82.

45. Ibid. p. 120.

46. *Kanz*, I: 108, 125–126, 129, 134. *Um al Qura*, p. 177.

47. *Ta'lim*, pp. 11–12. *Mukhtarat*, I: 144.

48. *Al-Islam*, I: 93–95. *Rihla*, pp. 40–47.

49. *Al-Rasa'il*, I: 45, 59, 171–172, 215–217.

50. *Al-Nisa'iyyat*, I: 107–110.

51. Ibid. I: 140–142.

52. See: Tucker, *Women in Nineteenth Century Egypt*.

53. *Tahrir*, in: *Complete Works*, II: 20. *Al-Mar'a*, p. 72.

54. *Al-Mar'a al-Jadida*, June 1924, (vol.6), pp. 230–232.

55. Ibid. Nov. 1921 (vol. 8), p. 233. Feb. 1923 (vol. 2), p. 39. March 1923 (vol.3), pp. 74–76. April 1923 (vol. 4) p. 111. May 1923 (vol.5), p. 146.

56. Ibid. Aug. 1924 (vol. 8), p. 330.

57. Ibid. Oct. 1921 (vol. 7), pp. 199–201.

58. *Al-Sufur*, pp. 279, 288–289.

59. Ibid. pp. 122–123. See also: pp. 136–138, 289–290.

60. Ibid. pp. 286, 288.
61. *Mukhtarat*, I: 168. *Rihla*, p. 120.
62. *Al-Saq*, I: 273. II: 201.
63. *Al-Rasa'il*, I: 24. *Al-Nisa'iyyat*, II: 22.
64. *Al-Mar'a al-Jadida*, Aug. 1923 (vol.8), pp. 266–268.
65. *Al-Fatat*, p. 82.
66. *Al-Mar'a*, pp. 14–20, 54–55. *Muntakhabat*, I: 80–81.
67. Ahmed, *Women and Gender in Islam*, pp. 148–168.
68. *Al-Nisa'iyyat*, I: 26–28.
69. Ibid. I: 102–103, 115–116.
70. *Al-Sufur*, p. 133.
71. Ibid. p. 51.
72. *Al-Fatat*, pp. 345–352, 358–363.
73. *Al-Sufur*, p. 62.
74. Ibid. pp. 110–111, 117–119.
75. Ibid. pp. 246–249.
76. Ibid. pp. 159–162. *Al-Fatat*, p. 85.
77. *Tahrir*, in: *Complete Works*, II: 43–68.
78. *Al-Mar'a*, pp. 34–35, 47–49, 50–51.
79. Ibid. p. 128.
80. *Muntakhabat*, I: 130.
81. *Al-Islam*, I: 88–93.
82. *Al-Saq*, II: 161,138.
83. *Al-Durar*, pp. 276–278.
84. *Tahrir*, in: *Complete Works*, II: 89–94.
85. Ibid. II: 83–87.
86. Women, verse 34.
87. *Tahrir*, in: *Complete Works*, II: 25–30, 38, 41, 84–86.
88. *Al-Rasa'il*, I: pp. 192–193, 202.
89. *Al-Nisa'iyyat*, I: 20, 37–44.
90. Ibid. I: 44.
91. Ibid. I: 136.
92. *Al-Qadim*, pp. 50–51.
93. *Al-Islam*, I: 82–88.
94. Bustani, *Ta'lim*, p. 20. Fawwaz, *al-Rasa'il*, I: 10, 34. Kawakibi, *Um al-Qura*, pp. 167, 179. Amin, *Tahrir*, in: *Complete Works*, II: 14, 78, 82. *Al-Mar'a*, p. 14. Bahithat al-Badiya, *al-Nisa'iyyat*, I: 105. Zaydan, *Mukhtarat*, I: 125–129. II: 32–33. Kurd 'Ali, *Ghara'ib*, I: 188, 324, 328. Dimashqiyya, *al-Mar'a al-Jadida*, Aug.1923 (vol. 8), pp. 266–268. Nazira, *al-Sufur*, pp. 62, 109. Al-Sayyid, *Muntakhabat*, I: 130. *Qissat*, p. 191.
95. *Tahrir*, in: *Complete Works*, II: 82.
96. *Al-'Irfan*, II: (1910), pp. 220–221.
97. *Al-Manar*, vol. 13, part 6, (1377 AH/1909 AD), pp. 405–409.
98. *Al-Sufur*, pp. 95,113. Women, verse 34.

Chapter 6

1. *Al-Jinan,* July 15, 1873, pp. 626–627. *La Syrie.* p. 208.
2. *Al-Saq,* I: 16–17.
3. *Al-Durar,* p. 72.
4. Al-Shummayyil, *Kitabat Siyasiyya,* pp. 93–94. Antun, *al-Jami'a,* vol.II, part 1(April 1900), p. 21. vol IV, part 2 (March 1903), p. 83 and parts 6, 7, 8, p. 337. Sarruf, *al-Muqtataf,* vol.IX (1885), p. 471.
5. *Al-Muqtataf,* vol. IX (1885), p. 469.
6. Ibid. p. 471. In the Auguast 1882 issue the *Muqtataf* published the speech in Arabic. A full account of the case is given by Nadia Farag, 'The Lewis Affair and the Fortunes of al-Muqtataf in *Middle Eastern Studies,* vol. VIII, N° 1 (1972), pp. 76–82.
7. *Al-Mar'a al-Jadida,* July 1924 (vol.7), p. 279. Aug. 1925 (vol.8), pp. 309–310.
8. *Um al-Qura,* pp. 173–174.
9. *Al-Mar'a,* pp. 74–79.
10. *Al-Qadim,* p. 24 (1906).
11. Ibid. p. 51.
12. *Ghara'ib,* II: 251.
13. *Safahat,* p. 170.
14. *Al-Islam,* I: 382.
15. *Al-Saq,* I: 17. *Kanz,* I: 86, 88, 120. *Kashf,* pp. 128–135. *Mashhad,* p. 34. *Al-Mudhakkirat,* II: 652; III:986.
16. *Kashf,* pp. 148, 174.
17. *Taba'i',* pp. 90, 97–99.
18. *Rihlat Paris,* p. 37.
19. *Ghabat al-Haq,* pp. 46–48, 50, 72.
20. *Al-Durar,* pp. 45–46.
21. *Al-Durar,* pp. 244–250, 255–256. *Mukhtarat,* III: 5. *Ghara'ib,* I: 37, 218–219. *Muntakhabat,* I: 78. *Mustaqbal,* pp. 76, 78.
22. *Tahrir,* in: *Complete Works,* II: 35, 75.
23. *Al-Mar'a,* p. 42.
24. Ibid. p. 5.
25. *Tahrir,* in: *Complete Works,* II: 76–77.
26. *Complete Works,* I: 347.
27. *Mukhtarat,* I: 128, 142. II: 3. *Urushalim,* p. 161.
28. *Mukhtarat,* III: 17, 24. *Al-Jami'a,* vol. II, part 3 (June 1900), p. 152. *Al-Muqtataf,* vol IX (1885), p. 471.*Kitabat Siyasiyya,* p. 93. *Majmu'at,* II: 176.
29. *Al-Muqtataf,* vol. IX (1885), p. 469.
30. *Mu'dilat al-Madaniyya al-Haditha,* p. 203.
31. *Urushalim,* p. 225. *Majmu'at,* I: 2.
32. *Al-Jami'a,* vol. V, part 9 (Nov. 1906), p. 336.
33. *Majmu'at,* I: 313–314.
34. Ibid.I: 55.
35. *Ibid.* I: 8.
36. *Kitabat Siyasiyya,* p. 138.
37. *Al-Nisa'iyyat,* I: 35, 45, 53, 61, 79–80, 142–143.

38. Ibid. I: 146.
39. *Al-Fatat.*, p. 90.
40. *Al-Mudhakkirat*, II: 396–398, 437.
41. Ibid. III: 769, 891.
42. *Ghara'ib*, I: 166.
43. Ibid. II: 254.
44. Ibid. I: 48, 50, 71.
45. Ibid. I: 38.
46. Ibid. I: 329.
47. *Al-Mar'a al-Jadida*, Aug. 1925 (vol. 8), p. 308.
48. *Muntakhabat*, II: 194. *Min Ba'id*, p. 246.
49. *Safahat*, p. 20. *Mustaqbal*, p. 130.
50. *Safahat*, pp. 115–116.
51. *Muntakhabat*, II: 78.
52. *Qissat*, p. 196.
53. *Muntakhabat*, II: 7.
54. *Mustaqbal*, p. 323.
55. *Qissat*, pp. 176, 195, 213. *Muntakhabat*, II: 38. *Mustaqbal*, p. 161.
56. *Min Laghu al-Saif wa Jid al-Shita'*, pp. 49–50.
57. *Fi al-Saif*, p. 55.
58. *Mustaqbal*, pp. 35, 44.
59. Ibid. pp. 79–81, 82–96, 104.
60. Ibid. pp. 210, 215.
61. Ibid. p. 49.
62. *Min Ba'id*, p. 258. *Al-Nisa'iyyat*, I: 113.
63. *Ibn Rushd*, p. 123. *Majmu'at*, I: 358.
64. *'Ala Hamish al-Sira*, in: *Complete Works*, III: 221.
65. *Fi al-Shi'r al-Jahili*, p. 70.
66. *Al-Nisa'iyyat*, I: 111. *Al-Mar'a al-Jadida*, Febr. 1925 (vol. 2), p. 51.
67. *Al-Jami'a*, vol. IV, part 2 (March 1903), p. 81. See also: al-Shummayyil, *Majmu'at*, I: 238.
68. *Min Ba'id*, p. 65.
69. *Mustaqbal*, p. 420.
70. *Al-Jinan*, vol. I (1870), pp. 562–565.
71. *Qissat*, p. 189.
72. Bustani, *Adaab al-'Arab*, in: *Rawai'*, XXII: 26. *Kanz*, I: 254. *Ghabat al-Haq*, pp. 48–53. *Al-Muqtataf*, vol. IX (1885), p. 471. Zaydan, *Rihla*, pp. 122–123. *Al-Mar'a al-Jadida*, Aug. 1925 (vol. 8), p. 308. *Tahrir al-Mar'a*, in: *Complete Works*, II: 24, 34, 41, 62–64, 66. *Al-Mar'a*, pp. 121–123. *Ghara'ib*, I:190. *Safahat*, p. 113.
73. *Rihlat Paris*, p. 47.
74. *Al-Mar'a*, p. 122.
75. *Al-Saq*, II: 153, 159.
76. *Rihlat Paris*, p. 47. *Taba'i'*, pp. 90, 97–99.*La Syrie*, p. 108. *Al-Muqtataf*, vol. IX (1885), p. 470. *Majmu'at*, II: 125. *Mukhtarat*, III: 5, 11–17. *Ibn Rushd*, p. 31. *Ghara'ib*, I: 37. *Al-Nisa'iyyat*, I: 118. *Al-Mar'a al-Jadida*, Aug. 1925 (vol.8), p. 308. Nov. 1925 (vol

11), p. 440. *Al-Durar*, pp. 157, 159, 194, 255, 256. *Al-Kitabat*, pp. 79, 81, 109–111. *Qissat*, pp. 177, 194. *Muntakhabat*, I: 56, II: 6, 9. *Safahat*, pp. 8–9, 113–115. *Ta'ammulat*, pp. 50–54. *Min Ba'id*, pp. 59–60, 246. *Mustaqbal*, pp. 76, 78.

77. *Min Ba'id*, p. 246.

78. *Muntakhabat*, I: 329–330. See also: *Qissat*, p. 190. *Muntakhabat*, I: 123. II: 23. *Safahat*, pp. 119–120.

79. *Mukhtarat*, III: 4. Bustani, *al-Jinan*, July 15, 1873, pp. 626–627. Al-Shummayyil, *Majmu'at*, II: 191. Antun, *Urushalim*, p. 225. Samné, *La Syrie*, p. 208.Dimashqiyya, *al-Mar'a al-Jadida*, July 1924 (vol.7), p. 279. Aug. 1925 (vol. 8), pp. 309–310.

Chapter 7

1. *Um al-Qura*, pp. 142–143.

2. *Taba'i'*, p. 66.

3. Ibid. p. 83.

4. *Al-Mudhakkirat*, III: 924. IV: 1169.

5. *Al-Islam*, I: 80.

6. *Al-Mudhakkirat*, IV: 1086.

7. *Al-Durar*, pp. 196–197.

8. *Mukhtarat*, III: 73.

9. *Ara' al-Doctor Shibli al-Shummayyil*, p. 39.

10. *Al-Mar'a al-Jadida*, Dec. 1921 (vol.9), p. 264. May 1924 (vol. 5), pp. 182–184.

11. *Um al-Qura*, pp. 145–147.

12. *Al-Sufur*, p. 45.

13. Ibid. pp. 52, 244.

14. Brown, *Rethinking Tradition*, p. 75.

15. Yared, *Arab Travellers*, pp. 29–54, 60–64.

16. *The Muqaddimah*, especially Chapter Three.

17. *Al-Mar'a*, pp. 109–110.

18. Ibid. pp. 112–114.

19. *Al-Jami'a*, vol.VI, part 5 (June 1908), p. 120.

20. *Ghara'ib*, I: 178.

21. *Al-Mudhakkirat*, II: 652. III: 863.

22. *Fi al-Shi'ir al-Jahili*, pp. 128–131. In his later years, Hussein wrote his Islamic books because he believed that the history of Islam contained moral and social lessons that were still valid for the present. See Chapter Three.

23. *Ta'ammulat*, pp. 77, 78.

24. *Majmu'at*, II: 202. 293.

25. *Um al-Qura*, p. 141.

26. *Tahrir al-Mar'a*, in: *Complete Works*, II: 76, 112.

27. Ibid. II: 13.

28. Ibid. II: 70.

29. *Al-Mar'a*, p. 129.

30. *Al-Nisa'iyyat*, I: 58, 116, 118.

31. *Al-Sufur*, pp. 82, 121.

32. Ibid. p. 150.

33. *Al-Fatat*, p. 78.
34. *Mashhad al-Ahwal*, p. 32.
35. *Da'irat al-Ma'arif*, Introduction, p. 2.
36. *Rihlat Paris*, p. 69. *Ghabat al-Haq*, pp. 15–16. *Mashhad*, pp. 53–54.
37. *Al-Mar'a*, p. 109.
38. Ibid. pp. 114–115.
39. Zaydan, *Mukhtarat*, I: 132. Al-Shummayyil, *Majmu'at*, I: 56. II: 197. *Kitabat Siyasiyya*, p. 12. Antun, *Ibn Rushd*, p. 143.
40. *Ara' al-Doctor*, p. 25.
41. *Majmu'at*, I: 56. II: 191.
42. Ibid. I: 358.
43. Ibid. I: 285.
44. Ibid. I: 11.
45. Ibid. II: 91.
46. *Al-Din*, pp. 67, 70.
47. *Ibn Rushd*, p. 191.
48. Ibid. p. 143.
49. *Majmu'at*, I: 237.
50. Ibid. II: 41–42.
51. *Ghara'ib*, I: 44, 159, 162–164, 172, 236. *Al-Qadim*, pp. 66, 308, 343–344.
52. *Ghara'ib*, I: 190.
53. *Mustaqbal*, p. 9.
54. Ibid. pp. 39, 76–77.
55. Ibid. p. 41. The translation is from Hourani, p. 330.
56. *Rihlat Zaydan*, p. 47. *Ghara'ib*, I: 326–327.
57. *Mustaqbal*, p. 44.
58. *Naqd*, p. 166.
59. *Safahat Matwiyya*, p. 113.
60. *Ta'ammulat*, pp. 56, 84.
61. Ibid. p. 83.
62. *Muntakhabat*, II: 24.
63. Ibid. II: 103.
64. *Al-Fatat*, pp. 22–23, 39, 113.
65. Ibid. p. 46.
66. Ibid. p. 111.
67. Yared, *Arab Travellers*, p. 23.
68. *Al-Saq*, II: 223–230.
69. *Kashf*, p. 204.
70. *Ghabat al-Haq*, p. 38.
71. Ibid. pp. 44, 75–76.
72. Ibid. pp. 45–46.
73. *Al-Kitabat*, pp. 120–121.
74. *Al-Durar*, pp. 156–157.
75. Ibid. pp. 231–234.
76. Ibid. pp. 473–474.

77. Ibid. p. 333.
78. *Taba'i'*, p. 57.
79. Ibid. p. 62.
80. *Les Egyptiens: Réponse à M. le Duc d'Harcourt*, in: *Complete Works*, I: 260–261.
81. *Mukhtarat*, I: 79, 111.
82. *Rihla*, p. 36.
83. *Mukhtarat*, II: 88.
84. Ibid. II: 49.
85. Ibid. II: 85–110.
86. Ibid. II: 103.
87. Ibid. III: 6.
88. *Rihla*, p. 116.
89. *Majmu'at*, II: 147–148, 156, 158. *Al-Wahsh*, p. 143.
90. *Majmu'at*, II: 120, 129–130. *Al-Wahsh*, pp. 68–69.
91. *Majmu'at*, II: 123.
92. *Al-Din wa al-'Ilm*, p. 66.
93. Ibid. p. 61.
94. *Al-Jami'a*, vol. II (April 1901), parts 22, 23, 24.
95. Ibid. vol. VI, part 8 (Sept. 1908), pp. 206–207.
96. *Majmu'at*, II: 152–157, 179–189.
97. Ibid. II: 154.
98. Ibid. II: 183–186.
99. *Al-Jami'a*, vol. V, part 4 (Sept. 1906), p. 157.
100. *Majmu'at*, II: 131.
101. *Al-Din*, pp. 80–81.
102. *Majmu'at*, II: 146.
103. *Majmu'at*, II: 152–157, 181–182, 184–186, 189. *Al-Din*, pp. 61–65.
104. *Majmu'at*, II: 203.
105. *Al-Din*, p. 43.
106. Ibid. pp. 67–68.
107. *Al-Jami'a*, vol. I (Jan.1, 1900), part 20.
108. *Arab Intellectuals*, p. 85.
109. *Le Réveil*, p. 106.
110. *Al-Mudhakkirat*, III: 705.
111. *Ghara'ib*, I: 99.
112. *Al-Mudhakkirat*, II: 547–548.
113. *Ghara'ib*, I: 224.
114. *Al-Mudhakkirat*, II: 547–548, 627–629.
115. Ibid. III: 949–951.
116. *Ghara'ib*, I: 130.
117. Ibid. I: 176.
118. *Ghara'ib*, II: 245–247. *Al-Mudhakkirat*, II: 547–548.
119. *Al-Islam*, I: 105–110 (1939).
120. *Al-Mudhakkirat*, IV: 1259.
121. *Bayna Bayn*, pp. 50–51.

122. *Mustaqbal*, pp. 181–182.

123. Ibid. pp. 105–106.

124. Ibid. pp. 125–127.

125. Ibid. p. 43.

126. *Ta'ammulat*, p. 107.

127. *Muntakhabat*, I: 180–182.

128. Ibid. I: 272–279, 281–283.

129. Ibid. II: 108–111.

Chapter 8

1. *Al-Saq*, II: 171–173. See also: *al-Saq*, I: 73, 156–157, 195. *Kashf*, p. 151. In traditional Muslim political thought it was God who revealed the Qur'an and its laws and who possessed real sovereignty. He chose a ruler to implement these laws, and as a result this ruler was considered to be God's representative on earth, accountable to none but God himself and his own conscience. It was therefore the duty of every Muslim to obey God's law, even if the ruler were unjust. See: Badr al-Din Ibn Jama'a, *Tahrir al-Ahkam fi Tadbir Ahl al-Islam*, pp. 355–357. Macdonald, *Muslim Theology*, pp. 3–67.

2. *Kanz*, II: 91.

3. Ibid. II: 77.

4. Kayyali, *Muhadarat*, pp. 83–84.

5. *Dalil al-Hurriyya*, p. 2.

6. *Rihla ila Paris*, pp. 2, 35.

7. *Al-Durar*, pp. 4, 93–99, 123, 155–157, 175–178, 455.

8. *Mathew* 5: 39.

9. *Women*, 59. Mawardi, *al-Ahkam*, pp. 3–4.

10. *Um al-Qura*, pp. 29, 37, 183.

11. Ibid. p. 29.

12. *Taba'i'*, pp. 10–12, 37.

13. *The Light*, 32.

14. *Taba'i'*, p. 94.

15. *Tahrir*, in: *Complete Works*, II: 16.

16. *Mukhtarat*, II: 63.

17. *Majmu'at*, I: 58–60.

18. Ibid. II: 43.

19. *Kitabat Siyasiyya*, pp. 10–11, 13–16.

20. Ibid. pp. 58–59, 85–90.

21. Al-*Mudhakkirat*, I: 75, 96.

22. *Le Réveil*, pp. 57, 91, 96.

23. *Al-Jami'a*, vol III, part 4, (Nov. 1901), pp. 252–254.

24. Ibid. vol. IV, part, 3 (May 1903), p. 219.

25. Ibid. vol. IV, part 6–8 (1903), p. 332.

26. *La Syrie*, p. 389.

27. Ibid. pp. 544 & 553.

28. *Al-Islam*, pp. 36–40.

29. *Min Ba'id*, p. 6.

30. *Al-Sufur*, p. 61.
31. *Safahat Matwiyya*, p. 30.
32. *Muntakhabat*, I: 22.
33. *Ta'ammulat*, pp. 101–102.
34. *Muntakhabat*, I: 50, 90–100, 198–200, 220, 263.
35. *Qissat*, p. 169.
36. *Muntakhabat*, II: 67.
37. *Ta'ammulat*, pp. 89–90.
38. *Muntakhabat*, II: 65.
39. *Kashf*, p. 71.
40. *Kanz*, II: 202–216, 221–234.
41. *Taba'i'*, p. 133.
42. *Mukhtarat*, II: 70–72.
43. *Al-Durar*, pp. 103–106, 111, 159–161, 164–165, 172–174, 187–189.
44. Ibid. p. 418.
45. *Muntakhabat*, I: 264–265.
46. *Ghabat*, pp. 10–12.
47. Kayyali, *Muhadarat*, pp. 84–85.
48. *Al-Durar*, pp. 251, 444.
49. *Taba'i'*, pp. 131–132.
50. Ibid. pp. 29–30.
51. *Mukhtarat*, III: 3.
52. Ibid. III: 112–120, 125.
53. *Kitabat*, p. 10.
54. Ibid. pp. 111–112, 115.
55. *Le Réveil*, p. 96.
56. *Al-Qadim*, p. 307.
57. Al-*Mudhakkirat*, III: 979.
58. Ibid. III: 664–665.
59. Ibid.I: 198.
60. *Safahat*, p. 197.
61. *Hadith al-Arbi'a'*, II: 138.
62. *Al-Manar*, vol. 10. part 3 (1325 AH/1907 AD), pp. 283–284.
63. *Al-Mar'a*, p. 110. *Al-Islam wa al-Hadara*, I: 377. *Al-Islam*, p. 34. *Mustaqbal*, pp. 33, 35. *Muntkhabat*, I: 29, 325.
64. *The Family of 'Imran*, 104. *Taba'i'*, p. 88.
65. *Taba'i'*, pp. 19–22.
66. *Masadir al-Thaqafa*, p. 106.
67. *Muntakhabat*, I: 23.
68. *Al-Kitabat al-Siyasiyya*, pp. 198–199.
69. *Kanz*, I: 63–64.
70. Ibid. I: 176, 178.
71. Ibid. I: 66.
72. *Kashf*, p. 149.
73. Raven, *Christian Socialism*, p. 63.

74. *Nafir,* p. 22.
75. Ibid. p. 56.
76. *Kanz,* I: 60–67.
77. *Kashf,* pp. 146, 314, 339.
78. Ibid. p. 136.
79. Ibid. p. 113.
80. Ibid. p. 105.
81. *Al-Wasita,* p. 47.
82. *Ghabat,* p. 44.
83. Ibid. p. 73.
84. Ibid. pp. 65–71.
85. Ibid. pp. 25, 29–30.
86. Kayyali, *Muhadarat,* pp. 84–85.
87. *Al-Kitabat,* p. 120.
88. *Al-Durar,* pp. 48, 127, 187, 248.
89. Ibid. p. 151. *Al-Kitabat,* pp. 115, 122.
90. *Al-Durar,* pp. 442–443.
91. Ibid. pp. 378–379.
92. Ibid. p. 111.
93. *Al-Rasa'il al-Zaynabiyya,* p. 7.
94. Ibid. pp. 89–91.
95. *Um al-Qura,* p. 184.
96. Ibid. pp. 32, 160. *Taba'i',* pp. 118, 119, 129.
97. *Taba'i',* p. 19.
98. *Um al-Qura,* Chapter I, 2nd and 11th case issues.
99. Ibid. p. 32.
100. Ibid. p. 37.
101. *Taba'i',* pp. 128, 135–136.
102. *Um al-Qura,* pp. 32, 166.
103. *Complete Works,* II: 75.
104. Ibid. I: 260.
105. *Al-Mar'a,* p. 110.
106. Ibid. p. 96.
107. Ibid. p. 29.
108. Ibid. p. 121.
109. *Mukhtarat,* II: 66–67.
110. Ibid. I: 41. II: 75.
111. *Rihla,* p. 48.
112. Ibid. pp. 37–38.
113. *Majmu'at,* II: 27–28, 55. *Kitabat,* pp. 16–20. *Le Réveil,* pp. 98, 245. *Al-Jami'a,* vol. III, part 4, (Nov. 1901), pp. 252–254. Vol.IV, part 7 (Oct. 1906), pp. 257–269. *Ibn Rushd,* pp. 151–152.
114. *Le Réveil,* p. 245.
115. *Kitabat,* p. 20.
116. *Majmu'at,* I: 61 (footnote 1).

117. *La Syrie*, pp. 599–620.
118. Ibid. pp. 601, 608.
119. *Al-Islam wa al-Hadara*, I: 377.
120. *Ghara'ib*, I: 93.
121. Ibid. I: 143–144.
122. *Al-Qadim*, p. 187.
123. *Ghara'ib*, I: 271–277.
124. *Al-Mudhakkirat*, III: 661.
125. *Al-Islam*, pp. 34–35, 41.
126. Ibid. p. 138.
127. *Al-Sufur*, p. 61.
128. Ibid. p. 281.
129. *Mustaqbal*, pp. 32–33. *Ara' Hurra*, p. 167. *Muntakhabat*, II: 62, 80–85.
130. *Min Ba'id,* p. 73. *Mustaqbal*, p. 34. *Qissat*, p. 49.
131. *Ara' Hurra*, p. 131. *Rihlat al-Rabi'*, p. 8. *Mustaqbal*, pp. 39–40.
132. *Mustaqbal*, p. 111.
133. *Al-Fitna al-Kubra*, in: *Complete Works*, IV: 219.
134. *Muntakhabat*, II: 65.
135. *Qissat*, pp. 176, 178, 214.
136. *Muntakhabat*, I: 296.
137. Ibid. II: 73–74.
138. *Mushkilat al-Hurriyya*, p. 10.
139. *Safahat*, p. 197.
140. See: Yared, *Arab Travellers*, pp. 39–41. Al-Azmeh, al-'*Ilmaniyya, pp.* 112–116.
141. Tucker, *Women in the Nineteenth Century*, pp. 12–13.
142. *Kanz*, I: 175.
143. Ibid. I: 195.
144. *Ghabat*, pp. 38, 44.
145. Ibid. pp. 39–40.
146. *Al-Kitabat*, p. 271. *Mukhtarat*, II: 9. *Majmu'at*, II: 24, 210.
147. *Majmu'at*, II: 119.
148. Ibid. II: 67.
149. Ibid. II: 11–13.
150. *Taba'i'*, p. 139.
151. Ibid. p. 122.
152. Ibid. pp. 86–87.
153. *Al-Mar'a*, p. 111.
154. Ibid. pp. 96, 108.
155. *Al-Sufur*, p. 66. *Al-Fatat*, p. 79.
156. *Al-Sufur*, p. 293.
157. Ibid. p. 294.
158. Brown, *Rethinking Tradition*, p. 113. The italics are mine.
159. *Al-Qadim*, pp. 272, 281.
160. *Al-Islam wa al-Hadara*, II: 17–18.
161. *Ghara'ib*, I: 130.

162. Al-*Mudhakkirat*, II: 475.
163. Ibid. III: 917.
164. Ibid. III: 659.
165. Ibid. I: 168.
166. *Safahat*, p. 204.
167. *Muntakhabat*, II: 69–74.
168. *Min Ba'id*, pp. 117–118.
169. *Mustaqbal*, p. 32.
170. Ibid. p. 34.

Chapter 9

1. *Nafir*, (Oct. 25, 1860), p. 21.
2. Ibid. (July 29, 1860), p. 10.
3. Ibid. p. 50.
4. *Al-Saq*, I: 198.
5. *Kanz*, II: 9, 92, 100.
6. Ibid. I: 109, 112.
7. Ibid. I: 55. Sultan 'Abdülhamid had tried to rally the Muslims around him as their caliph in order to appear to be a powerful ruler over a united Empire when attacked by Europe.
8. *Dalil*, p. 10.
9. Book IV, Ch. V, p. 542.
10. *Al-Durar*, p. 102.
11. Ibid. p. 453.
12. Ibid. pp. 100–101, 119–120.
13. *Nafir*, (Febr. 22, 1861), p. 60. *Kanz*, I: 112. II: 8.
14. *Al-Durar*, p. 100.
15. Ibid. p. 149.
16. *Al-Jinan*, (Jan. 1870), p. 1.
17. *Nafir*, (July 29, 1860), pp. 9, 10, 17–19, 25–28, 29–46.
18. *Ghabat*, p. 70.
19. *Nafir*, p. 52.
20. *Adaab al-'Arab.* in: *Rawa'i'*, XXII: 38.
21. *Al-Saq*, I: 39.
22. Ibid. I: 57–58, 171–173, 194, 208–211.
23. *Al-Durar*, pp. 113, 118, 168–171, 175–178, 180–182, 203–207, 374–376. *Al-Kitabat*, pp. 200–207, 259–261.
24. *Al-Durar*, pp. 120–123, 166–168, 168–171.
25. Ibid. pp. 373–376.
26. Ibid. p. 247.
27. Ibid. pp. 220–223.
28. Ibid. pp. 144–146, 199–200, 213–214.
29. *Al-Kitabat*, pp. 243–245.
30. *Al-Durar*, pp. 199–200.
31. *Al-Kitabat*, p. 183.

32. *Arab Intellectuals*, p. 183.
33. *Al-Jinan*, (Oct. 1870), p. 627.
34. *Al-Durar*, pp. 371, 451–452.
35. Ibid. p. 96.
36. *Nafir*, (Dec. 14, 1860), p. 42. *Al-Wasita*, p. 21.
37. *Al-Saq*, I: 162–164.
38. *Ghabat*, p. 70.
39. *Al-Wasita*, p. 17. *Mashhad al-Ahwal*, p. 40.
40. *Al-Jinan*, vol. III (1873) p. 153.
41. *Rihla ila Paris*, p. 34. About the first Arab independence movements see: Amtonius, *The Arab Awakening*, pp. 53–55, 79–100.
42. *Kanz*, I: 20, 55–57.
43. *Al-Makshuf*, no. 170 (1938), p. 11.
44. *Adaab*, in: *Rawa'i'*, XXII: 32–33. *Kashf al-Mukhabba*, pp. 217–218. *Mir'at al-Hasna'*, pp. 44–46. *Al-Durar*, p. 200.
45. *Adaab*, in: *Rawa'i'*, XXII: 32–33, 41–43. *Al-Saq*, I: 19, 171. *Durr al-Sadaf*, p. 27.
46. *Durr*, p. 92.
47. *Al-Jinan*, (July 15, 1873), p. 626.
48. *Nafir*, (Febr. 22, 1861) p. 60.
49. *Al-Saq*, I: 94, 162–164, 168, 171–174. *Kashf*, pp. 120–127.
50. *Kanz*, I: 122, 250.
51. *Adaab*, in: *Rawa'i'*, XXII: 30–32.
52. *Mashhad*, p. 32.
53. *Al-Durar*, pp. 200–203. *Al-Kitabat*, pp. 180, 182–183.
54. *Al-Rasa'il*, pp. 198–200, 203–206, 213–214.
55. Ibid. pp. 199–200.
56. *Al-Nisa'iyyat*, I: 29.
57. Ibid. I: 99.
58. *Athaar Bahithat al-Badiya*, pp. 293–296.
59. *Al-Nisa'iyyat*, I: 30–31, 118–119.
60. *Taba'i'*, p. 125.
61. Ibid. p. 110.
62. *Um al-Qura*, p. 221.
63. Ibid. pp. 164, 169–170.
64. Ibid. pp. 238, 243.
65. Ibid.p. 240.
66. Ibid. Ch. I, case issues 2 & 11.
67. *Complete Works*, I: 257–258.
68. *Mukhtarat*, II: 43.
69. Ibid. II: 18, 23.
70. Ibid. II: 147–148, 152–153.
71. Ibid. II: 123–124, 133–137.
72. *Kitabat Siyasiyya*, p. 103.
73. *Al-Jami'a*, vol. V, part 7 (Oct. 1906), p. 288.
74. *Ibn Rushd*, p. 37.

75. *Al-Jami'a*, vol. V, part 8, (Nov. 1906), p. 316.

76. *Le Réveil*, p. 165.

77. Ibid. p. 145.

78. *Mukhtarat*, II: 72. *Kitabat*, p. 144. *Al-Jami'a*, vol. V, part 7(Oct. 1906), p. 288.

79. Letters in: *The Autobiography of Jurji Zaidan*, trans. by T. Philipp, p. 78.

80. Ibid. pp. 79–80.

81. *Majmu'at Shibli al-Shumayyil*, II: 190–203.

82. *Kitabat*, pp. 64–65.

83. Ibid. p. 63.

84. Ibid. p. 102.

85. Ibid. pp. 144, 149, 154–156.

86. *Kitabat*, p. 148, footnote 2. For details of this party and that of the Arab Congress in Paris, see: Hourani, *Arab Thought*, pp. 282–283.

87. *Kitabat*, p. 155.

88. *Mukhtarat*, III: 90–93.

89. Ibid. III: 94.

90. *Rihla*, pp. 93–94, 149. *Mukhtarat*, III: 95.

91. *Kitabat*, pp. 106–107.

92. Ibid. pp. 109–110.

93. Ibid. pp. 181–187.

94. Ibid. p. 202.

95. *Le Réveil*, pp. 25, 37–42, 103, 181–257.

96. Ibid. pp. 100, 129.

97. *Urushalim*, pp. 182–183.

98. *Mukhtarat*, III: 88.

99. Ibid. III: 130–131.

100. Ibid. III: 135–138.

101. Ibid. III: 139, 147–149.

102. See, e.g. Ch. 7.

103. *Al-Manar*, vol. 17, p. 638.

104. Philipp, *Jurji Zaidan*, p. 120.

105. *Le Réveil*, pp. 164–165. The italicas are mine.

106. Ibid. pp. 211–212, 234.

107. Ibid. p. 246.

108. Ibid. pp. 5–8.

109. Ibid. pp. 44–49.

110. Ibid. pp. 210, 232–234.

111. Ibid. p. 144.

112. Ibid. pp. 151–156.

113. Ibid. pp. 102, 108–113.

114. Ibid. pp. 86–90.

115. Ibid. pp. 104–105.

116. Ibid. pp. 101–102.

117. Ibid. p. 242.

118. *Mukhtarat*, III: 123. *Al-Muqtataf*, vol. 8 (1884), p. 472, vol. 9 (1885), pp. 284–288. *Majmu'at*, II: 207.

119. *Rihla*, pp. 114–119, 121–122.

120. Ibid. pp. 72–73, 139–142, 143, 145.

121. *Majmu'at*, II: 227.

122. *Kitabat*, p. 187. See also: pp. 190–191, 206–209.

123. *Majmu'at*, II: 60, 88–91, 207.

124. Ibid. II: 199.

125. Ibid. II: 286, 295.

126. Ibid. I: 360–361. II: 224.

127. Huxley, *Science, Liberty and Peace*, pp. 33–35.

128. *Majmu'at*, I: 361–362.

129. Ibid. I: 358.

130. Ibid. II: 295–296.

131. Ibid. II: 332.

132. *Al-Mudhakkirat*, I: 251, 253.

133. *Al-Qadim*, p. 263.

134. *Al-Bi'tha al-Islamiyya*, pp. 66–67, 146–147.

135. *Al-Qadim*, pp. 261–262.

136. *Al-Islam*, I: 356.

137. *Al-Mudhakkirat*, I: 201–208, 236–241.

138. Ibid. I: 206.

139. *Ghara'ib al-Gharb*, I: 169.

140. *Al-Mudhakkirat*, I: 156–157, 169–171. Jamal Pasha was the Ottoman governor of Syria who ordered the hanging of Syrian and Lebanese nationalists in 1915 and 1916. Khoury asserts that Jamal Pasha paid Kurd 'Ali to praise the Unionists. *Urban Notables*, p. 75.

141. *Al-Qadim*, pp. 266–268.

142. *Ghara'ib*, I: 141, 143–144.

143. *Al-Islam*, I: 326–329, 332–336.

144. *Al-Mudhakkirat*, I: 75–76.

145. *Ghara'ib*, I: 160–161.

146. *Al-Mudhakkirat*, II: 525.

147. *Al-Islam*, I: 377–378.

148. Ibid. I: 47.

149. *Al-Qadim*, p. 25.

150. *Al-Islam*, I: 52. Ibn Sina died in 1037, al-Biruni after 1050, al-Razi in 1068, Jahez in 869, Ibn Rushd in 1198 and Ibn Khaldun in 1382.

151. *Ghara'ib*, II: 142–171, 175–180.

152. Mainly: *al-Islam wa al-Hadara al-'Arabiyya*, (2vols), *Ghaber al-Andalus wa Hadiruha*, *al-Idara al-Islamiyya fi 'Izz al- 'Arab*, *Umara' al-Bayan*.

153. *Al-Mudhakkirat*, I: 84–85.

154. Ibid. I: 24. III: 712.

155. Ibid. I: 129. III: 910–914.

156. Ibid. II: 539–544, 561–562. III: 736–739.

157. *Al-Mudhakkirat*, I: 46.
158. *Al-Islam*, I: 46.
159. *Al-Mudhakkirat*, II: 368–369, 373.
160. *Al-Mar'a al-Jadida*, May 1926 (vol. 5), p. 187. The italics are mine.
161. *La Syrie*, p. 484.
162. Ibid. pp. 309–314.
163. Ibid. p. 314.
164. Ibid. pp. 304, 306.
165. Ibid. p. 523.
166. Ibid. p. 232.
167. Ibid. p. 254. This is the Greater Lebanon that the French mandate formed two years later, in 1920, and which is the Lebanon of today. One might well ask how far French foreign policy lay behind Samné's ideas here.
168. Ibid. pp. 289–290.
169. Ibid. pp. 396–426.
170. Ibid. p. 411.
171. Ibid. p. 301.
172. Ibid. p. 320.
173. Ibid. p. 319.
174. Ibid. p. 287.
175. Ibid. pp. 69–96.
176. Ibid. pp. 387–389.
177. Khoury, *Urban Notables*, p. 77.
178. *La Syrie*, p. 534.
179. Ibid. pp. 584–591.
180. Ibid. p. 661.
181. *Al-Fatat*, pp. 72–75.
182. Ibid. p. 76.
183. Ibid. pp. 66–67.
184. *Ta'ammulat*, p. 21.
185. Ibid. pp. 18, 19.
186. *Mustaqbal*, p. 378.
187. *Ta'ammulat*, p. 65.
188. Ibid. p. 66.
189. *Safahat Matwiyya*, pp. 33–34.
190. *Qissat Hayati*, p. 138.
191. *Mustaqbal*, p. 344.
192. Ibid. p. 345.
193. Ibid. p. 74.
194. Ibid. pp. 18–19.
195. *Ta'ammulat*, p. 69.
196. *Qissat*, p. 80.
197. *Safahat*, pp. 36–38.
198. *Muntakhabat*, I: 166.
199. *Qissat*, p. 132.

200. *Safahat*, p. 138.
201. *Mustaqbal*, p. 27.
202. *Ta'ammulat*, pp. 73–74.
203. *Al-Hilal*, 31 (Jan. 1923), p. 347.
204. *Mustaqbal*, p. 378.
205. Ibid. p. 23.
206. *Muntakhabat*, I: 250–251.
207. *Qissat*, p. 138.
208. *Muntakhabat*, I: 170–173.
209. Wendell, *The Evolution of the Egyptian National Image*, p. 270. For Mill's definition of nationalism, see, ibid. pp. 270–271.
210. *Muntakhabat*, II: 165.
211. *Qissat*, p. 172.
212. Ibid. pp. 178–181.
213. *Muntakhabat*, I: 27–32, 71–112, 121–160.
214. *Qissat*, pp. 67–68, 72.
215. Ibid. pp. 53–55, 59.
216. *Safahat*, p. 179.
217. *Muntakhabat*, I: 305.
218. *Mustaqbal*, pp. 60–65.
219. *Muntakhabat*, I: 83–86.
220. *Mustaqbal*, p. 17.
221. Ibid. p. 28.
222. Ibid. p. 54.
223. Ibid. pp. 57–58.
224. Ibid. p. 56.
225. Ibid. p. 54.
226. *Qissat*, p. 209.
227. Ibid. pp. 213–214.
228. *Fi al-Saif*, p. 77.

Chapter 10

1. In the opening article of his periodical *al-Jinan*, Bustani writes that the aim of his journal was to improve and revive the Arabic language. *Al-Jinan*, January, 1870.
2. Sharabi, *Arab Intellectuals*, pp. 17–18.
3. *Adaab al-'Arab*, in: *Rawa'i'*, XXII: 35–37.
4. *Kanz*, I: 202–296.
5. *Sirr al-Layal*, p. 25.
6. *Adaab*, in: *Rawa'i'*, XXII: 33–37, 41.
7. *Al-Saq*, II: 206.
8. *Nafir Suriyya*, 1860, Oct. 15. Nov., 1,8,19. Dec. 14, pp. 17–19, 25–28, 29–46.
9. *Al-Saq*, I: 70–72, 203, 215.
10. Ibid. I: 200, 215, 310.
11. *Kashf*, pp. 232, 312.
12. *Al-Saq*, I: 33.

13. *Kashf*, pp. 309–310.
14. See for example pp. 18, 21, 22, 23, 25, 29. Marrash wrote his book in 1880 before this style became famous through Kahlil Gibran.
15. Quoted in Khaki, *Qasim Amin*, p. 124.
16. Bustani, *Adaab*, in: *Rawa'i'*, XXII: 37. Al-Shidyaq, *al-Jasus 'ala al-Qamus*, p. 3.
17. Khaki, *Qasim Amin*, pp. 123–125.
18. Zaydan, *al-Lugha al-'Arabiyya Ka'inun Hayy*, p. 21. Al-Shumayyil, *Majmu'at*, I: 366, footnote 2. Sarruf, *al-Muqtataf*, vol. 72 (1928), p. 481. Kurd 'Ali, *al-Mudhakkirat*, IV: 1089.
19. Zaydan, *Mukhtarat*, III: 105–112. Al-Shumayyil, *Kitabat*, pp. 137–138.
20. *Ghara'ib*, I: 82.
21. *Al-Qadim*, p. 66.
22. *Mukhtarat*, III: 139, 147–149. *Al-Muqtataf*, vol. 9 (1885), pp. 471, 633–636.
23. *Al-Muqtataf*, vol. 72 (1928), p. 481.
24. *Al-Lugha*, pp. 28–61.
25. Ibid. pp. 64–79.
26. *Al-Islam*, I: 170–183.
27. *Al-Mudhakkirat*, IV: 1096–1108.
28. Ibid. II: 502. III: 793–796.
29. *Al-Qadim*, p. 107. The italics are mine.
30. *Al-Muqtataf*, vol. 74 (1929), pp. 361–362.
31. *Majmu'at*, I: 366, footnote 2.
32. *Kitabat*, pp. 137–138.
33. *Al-Lugha*, pp. 88–89.
34. Ibid. p. 21.
35. Ibid. pp. 139–140.
36. *Mukhtarat*, III: 105–112.
37. *Al-Mudhakkirat*, II: 603–604.
38. *Ghara'ib*, I: 83.
39. Ibid. I: 89.
40. *Mukhtarat*, I: 106–107.
41. *Ghara'ib*, II: 34.
42. Ibid. I: 47, 52–53, 232.
43. Ibid. I: 138.
44. Ibid. I: 208.
45. *Al-Mudhakkirat*, IV: 1171.
46. *Ghara'ib*, I: 96–98, 110–111, 231, 239–240.
47. *Al-Islam*, I: 110–115.
48. *Le Réveil*, p. 178.
49. *Al-Mar'a al-Jadida*, Dec. 1925 (vol. 12), p. 485.
50. Ibid. Oct. 1922 (vol. 10), p. 200.
51. Ibid. Nov. 1925 (vol. 11), p. 440. Dec. 1925 (vol. 12), p. 485.
52. *Qissat*, p. 190.
53. *Min Ba'id*, pp. 263, 284–286.
54. *Mustaqbal*, p. 224.

55. Ibid. p. 66.
56. Ibid.p. 188.
57. Ibid. pp. 225–226.
58. Ibid. p. 226. The italics are mine. Al-Khalil died 776?/786?/791. Sibawayh died 796?, al-Akhfash between 825 and 835, al-Mubarrad in 900?
59. *Mustaqbal*, pp. 226, 228.
60. Ibid. p. 229. The italics are mine.
61. Ibid. pp. 235–236.
62. *Muntakhabat*, I: 246.
63. Ibid. I: 247.
64. Ibid. II: 145, 146.
65. Ibid. II: 126–146.
66. Ibid. II: 133.
67. Ibid. II: 141.
68. Ibid. II: 129, 135.
69. Ibid. II: 137, 143.
70. *Mustaqbal*, pp. 231–232.
71. *Fi al-Shi'r*, pp. 12–13.
72. *Min Ba'id*, p. 37.
73. Kurd 'Ali, *al-Mudhakkirat*, II: 608. Hussein, *Mustaqbal*, p. 360.
74. *Hadith al-Arbi'a'*, II: 62–66.
75. *Qissat*, p. 190. *Rihlat al-Rabi'*, pp. 83–86.
76. *Rihlat*, pp. 84–86.
77. *Saut Paris*, I: 131–136, 166–176. II: 21–27, 73–75.
78. Ibid. I: 29.
79. *Fi al-Saif*, p. 15.

Bibliography

'Abbud, Marun. *Judud wa Qudama'*, Dar al-Thaqafa, Beirut, 1954.

—— *Ruwwad al-Nahda al-Haditha*, Dar al-'Ilm lil-Malayin, Beirut, 1952.

'Abbud, Nazir. *Jurji Zadan, Hayatuhu, A'maluhu, Ma qila fihi*, Dar al-Jil, Beirut, 1983.

'Abd al-Raziq, 'Ali. *Al-Islam wa Usul al-Hukm*, Dar al-Ma'arif li al-Tiba'a wa al-Nashr, Sousa, Tunis, 1999.

—— *Hukm Hay'at Kibar al-'Ulama' fi Kitab al-Islam wa Usul al-Hukm, wa Hukm Majlis Ta'dib al-Qudat al-Shar'iyyin fi Wizarat al-Haqqaniyya bi Fasl Mu'allifihi min al-Qada' al-Shar'i*, al-Matba'a al-Salafiyya, Cairo, 1344 AH/1925 AD.

Abu-Lughod, Ibrahim. *Arab Rediscovery of Europe. A Study in Cultural Encounters*, Princeton University Press, Princeton, New Jersey, 1963.

Abu-Khalil, Shawqi. *Jurji Zaidan fi al-Mizan*, Dar al-Fikr, Damascus, 1981.

Ahmed, Leila. *Women and Gender in Islam. Historical Roots of a Modern Debate*, Yale University Press, New Haven and London, 1992.

Al-Alussi, Jamal al-Din. *Muhammad Kurd 'Ali*, Dar al-Jumhuriyya, Baghdad, 1966.

Amin, Ahmad. *Fayd al-Khater*, Maktabat al-Nahda al-Misriyya, Cairo, 1948.

—— *Zu'ama' al-Islah fi al-'Asr al-Hadith*, Matba'at al-Nahda al-Misriyya, Cairo, 1948.

Amin, Qasim. *Al-A'mal al-Kamila*, (*Complete Works*) 2 vols., with an introduction and notes by Dr. Muhammad 'Amara, al-Mu'assasa al-'Arabiyya li al-Dirasat wa al-Nashr, Beirut, 1976.

—— *Al-Mar'a al-Jadida*, al-Hay'a al-Misriyya al-'Amma li al-Kitab, Cairo, 1993.

—— *Tahrir al-Mar'a, in: Complete Works*, vol. II: 9–114.

—— *The Liberation of Women*, Translated by Samiha Sidham Peterson, The American University Press, Cairo, 1992.

Ammoun, Denise. *Histoire du Liban Contemporain*, 1860–1943, Fayard, Paris, 1997.

Antonius, George. *The Arab Awakening*, Capricorn Books, New York, 1965.

Antun, Farah. *Ibn Rushd wa Falsafatuhu, ma' Nusus al-Munazara baina Muhammad 'Abdo wa Farah Antun*, with an introduction by Dr. Adonis al-'Akra, Dar al-Tali'a, Beirut, 1981.

—— *Al-Jami'a* (periodical), Alexandria, 1899–1903, New York, 1906–1908.

—— *Al-Din wa al-'Ilm wa al-Mal*, (1903)

Al-Wahsh, al-Wahsh, al-Wahsh, (1903)
Urushalim al-Jadida, aw Fath al-'Arab Bait al-Maqdis, (1904)
all three novels in one volume with an introduction by Dr. Adonis al-'Akra, Dar al-Tali'a, Beirut, 1979.

Al-Attas, Sayyid M. *Islam, Secularism and the Philosophy of the Future*, Mansell Publishing Limited, London, 1985.

Al-'Aqqad, 'Abbas Mahmud.*Rijal 'Araftuhum*, Dar al-Hilal, Cairo (n.d.)

Al-'Azawi, 'Abbas. *Tarikh al-Adab al-'Arabi fi al-'Iraq*, vol. 2, Matba'at al-Majma' al-'Ilmi al-'Iraqi, 1382 AH/1962 AD.

Al-Azmeh, Aziz. *Al-'Ilmaniyya min Manzur Mukhtalif*, Markaz Dirasat al-Wihda al-'Arabiyya, Beirut, 1998.

Azoury, Negib. *Le Réveil de la Nation Arabe dans l'Asie Turque*, Paris, Plon, 1905.

Badran, Margot, & Cooke, Miriam (eds). *Opening the Gates, A Century of Arab Feminist Writing*, Indiana University Press, Bloomington and Indianapolis, 1990.

Bayhum, Muhammad Jamil. "'Ahd al-Kawakibi fi al-'Alam al-'Arabi', in: *Majallat al-Hadith*, September-October, 1952, pp. 559–563.

Birnbaum, Milton. *Aldous Huxley's Quest for Values*, University of Tennessee Press, Knoxville, 1971.

Bullata, Issa. *Trends and Issues in Contemporary Arab Thought*, SUNY Series in Middle Eastern Studies, State University New York, 1990.

Brockelmann, Carl. *Geschichte der Arabischen Literatur* (GAL), supplement to vol. I, Leiden, Brill, 1937. Supplement to vol. II, Leiden, Brill, 1938. Supplement to vol. III, Leiden, Brill, 1942.

Brown, Daniel. *Rethinking Tradition in Modern Islamic Thought*, Cambridge University Press, Cambridge, 1999.

Al-Bustani, Butrus. *Aadab al-'Arab*, in: Fuad Afram al-Bustani, *Rawa'i'*, vol. XXII, pp. 25–43, al-Matba'a al-Cathulikiyya, Beirut, 1929,

—— *Da'irat al-Ma'arif*, Dar al-Ma'rifa, Beirut, (n.d.)

—— *Al-Jinan* (periodical from 1870–1883 on microfilm), Matba'at al-Ma'arif, Beirut, 1870–1883.

—— *Nafir Suriyya*, Dar al-Fikr li al-Abhath wa al-Nashr, Beirut, 1990.

—— *Ta'alim al-Nisa'*, in: Fuad Afram al-Bustani, *Rawa'i'*, vol. XXII, pp. 1–24, al-Matba'a al-Cathulikiyya, Beirut, 1929.

—— *Qissat As'ad al-Shidyaq*, Dar al-Hamra', Beirut, 1992.

Cachia, Pierre. *Taha Hussein, His Place in the Egyptian Literary Renaissance*, Luzac & Co. Ltd., London, 1956.

Chevalier, Dominique; Guellouz,Azzedine; Miquel, André.*Les Arabes, l'Islam et l'Europe*, Flammarion, Paris, 1991.

Committee of Officials. *Kingdom of Iraq*, The Lord Baltimore Press, Baltimore, Maryland, U.S.A., 1946.

Dagher, Yusef As'ad. *Masadir al-Dirasa al-Adabiyya* (2 vols). Jam'iyyat Ahl al-Qalam fi Lubnan, Matabi' Lubnan, Beirut, 1956.

—— *Qamus al-Sahafa al-Lubnaniyya*, Manshurat al-Jami'a al-Lubnaniyya, Beirut, 1972.

Daher, 'Adel. *Al-Ussus al-Falsafiyya li al-'Alamaniyya*, Dar al-Saqi, London, 1998.

Dahhan, Sami. *'Abd al-Rahman al-Kawakibi*, Dar al-Ma'arif, Cairo, (n.d.)

—— *Muhammad Kurd 'Ali*, Damascus, 1347 AH/ 1955 AD.

Dimashqiyya, Julia Tohmi. *al-Mar'a al-Jadida* (periodical), 6 vols., Matba'at Tabbara, Beirut, 1921–1926.

Durkheim, Emile. *Les Règles de la Méthode Sociologique*, Librairie Félix Alcan, Paris, 1927.

Encyclopedia of the Modern Middle East, Macmillan Reference USA, New York, 1996.

Encyclopédie de l'Islam (new edition), Brill, Leiden, 1960–1971.

Fawwaz, Zaynab. *Al-Rasa'il al-Zaynabiyya* (vol. I), al-Matba'a al-Mutawassita, Cairo, (n.d.)

le Gassick, Trevor J. *Major Themes in Modern Arabic Thought: an Anthology*, College Audience Trade, 1997.

Al-Ghazzi, Kamel. "Abd al-Rahman al-Kawakibi,' in: *Majallat al-Hadith*, Aleppo, June-July, 1929, pp. 405–420, 445–450.

Haddad, al-Taher. *Imra'atuna fi al-Shari'a wa al-Mujtama'*, al-Dar al-Tunisiyya li al-Nashr, Tunis, 1972.

Al-Hilal, *al-Kitab al-Dhahabi, 1892–1942*, Dar al-Hilal, Cairo, 1942.

Harris, George L., in collaboration with Mukhtarani, Mildred C. Bigelow, John Cookson, Sheila C. Gillen, George A. Lipsky, Charles H. Royce. *Iraq, its People, its Society, its Culture*, Hraf Press, New Haven, 1958.

Al-Hashimi, Muhammad Yehia. 'al-Kawakibi Ba'ith al-Nahda al-'Ilmiyya' in: *Majallat al-Hadith*, Aleppo, Sept-Oct., 1952, pp. 579–584.

Holt, P.M. *Egypt and the Fertile Crescent 1516–1922, a Political History*, Cornell University Press, Ithaca, New York, 1967.

Al-Homsi, Qustaci. *Al-Sihr al-Halal fi Shi'r al-Dallal*, Matba'at al-Ma'arif, Cairo, 1903.

Houranil Albert. *Arabic Thought in the Liberal Age, 1789–1939*, Cambridge University Press, Cambridge, 1991.

Hussein, Taha. *'Ala Hamish al-Sira* (2vols), Dar al-Kitab al-Lubnani, Beirut, 1973.

—— *Al-Ayyam*, vols, I & II, Dar al-Ma'arif, Cairo, 1952, vol. III, Dar al-Ma'arif, Cairo, 1972.

—— *Ara' Hurra* (includes aritcles by Kurd 'Ali, Taha Hussein and 'Ali Musharrafa), al-Matba'a al-'Asriyya, Cairo (n.d.).

—— *Bayna Bayn*, Dar al-'Ilm li al-Malayin, Beirut, 1952.

—— *Fi al-Saif*, Dar al-Kitab al-Lubnani, Beirut, (n.d.).

—— *Fi al-Shi'r al-Jahili*, Matba'at Dar al-Kitab al-Misriyya, Cairo, 1926 AD/1344 AH.

—— *Al-Fitna al-Kubra*, in: *Complete Works*, IV, Dar al-Kitab al-Lubnani, Beirut, 1973.

—— *Fusul fi al-Adab wa al-Naqd*, in: *Complete Works*, V, Dar al-Kitab al-Lubnani, Beirut, 1973.

——— *Hadith al-Arbi'a'* (3 vols.), Dar al-Ma'arif, Cairo, 1059–1962.

——— *Min Ba'id*, al-Matba'a al-Rahmaniyya, Cairo, 1935.

——— *Min Laghu al-Saif ila Jadd al-Shita'*, Dar al-'Ilm li al-Malayin, Beirut, 1967.

——— *Mustaqbal al-Thaqafa fi Misr*, al-Hay'a al-Misriyya al-'Amma li al-Kitab, Cairo, 1993.

——— *Naqd wa Islah*, Dar al-'Ilm li al-Malayin, Beirut, 1977.

——— *Rihlat al-Rabi'*, Dar al-Ma'arif li al-Tiba'a wa al-Nashr, Cairo, 1948.

——— *Sawt Paris* (2vols), Matba'at al-Ma'arif, Cairo, 1943.

——— *Tajdid Dhikra Abi-'Ala'*, in: *Complete Works*, X, Dar al-Kitab al-Lubnani, Beirut, 1973–1974.

Huxley, Aldous. *After Many a Summer Dies the Swan*, Harper and Brothers, New York and London, 1939.

Ibn Jama'a, Badr al-din. Tahrir al-Ahkam fi Tadbir Ahl al-Islam, in: *Islamica*, vols. VI & VII, Leipzig, 1934, pp. 353–414.

Ibrahim, Emily Faris. *Al-Haraka al-Nisa'iyya al-Lubnaniyya*, Dar al-Thaqafa, Beirut, (n.d.)

Ishaq, Adib. *Al-Durar* (compiled by his brother 'Awny Ishaq), al-Matba'a al-Adabiyya, Beirut, 1909.

——— *Al-Kitabat al-Siyasiyya wa al-Ijtima'iyya* (compiled and with an introduction by Naji 'Alloush), Dar al-Tali'a li al-Tiba'a wa al-Nashr, Beirut, 1978.

Isma'il, Haidar Haj. *Al-Mujtama' wa al-Din wa al-Ishtirakiyya, Farah Antun*, Beirut, 1972 (no publisher mentioned).

——— *Taba'i' al-Istibdad wa Ahwal al-Thawra*, Matba'at Samia, 1972 (no city mentioned).

Al-Jabri, 'Abd al-Muta'al Muhammad. *Al-Muslima al-'Asriyya 'Inda Bahithat al-Badiya, Malak Hifni Nasif*, Matba'at Dar al-Bayan, 1976 (no city mentioned).

Jabri, Shafiq. *Muhadarat 'an Muhammad Kurd 'Ali*, Ma'had al-Dirasat al-'Arabiyya al-'Aliya, Arab League, 1957.

Jad'an, Fahmi. *Usus al-Taqaddum 'inda Mufakkiri al-Islam fi al-'Alam al-'Arabi al-Hadith,* al-Mu'assasa al-'Arabiyya li al-Dirasat wa al-Nashr, Beirut, 1979.

Kahhali, 'Umar Rida. *A'lam al-Nisa'*, al-Matba'a al-Hashimiyya, Damascus, 1940 AD,/1359 AH.

Kallas, George. *Al-Haraka al-Fikriyya al-Nasawiyya fi 'Asr al-Nahda (1849–1928),* Dar al-Jil, Beirut, 1996.

Al-Kawakibi, 'Abd al-Rahman. *Taba'i' al-Istibdad wa Masari' al-Isti'bad*, al-Matba'a al-'Umumiyya, 1321 AH (no city mentioned).

——— *Um al-Qura*, al-Matba'a al-'Asriyya, Aleppo, 1959.

Al-Kawakibi, As'ad. "Abd al-Rahman al-Kawakibi' in: *Majallat al-Hadith*, Aleppo, Sept.-Oct. 1952, pp. 542–554.

Al-Kayyali, 'Abd al-Rahman. ' 'Almabadi' al-Khalida fi Kitabai Taba'i' al-Istibdad wa Um al-Qura' in: *Majallat al-Hadith*, Aleppo, Sept.-Oct. 1952, pp. 564–578.

Kayyali, Sami. *Muhadarat 'an al-Haraka al-Adabiyya fi Halab (1800–1950),* Matba'at Nahdat Misr, Cairo, 1957.

—— *Al-Adab al-'Arabi al-Mu'asir fi Suriyya (1850–1950),* Dar al-Ma'arif, Cairo, 1959.

—— 'Dhikra al-Kawakibi', in: *Majallat al-Hadith,* Aleppo, Sept.-Oct. 1952, pp. 537–541.

Khalaf Allah, Muhammad Ahmad. *Al-Kawakibi, Hayatuhu wa Ara'uhu,* Maktabat al- 'Arab, Cairo, (n.d.).

Khaki, Ahmad. *Qasim Amin, Tarikh Hayatihi al-Fikri,* Maktabat al-Anglo al-Misriyya, Cairo, 1973.

Al-Khoury, Maroun 'Issa. *Fi al-Yaqza al-'Arabiyya, al-Khitab al-Socio-Siyasi 'ind Farah Antun,* Jarrous Press, Tripoli, Lebanon, 1994.

Khoury, Philip S. *Urban Notables and Arab Nationalism, the Politics of Damascus 1860–1920,* Cambridge University Press, Cambridge, 1983.

Kirk, George E. *A Short History of the Middle East (from the Rise of Islam to Modern Times),* Methuen & Co. Ltd., London, 1959.

Al-Kitab al-Dhahabi li Yubil al-Muqtataf al-Khamsini (1876–1926), Matba'at al-Muqtataf, Cairo, 1926.

Kurd 'Ali, Muhammad. *Ara' Hurra* (includes articles by Kurd 'Ali, Taha Hussein and 'Ali Musharrafa), al-Matba'a al-'Asriyya, Cairo, (n.d.)

—— *Al-Bi'tha al-Islamiyya ila Dar al-Khilafa al-Islamiyya* (together with Muhammad al-Batir, Hussein al-Habbal & 'Abd al-Basit al-Unsi), Yusef Sader, al-Matba'a al-Islamiyya, Beirut, 1916.

—— *Ghara'ib al-Gharb* (2vols), al-Maktaba al-Rahmaniyya, Cairo, 1341 AH/1923 AD.

—— *al-Islam wa al-Hadara al-Gharbiyya* (2vols.), vol. I, Matba'at Lajnat al-Ta'lif wa al-Tarjama wa al-Nashr, Cairo, 1950. vol. II, Matba'at Dar al-Kutub al-Misriyya, Cairo, 1354 AH/1936 AD.

—— *Khitat al-Sham* (6vols.), al-Matba'a al-Haditha, Damascus, 1925–1928.

—— *Masadir al-Thaqafa al-'Arabiyya wa ta'thiruha fi al-Hadara al-Haditha,* al-Matba'a al-'Asriyya, Cairo, (n.d.)

—— *Al-Mudhakkirat,* (4 vols.), Matba'at al-Taraqqi, Damascus, vols. 1&2, 1948; vol.3,1949; vol. 4, 1951.

—— *Al-Qadim wa al-Hadith,* al-Matba'a al-Rahmaniyya, Cairo, 1343 AH/1925 AD.

—— 'al-Sayyid 'Abd al-Rahman al-Kawakibi' in: *al-Muqtataf,* July 1902, pp.622–623.

Longrigg, Stephen Hemsley. *Syria and Lebanon under French Mandate,* Oxford University Press, London, 1958.

Macdonald, D.B. *Development of Muslim Theology, Jurisprudence and Constitutional Theory,* New York, 1903.

Majmu'at Mu'allifin min Adib Ishaq wa al-Afghani ila Nasif Nassar, *Adwa' 'Ala al-Ta'assub,* Dar Amwaj, Beirut, 1993.

Al-Maqdisi, Anis. *Al-Ittijahat al-Adabiyya fi al-'Alam al-'Arabi al-Hadith,* Beirut, 1963 (no publisher mentioned).

Makdisi, Ussama. *The Culture of Sectarianism, Community, History and Violence in Nineteenth-Century Ottoman Lebanon*, University of California Press, Berkeley, Los Angeles, London, 2000.

Marrash, Francis. *Dalil al-Hurriyya al-Insaniyya*, Aleppo, 1861.

—— *Diwan Mir'at al-Hasna'*, Matba'at al-Ma'arif, Beirut, 1872.

—— *Durr al-Sadaf fi Ghara'ib al-Sudaf*, Matba'at al-Ma'arif, Beirut, 1872.

—— *Ghabat al-Haq, Kitab Siyasi, Ijtima'i*, Dar al-Hamra', Beirut, 1990.

—— *Mashhad al-Ahwal*, al-Matba'a al-Kulliyya, Beirut, 1883.

—— *Rihlat Paris*, al-Matba'a al-Sharqiyya, Beirut, 1867.

—— *Shahadat al-Tabi'a fi Wujud Allah wa al-Shari'a*, Matba'at al-Amerikan, Beirut, 1892.

Mas'ad, Bulos. *Faris al-Shidyaq*, Matba'at al-Ikha', Cairo, 1934.

Al-Mawardi, Abu al-Hasan 'Ali. *Al-Ahkam al-Sultaniyya*. Matba'at al-Watan, Cairo, 1298 AH.

Mazhar, Isma'il. *Mu'dilat al-Madaniyya al-Haditha, wa Maqalat Ukhra*, Dar al-'Asr li al-Tiba'a wa al-Nashr, Cairo, 1928.

Meier, Olivier. *Al-Muqtataf et le debat sur le Darwinism, Beyrouth 1876–1885*, CEDEJ, Cairo, 1996.

Mohammad, Fathiyya. *Balaghat al-Nisa' fi al-Qarn al-'Ishrin*, Hussein Hasanayn, Cairo (n.d.)

Montesquieu, C.de S. *L'Esprit des Lois*, Oeuvres complètes, Ed. du Seuil, Paris, 1964.

Al-Mu'min, Makki Habib & Manhal, 'Ali 'Ujayl. *Min Taba'i' Yaqzat al-Umma al-'Arabiyya*, Manshurat Wizarat al-Thaqafa wa al-I'lam, Iraq, 1981.

Al-Najjar, Hussein Fawzi. *Ahmad Lutfi al-Sayyed, Ustadh al-Jeel*, al-Mu'assasa al-Misriyya al-'Amma li al-Ta'lif wa al-Anba' wa al-Nashr, Cairo, 1384 AH/ 1965 AD.

—— *Lutfi al-Sayyid wa al-Shakhsiyya al-Misriyya*, Maktabat al-Qahira al-Haditha, Cairo, (n.d.)

Najjar, Ibrahim Salim. 'Min Dhikrayat al-Madi: 'Abd al-Rhman al-Kawakibi', *Majallat al-Hadith*, Aleppo, January 1940.

Najm, Muhammad Yusef. *Al-Qissa fi al-Adab al-'Arabi al-Hadith*, Dar Misr li al-Tiba'a, Cairo, 1952.

Nasif, Malak Hifni (Bahithat al-Badiya). *Al-Nisa'iyyat* (2vols.), Matba'at al-Taqaddum, Cairo, second ed. (n.d.)

—— *Athar Bahithat al-Badiya* (with an introduction by Dr. Suhair Qalamawi), al-Mu'assasa al-Misriyya al-'Amma li al-Ta'lif wa al-Tarjama wa al-Tiba'a wa al-Nashr, Cairo, 1962.

Nasif, Majd al-Din Hifni. *Tahrir al-Mar'a fi al-Islam*, Matba'at Abi al-Hol, Cairo, 1342 AH/1924 AD.

Nasr, Anis. *Al-Nubugh al-Lubnani fi al-Qarn al-'Ishrin*, Aleppo, 1938 (no ed. mentioned)

Nuwaiyhed, Nadia al-Jurdi. *Nisa' min Biladi*, al-Mu'assasa al-'Arabiyya li al-Dirasat wa al-Nashr, Beirut, 1986.

Owen, Roger. *The Middle East in the World Economy, 1800–1914,* Methuen, London & New York, 1981.

Pérès, H. *L'Espagne vue par les Voyageurs Musulmans, de 1610 à 1930.* Librairie d'Amérique et d'Orient, Paris, 1937.

Philipp, Thomas. *The Autobiography of Jurji Zaidan, including four letters to his Son,* translated, edited and introduced by Thomas Philipp, Three Continents Press, Inc., Washington D.C., 1990.

—— *Gurgi Zaidan, His Life and Thought,* In Kommision bei Franz Steiner Verlag, Wiesbaden, Beirut, 1979.

Pickthall, Muhammad Marmaduke. *The Meaning of the Glorious Koran, an Explanatory Translation,* New American Library, New York, (n.d.)

Ramadan, Tariq. Aux sources du Renouveau Musulman (d'al-Afghani à Hasan al-Banna, un siècle de Reformisme Islamique), Bayard Edition/Centurion, Paris, 1998.

Al-Rasi, Georges. *Al-Islam al-Jaza'iri, min al-Amir 'Abd al-Qadir ila Umara' al-Jama'at,* Dar al-Jadid, Beirut, 1997.

Raven, C.E. *Christian Socialism,* 1848–1854, Macmillan, London, 1920.

Ruedy, John (ed.). *Islamism and Secularism in North Africa,* St. Martin's Press, New York, 1994.

Al-Sa'id, Rif'at. *Thalathatu Lubnaniyyin fi al-Qahira: Shibli al-Shumayyil, Farah Antun, Rafiq Jabbur,* Dar al-Tali'a li al-Tiba'a wa al-Nashr, Beirut, 1973.

Salibi, Kamal S. *The Modern History of Lebanon,* Caravan Books, Delmar, New York, 1977.

Samné, Georges Dr. La Syrie, preface by Chekri Ganem, Bossard, Paris, 1920.

Sarkis, Yusif Lyan. *Mu'jam al-Matbu'at al-'Arabiyya wa al Mu'arraba,* Matba'at Sarkis, Cairo, 1346 AH/ 1928 AD.

Al-Sayyid, Ahmad Lutfi. *Mabadi' fi al-Siyassa wa al-Adab wa al-Ijtima',* with an introduction by Taher al-Tanahi, Dar al-Hilal, Cairo, 1963.

—— *Madhhab al-Hurriya, ila Nuwwabina,* Matba'at al-Jarida, Cairo, (n.d.)

—— *Al-Muntakhabat* (2 vols.), Dar al-Nashr al-Hadith, Cairo, 1937.

—— *Mushkilat al-Hurriyyat fi al-'Alam al-'Arabi,* Dar al-Rawa'i', Beirut, 1959.

—— *Safahat Matwiyya min Tarikh al-Haraka al-Istiqlaliyya fi Misr,* Hadiyyat al-Muqtataf al-Sanawiyya, Cairo, 1946.

—— *Ta'ammulat fi al-Falsafa wa al-Adab wa al-Siyasa wa al-Ijtima',* Dar al-Ma'arif, Cairo, 1965.

—— *Qissat Hayati,* with an introduction by Taher al-Tanahi, Dar al-Hilal, Cairo, (n.d.).

Sharaf, 'Abd al-'Aziz. *Lutfi al-Sayyid, Failasuf Ayqaza Umma.* Maktabat Misr, Cairo, 1991.

Sharabi, Hisham. *Arab Intellectuals and the West, The Formative Years 1875–1914,* The Johns Hopkins Press, Baltimore and London, 1970.

Al-Shidyaq, Ahmad Faris. *Al-Jasus 'ala al-Qamus*, Matba'at al-Jawa'ib, Constantinople, 1299 AH.

—— *Sirr al-Layal fi al-Qalb wa al-Ibdal*, Matba'at al-Jawa'ib, Constantinople, 1284 AH.

—— *Kanz al-Ragha'ib fi Muntakhabat al-Jawa'ib* (7 vols.), Matba'at al-Jawa'ib, Constantinople, 1288–1298 AH.

—— *Al-Saq 'ala al-Saq fi ma hua al-Fariaq* (2 vols.), al-Maktaba al-Tijariyya, Cairo, 1920.

—— *Al-Wasita fi Ma'rifati Ahwal Malta*, and *Kashf al-Mukhabba 'an Tamaddun Urubba*, Matba'at al-Jawa'ib, Constantinople, 1299 AH.

Shikho, Rev. Louis. *Al-Adab al-'Arabi fi al-Qarn al-Tasi' 'Ashar* (2 vols.), Matba'at al-Aba' al-Yasu'iyyin, Beirut, 1926.

—— *Tarikh al-Adab fi al-Rub' al-Awwal min al-Qarn al-'Ishrin*, Matba't al-Aba' al-Yasu'iyyin, Beirut, 1926.

Al-Shumayyil, Shibli. *Ara' al-doctor Shibli al-Shumayyil*, Matba'at al-Ma'arif, Cairo, 1912.

—— *Falsafat al-Nushu' wa al-Irtiqa'* in: *Majmu'at al-Doctor Shibli al-Shumayyil*, vol.I, pp. 1–224, Matba'at al-Muqtataf, Cairo, 1910.

—— *Al-Haqiqa, wa hia Risala Tatadamman Rududan li Ithbat Madhhab Darwin fi al-Nushu' wa al-Irtiqa'*, in: *Majmu'at al-Doctor Shibli al-Shumayyil*, vol. I, pp. 227–306. Matba'at al-Muqtataf, Cairo, 1910.

—— *Kitabat Siyasiyya wa Islahiyya*, collected, prepared and studied by Dr. As'ad Razzuq, Dar al-Hamra', Beirut, 1991.

—— *Majmu'at al-Dotor Shibli al-Shumayyil*, vol II, (a collection of articles previously published in various journals), Matba'at al-Ma'arif, Cairo, 1908.

—— *Mulhaq Mabahith fi al-Hayat li ta'yid al-Ra'i al-Maddi min sanat 1878*, in: *Majmu'at al-Doctor Shibli al-Shumayyil*, vol I, pp. 310–367, Matba'at al-Muqtataf, Cairo, 1910.

Simon, Reeva, S. *Iraq Between the Two World Wars*, Columbia University Press, New York, 1986.

Al-Tabbakh, Muhammad Raghib. *A'lam an-Nubala' bi Tarikh Halab al-Shahba'* (7vols.), al-Matba'a al-'Ilmiyya, Aleppo, 1345 AH/1926 AD.

Tabierrot, Norbert. *Al-Kawakibi, al-Mufakkir al-Tha'ir*, translated by 'Ali Salami, Dar al-Adab, Beirut, 1968.

de Tarazi, Vicomte Philip. *Tarikh al-Sahafa al-'Arabiyya* (4 vols.), al-Matba'a al-Adabiyya, Beirut, 1913.

Tignor, Robert L. *Modernization and British Colonial Rule in Egypt, 1882–1914*, Princeton University Press, Princeton, New Jersey, 1966.

Toledano, Ehud, R. *State and Society in Mid-Nineteenth Century Egypt*, Cambridge University Press, Cambridge, 1990.

Tucker, Judith. *Women in Nineteenth-century Egypt*, Cambridge University Press, Cambridge, 1985.

Wendell, Charles. *The Evolution of the Egyptian National Image from its Origin to Ahmad Lutfi al-Sayyid*, University of California Press, Berkely, Los Angeles, London, 1972.

Yared, Nazik Saba. *Arab Travellers and Western Civilization*, Saqi Books, London, 1996.

Zaydan, Jurji. *'Aja'ib al-Khalq*, Matba'at al-Hilal, Cairo, 1912.

—— *Al-Lugha al-'Arabiyya Ka'inun Hayy*, revised by Dr. Murad Kamel, Dar al-Hilal, Cairo, (n.d.)

—— *Mudhakkirat*, ed. by Dr. Salah al-Din al-Munajjid, Dar al-Kitab al-Jadid, Beirut, 1968.

—— *Mukhtarat* (3 vols.), Matba'at al-Hilal, Cairo, vol. I,1919; vol II, 1920; vol. III, 1921.

—— *Tabaqat al-Umam*, Dar al-Turath, Beirut, 1389 AH/ 1969 AD.

—— *Rihlat Jurji Zaydan ila Uruppa*, Idarat al-Hilal, Cairo, 1923.

—— *Tarajim Mashahir al-Sharq fi al-Qarn al-Tasi' 'Ashar*, Dar Maktabat al-Hayat, Beirut, 3rd ed. (n.d.)

—— *Tarikh Aadab al-Lugha al-'Arabiyya*, new edition revised by Dr. Shawqi Dayf, Dar al-Hilal, Cairo, (n.d.)

—— *Al-Tarikh al-'Amm Mundhu al-Khaliqa ila Hadhihi al-Ayyam*, (edition, date and place unknown).

—— *Tabaqat al-Umam*, Matba'at al-Hilal, Cairo, 1912.

Zayn al-Din, Nazira. *Al-Fatat wa al-Shuyukh*, al-Mada, Damascus, 1998 (2nd ed.)

—— *Al-Sufur wa al-Hijab*, al-Mada, Damascus, 1998 (2nd ed.)

Ziadi, May. *Bahithat al-Badiya, Dirasa Naqdiyya*, Mu'assasat Naufal, Beirut, 1975.

Al-Zirkili, Khayr al-Din. *Al-A 'lam, Qamus Tarajim li Ashhar al-Rijal wa al-Nisa' min al 'Arab wa al-Musta'ribin wa al-Mustashriqin*, (10 vols.), Matba'at Kostatsumas wa Shurakah, 2nd. ed., 1373–1378 AH/ 1954–1959 AD.

Periodicals
Al-Hilal
Al-'Irfan
Islamic Culture
Al-Jami'a
Majallat al-Hadith
Al-Makshuf
Al-Manar
Al-Mar'a al-Jadida
Al-Mashriq
Middle Eastern Studies
Al-Muqtataf
Revue Egyptienne de Droit International

Index

'Abbas, Farhat, 11
'Abbas Hilmi I, Viceroy of Egypt, 13 'Abbas Hilmi II, Khedive of Egypt, 14–15
'Abbasid Caliphate, 26, 59, 96, 175
'Abdu, Sheikh Muhammad, 27, 29, 40, 59, 64, 78–9
'Abdülaziz Oglu Mahmud II, 13
'Abdülhamid II, Sultan, 18, 19, 26, 28, 130, 140, 141, 162, 164
Adham, Isma'il, 12
Al-Afghani, Jamal al-Din, 14–15, 27, 30, 152, 204
Ahmed, Leila, 89, 92
Al-Ahram, 18
Alexander the Great, 103
Algeria, 11
'Ali Pasha, Muhammad, 13
Allenby, Viscount Gen. E.H.H., 20
American University of Beirut, 18, 23
Amin, Qasim
    anticlericalism of, 63, 64
    change, attitude to, 111
    democracy, views on, 135
    despotism, attack on, 130
    on freedom, 139
    ignorance, criticism of, 98–9
    on individualism, 67, 71
    knowledge for the sake of, search for, 104
    on language, 184–5, 186
    on laws (of God and man), 145–6
    liberal attitude to past, 109–10
    on nationalism, 156–8

    protests against, 94
    reason, on limits of power of, 104
    on religion, 46–7, 56, 61
    scientific fundamentalism of, 113
    social inequality, preoccupation with, 120
    socio-political improvement, 106
    spiritual/temporal, on separation of, 27–8
    Western thought, influence of, 129
    on women's status, 82, 85–6, 89, 91, 92
Antun, Farah
    anticlericalism of, 63, 65
    on constitutional rule, 140
    education, views on, 98–9
    on individualism, 67–8, 72–7
    on intolerance, 106
    knowledge for the sake of, search for, 104
    on nationalism, 158, 159
    reason, on limitless power of, 103–4
    on religion, 47–57, 60–1
    scientific fundamentalism of, 113–15
    on secularism in education, 95–6
    socialism, influence on, 121–4
    spiritual/temporal, on separation of, 28–31
    stability through tyranny, a voice for, 131
    on women's status, 84
Arab Nationalism, 153–5, 162–3
The Arabic Language is a Living Being (Zaydan, J.), 185
Aristotle, 73, 103, 132, 135, 142

Ashkenazi Jews, 20
Atatürk, Mustafa Kamal, 34, 147
Averroes and his Philosophy (Antun, F.), 29
Al-Azhar University, 16, 64, 118, 190
'Azmi, Mahmud, 12
Azoury, Nejib
  anticlericalism of, 63
  on Arabism, 163–5
  on constitutional rule, 140
  on individualism, 77
  on language, 189
  on nationalism, 158, 159, 162
  on socialism, 124
  spiritual/temporal, on separation of,
  31–2

Al-Badiya, Bahithat *see* Nasef, Malak Hifni
Bakhit, Sheikh Muhammad, 59
Bakr, Abu, 35, 37, 38–9
Balfour Declaration, 20
Baring, Sir Evelyn (Lord Cromer), 14–15,
  55, 58
Al-Bashir, 51
Bashir III, Shehabi, 17
Al-Bazzaz, 'Abd al-Rahman, 11
Bentham, Jeremy, 158, 174
The Bible, 44, 45, 47–9, 59–60, 83
  see also Qur'an
Britain
  in Egypt, 14–16, 128, 151–2, 165–6
  religious tolerance of, 73
Brown, Daniel, 109
Büchner, Ludwig, 53
Al-Bukhari, 62
Al-Bustani, Butrus
  anticlericalism of, 63
  Arabic revival, part in, 19
  democracy, views on, 136–7
  education, on role of, 95
  on individualism, 75
  on intolerance, 106
  on language, 183
  morality and knowledge, 105
  on nationalism, 149, 151, 154–5
  on religion, 42, 46
  spiritual/temporal, on separation of,
  25, 28, 31

on women's status, 83, 85, 87
Al-Bustani, Saleem, 25

The Characteristics of Tyranny (al-Kawakibi,
  'A. al-R.), 26, 27, 98, 129
Christianity, 29–30, 42–7, 52, 58, 62–5, 73,
  76, 79, 91, 107–8, 194–5, 199–200
Comte, Auguste, 59, 68, 78, 98, 101, 105,
  109, 114, 139, 196
Constant, Benjamin, 49

Dabbas, Charles, 22
Dallal, Jubrail
  anticlericalism of, 63, 65
  democracy, views on, 137
  on religion, 44, 57
  revolutionary spirit of, 133
  tyranny, attack on, 128
Damascus University, 23
Darwin, Charles, 45–6, 55, 111
Darwinism, 47–8, 53, 91, 96
de Bonald, Louis-Gabriel, 49
De Re Publica (Aristotle), 132, 135, 142
Demolins, Edmond, 111–12
Descartes, René, 77, 101
Diderot, Denis, 101
Dimashqiyya, Julia Tohmi
  on education, role of, 96, 101
  on individualism, 69–70
  on intolerance, 106
  knowledge for the sake of, search for,
  104
  on language, 189
  on morality and knowledge, 105
  nationalism of, 169
  on socio-political improvement, 105
  spiritual/temporal, on separation of,
  35
  traditional values, criticism of, 108–9
  on women's status, 85–9
Al-Din, Kheir, 109
Al-Din, Nazira Zayn
  anticlericalism of, 64
  change, attitude to, 111, 112
  democracy, advocate of, 141–2
  on individualism, 69–70, 74, 77–80
  on laws (of God and man), 146

nationalism of, 172–3
opposition to, 94
on religion, 61–2, 64
religious fanaticism, criticism of, 117–18
spiritual/temporal, on separation of, 40–1
traditional values, criticism of, 109
on truth (and the search for), 101
tyranny, attack on, 131
on women's status, 82, 83, 85, 87, 88–90
Dodge, Bayard, 74
Druze communities, 16–18
Druze revolt, 21
Durkheim, Emile, 70

Edison, Thomas, 52
Egypt, 10, 12–16, 20, 85–6, 102–3, 119, 126, 148, 155, 173–80
L'Egypte et les Egyptiens (Harcourt), 157–8
Egyptian University of Cairo, 16, 28, 96, 105, 189
L'Esprit des Lois (Montesquieu), 139, 150
Ethics (Aristotle), 73

Farook, King of Egypt, 16
Al-Fasi, Alla, 10
Fawwaz, Zaynab
    anticlericalism of, 65
    criticism of, 94
    on freedom, 138
    on individualism, 67, 68
    on nationalism, 155–6
    on women's status, 82, 83, 85, 87–8, 89, 92
Feisal, Prince of Mecca, 171
Feisal I, King of Iraq, 11–12, 131
Feisal of Hijaz, Prince, 20–1
Ferdinand and Isabella, 26
The Forest of Justice (Marrash, F.), 83, 113, 137, 184
Fourier, Charles, 120–1
France
    Commune in, 132
    in Lebanon and Syria, 21–3, 128, 130, 136, 151, 152

religious persecution in, 74
Frederick II of Germany, 30
French Revolution, 44, 49, 67, 98, 119, 123, 128, 137
Fuad, Prince of Egypt, 15–16
The Future of Culture in Egypt (Hussein, T.), 117

Galileo, 63
Ghabat al-Haq (Marrash, F.), 83, 113, 137, 184
Ghali, Butrus Pasha, 58
Gorst, Sir Eldon, 15

Haddad, al-Tahar, 10
The Hadith, 35, 38, 62, 83, 90, 94, 101, 117, 195
Al-Haj, Massali, 11
Hanifa, Imam Abu, 79
Harcourt, Duke of, 139, 157–8
Harvey, William, 63
Hatti-i-Hümayun, 17, 143, 153
Haykal, Husein, 12
The Hijaz, 20, 32, 131, 155, 171
Al-Hilal, 18, 99, 163
The History of Arabic Literatures (Zaydan, J.), 187
The History of Islamic Civilization (Zaydan, J.), 163
Hizb al-Umma, 175
Al-Hizb al-Watani, 152
Hobbes, Thomas, 38, 196
Homer, 103
Hugo, Victor, 101
Human Rights, Declaration of, 76, 130
Al-Husri, Sati', 12
Huss, Jan, 63
Hussein, Sharif, 172
Hussein, Taha
    absolute rule, attack on, 130, 131
    anticlericalism of, 64
    change, attitude to, 111
    civilization, on source of, 116–17
    on constitutional rule, 142
    democracy, advocate of, 134–5
    democracy, views on, 135, 140
    education, views on, 98

on individualism, 70, 71, 72, 77–8, 79
knowledge for the sake of, search for, 104
on language, 189–92
on laws, secular attitude, 147–8
nationalism of, 173–6, 178–80
positivism of, 110–11
reason, on limits of power of, 104
on religion, 58–62
socio-economic change, attitude to, 125–6
socio-political improvement, 105–6
spiritualism/temporalism, on separation of, 39–40
teaching, concern at antiquated methods, 102–3
on women's status, 84
Hussein of Hijaz, Sharif, 20, 21
Huxley, Aldous, 67, 99, 114, 139, 166, 196

Ibrahim, 60–1, 104
Imprimerie Catholique, 18
Iraq, 11–12, 131, 155
Ishaq, Adib
on colonisation, 152
democracy, views on, 136, 137
despotism, attack on, 128, 129
on education, 98
France, attitude to, 152
on freedom, 138
on individualism, 73, 74, 75
on language, 183
on laws (of God and man), 144–5
on nationalism, 153
on religion, 44–5, 46, 49, 56
revolution, attitude to, 133
socio-political improvement, 105
spiritual/temporal, on separation of, 28
on women's status, 85, 92
Islam and the Principles of Government (al-R., 'A. 'A.), 10, 35
Isma'il, 60–1, 104
Isma'il, Khedive of Egypt, 13–14

Jamal Pasha, 20, 167
Al-Jami'a, 29, 99, 122, 158, 163

Al-Janna, 25
Al-Jarida, 15
Al-Jawa'ib, 43, 136
Al-Jaza'iri, Prince 'Abd el-Qadir, 17
Al-Jaza'iri, Prince Khaled, 11
Al-Jinan, 25
Judaism, 59, 60, 62
Julius Caesar, 103
Al-Junayna, 25

Kamil, Hussein, 15
Kamil, Mustafa, 12, 15
Al-Kawakibi, 'Abd al-Rahman
anti-revolutionary attitude, 133
anticlericalism of, 64–5
change, attitude to, 111
democracy, views on, 135–6
despotism, attack on, 129, 130
education, on power of, 133–4
on freedom, 138–9
on individualism, 67, 68, 70, 72, 75–6, 78–9
injustice suffered by, 128
on laws (of God and man), 145
on nationalism, 156–8
opposition to Pan-Islamism, 19
reason, on limits of power of, 104
on religion, 45–6, 52, 56, 59
socialism, influence on, 119–120
socio-political improvement, 105–6
spiritual/temporal, on separation of, 25–9, 31, 32
traditional education, condemnation of, 98
ulama, effect of, 107–8
Western thought, influence of, 129
on women's status, 85, 87
Khaldun, Ibn, 109
Al-Khattab, 'Umar ibn, 187
Kitchener, Horatio H., 15
Kurd 'Ali, Muhammad
absolute rule, attack on, 130
anticlericalism of, 63–4
on art, 188
capitalism, belief in, 124–5
change, attitude to, 111
contradictions in work of, 125

democracy, views on, 135, 136, 140, 141
economic independence, belief in, 124–5
education, on power of, 133–4
education, views on, 98
European experience, 110
on individualism, 67, 69, 70, 71, 72–6, 78
injustice suffered by, 128
knowledge, on quest for, 96–7
on language, 186, 187–8
on laws (of God and man), 146–7
nationalism of, 167–9, 172
progress, attitude to, 115–16
reason, on limits of power of, 104
on religion, 56–8, 60, 61
socio-political improvement, 105–6
spiritual/temporal, on separation of, 33–5
on superstition, 97
on truth (and the search for), 101
ulama, effect of, 107–8, 109
on women's status, 84, 87, 89, 91, 93

Lamennais, Felicité R., 49
The Leaders of Thought (Hussein, T.), 103
Lebanon, 10, 12, 16–23
Lebon, Gustave, 73
The Leg Over the Leg (al-Shidyaq, A.), 89, 118, 182
Legal Politics (Taymiyya, I.), 40
Lemaître, Jules, 192
The Liberation of Women (Amin, Q.), 82, 91, 111
Life of the Apostles (Renan, E.), 48
Lisan al-Maghreb, 10
Locke, John, 38, 139, 196
Louis-Philippe, King of France, 132
Ludlow, John, 136

McMahon, Sir Henry, 15, 20
Al-Madrassa al-Wataniyya, 95, 151
Al-Mahasin, Abu, 83
Majlis al-Mah'uthan, 134
Al-Majma' al-'Ilmi al-'Arabi, 186
Malta, 43
Manar, 74

Al-Mar'a al-Jadida, 101
Marconi, Guglielmo, 52
Maronites, 16–18, 21, 24, 42–3, 63, 73, 75
Marrash, Francis
change, attitude to, 113
democracy, views on, 137
on education, 98
on freedom, 137
French influence on, 113
on individualism, 66, 68, 72, 75
knowledge, on practical use of, 105
on language, 183–4
on laws (of God and man), 144
morality and knowledge, 105
on nationalism, 150, 151, 154–5
reason, on limits of power of, 104
on religion, 45–6, 51, 63
revolutionary spirit of, 133
Romanticism of, 128–9
socialism, influence on, 119
socio-political improvement, 105
on superstition, 97
on women's status, 85
The Marvels of Creation (Zaydan, J.), 47
Maurice, Frederick D., 118
Al-Mawardi, 26, 129
Mazhar, Isma'il, 12, 99
The Means of Knowing Malta's Circumstances (al-Shidyaq, A.), 183
Memoirs (Kurd 'Ali, M.), 168
Mill, John Stuart, 67, 139, 158, 174, 196
Montesquieu, 74, 101, 139, 144, 150
Morocco, 10, 155
Mother of Cities (al-Kawakibi, 'A. al-R.), 25–6, 138, 157
Mu'awiya I, Caliph, 31
Muhammad II, Sultan, 26
Muhammad the Prophet, 36–9, 61, 62, 79, 83, 136, 146, 186
see also Qur'an
Al-Muqattam, 18
Al-Muqtataf, 51, 76, 99, 163
Musa, Salama, 12
Mu'tazilites, 66, 67, 96, 195

Nabarawi, Zeiza, 12
Al-Nadim, 'Abd Allah, 12

Nafīr Suriyya, 25, 151
Nahhas, Mustafa, 16
Nasef, Malak Hifni
    change, attitude to, 112
    criticism of, 94
    on individualism, 71, 72, 75
    on knowledge, limitless nature of, 103
    knowledge for the sake of, search for, 104
    on nationalism, 155–6
    on polygamy, 92–3
    socio-political improvement, 105
    on superstition, 100
    on women's status, 83, 85, 86, 87–8, 89, 90, 91
Nature's Testimony (Marrash, F.), 45
The New Jerusalem (Antun, F.), 162
The New Women (Amin, Q.), 82, 91, 111
Nietsche, Friedrich W., 31, 50
Nimr, Faris, 51

Organic Regulation, 17–18
Ottoman Empire, 13–20, 44, 46, 73–4, 81, 128, 130–4, 140–4, 151–3, 159–60, 196
Ottomanism, 153, 159–60

Palestine, 19–20
Pan-Islamism, 30–1, 33
Pascal, Blaise, 101
Pasteur, Louis, 61
A Perspective of Circumstance (Marrash, F.), 45
Philipp, Thomas, 31, 163
The Philosophy of Evolution and Progress (al-Shummayyil, S.), 53
Plato, 103
Prague, Jerome, 63
On Pre-Islamic Poetry (Hussein, T.), 59, 104
The Proper Sphere of Government (Spencer, H.), 102
Protestantism, 42–3, 63, 101

The Qur'an
    belief in, 195
    al-Din on, 62, 78, 80, 83, 87
    on freedom, 77, 78, 80
    Hussein on, 59–60, 77

justice and equality, calls in, 138
Kurd 'Ali on, 56–7
language and, 181–2, 186
the law and, 143–8
'Obey Allah,' verse in, 129
political thought and, 222
on pre-destination, 66
on reason (and use of), 96
on religious matters, 35–6
Sura of the Djinn, 104
understanding of, 101
on veiling, 89–90
Western contradiction to, 118
on women's status, 92–3, 94
see also Bible; Muhammad

Rashid Bey, 131
Rashidun Caliphate, 26
Al-Raziq, 'Ali 'Abd
    absolute rule, attack on, 130, 131
    anticlericalism of, 64
    change, attitude to, 111
    democracy, views on, 135, 140, 141
    on individualism, 77, 79
    on religion, 59
    spiritual/temporal, on separation of, 26, 35–40
Religion, Knowledge and Money (Antun, F.), 122, 123
Renan, Ernest, 46, 48, 101, 114
The Reawakening of the Arab Nation (Azoury, N.), 31, 162
Rida, Muhammad Rashid, 27, 31, 50, 52, 55, 94, 135
Rushd, Ibn (Averroes), 29, 48, 50, 68, 96

Sa'id, Viveroy of Egypt, 13
Saint-Beuve, Charles, 192
Saladin, 33
Samné, Georges
    despotism, attack on, 131, 140–1
    on education, role of, 95
    on individualism, 77
    on intolerance, 106
    nationalism of, 169–72
    socio-political improvement, 105

spiritualism/temporalism, on
separation of, 31–2
San Remo, Treaty of, 11, 21
Sarrail, Gen. Maurice, 21
Sarruf, Ya'qub
education, views on, 98
on individualism, 67, 68, 72
on language, 185–6
morality and knowledge, 105
reason, on limits of power of, 104
on religion, 51, 53, 55, 57, 61
scientific fundamentalism of, 113
on secularism in education, 95–6
socio-political improvement, 105
on women's status, 84
Al-Sayyid, Ahmad Lutfi
capitalism, belief in, 126
change, attitude to, 111
civilization, on source of, 117
on constitutional rule, 142, 143
democracy, views on, 135, 136, 140
education, on power of, 134
education, views on, 98
on individualism, 69, 71, 72, 75, 77, 78
knowledge, on practical use of, 105
on language, 189–92
on laws, secular attitude, 147
nationalism of, 173, 174–80
positivism of, 110–11
on religion, 57–8, 60
on secularism in education, 96
socio-political improvement, 105
spiritualism/temporalism, on
separation of, 32–3, 39
teaching, concern at antiquated
methods, 102
tyranny, attack on, 131–2
on women's status, 83, 85–6, 89, 91
The Secret of National Progress (Demolins,
E.), 111
The Secret of the Anglo-Saxons' Progress
(Demolins, E.), 111–12
secularism
anticlericalism, 63–5
art and, 188
autonomy and, 66–79
belief, freedom of, 73–4

change and, 107–27
civilization and progress, 107–27
definition of, 9
economic progress and, 118–27
education and, 95–106
fanaticism, 106
fanaticism and, 63
free will and, 66–79
government and, 128–43
knowledge and, 95–106
language, literature and, 181–93
the law and, 143–8
Muslim/Christian differences on,
199–200
nationalism and, 149–80
political impetus towards, 197–8
press freedom, 75
progress and civilization, 107–27
religion and, 42–62
social values and, 195, 198–9
thought, freedom of, 74–80
Western influence on, 129, 194–6
women's' status, 81–94
see also Amin; Antun; Azoury; al-
Bustani; Dallal; Dimashqiyya; al-Din;
Fawwaz; Hussein; Ishaq; al-Kawakibi;
Kurd 'Ali; Marrash; Nasef; al-Raziq;
Samné; Sarruf; al-Sayyid; al-Shidyaq; al-
Shummayyil; Zaydan
Self-Help (Smiles, S.), 68
Al-Shadyaq, As'ad, 73
Shafi'i, Imam Abu 'Abd Allah, 79
Shahin, Tanius, 17
Al-Sharabi, Hisham, 55, 153, 181–2
Shari'a Law, 143–8
Al-Shidyaq, As'ad
anti-revolutionary attitude, 132–3
anticlericalism of, 63–5
on Arab nationalism, 154–5
Christian Socialism, influence on, 118,
137
democracy, views on, 136, 137
on individualism, 66, 72, 75
on language, 182–3
morality and knowledge, 105
on religion, 42, 46, 49, 56
on secularism in education, 95

spiritualism/temporalism, on separation of, 24–5, 28, 31
Tanzimat, defence of, 144
traditional education, condemnation of, 97
tyranny, attack on, 128–9
on women's status, 81–2, 85, 87, 92
Al-Shidyaq, Faris, 19, 24, 43–4, 73
Shikho, Louis, 31
Al-Shummayyil, Shibli
anti-nationalism of, 166–7
anticlericalism of, 64
Britain, praise for, 165–6
on constitutional rule, 140
education, views on, 98–9
evolutionary attitude to the past, 111
on individualism, 67, 68, 72, 73–5, 76
on intolerance, 106
knowledge for the sake of, search for, 104
on language, 185
on laws (of God and man), 144–5
on nationalism, 158–9, 160
on partiotism, 161–2
reason, on limitless power of, 103–4
on religion, 47, 48, 51–7, 60
revolutionary spirit of, 133
scientific fundamentalism of, 113–15
on secularism in education, 95–6
socialism, influence on, 121–4
socio-political improvement, 105
spiritualism/temporalism, on separation of, 28, 31
traditional values, criticism of, 108
on women's status, 84–5
Simon, Jules, 84, 101
Socrates, 75, 77, 103
Spanish Inquisition, 75
Spencer, Herbert, 67, 102, 139
The Story of As'ad al-Shidyaq (al-Bustani, B.), 24–5
Suez Canal, 13–14, 16
The Sunna, 62, 64, 78, 80, 87, 118
Sykes-Picot Agreement, 20, 21
Syria, 10, 12, 16–23, 34, 155, 159–61, 169–71
Syrian Protestant College, 76, 96, 165
La Syrie (Samné, G.), 32

Tahtawi, Rafa'a Rafi', 85, 109
Taine, Hyppolite, 192
Taleb, 'Ali Ibn Abi, 33
Tanzimat, 25, 143–4, 154
Taqla, Bishara, 18
Taqla, Saleem, 18
Tawfiq, Khedive of Egypt, 14
Taymiyya, Ibn, 40
Teaching Women (al-Bustani, B.), 85
The Throne and the Temple (Dallal, J.), 44, 128, 133, 137
Al-Tunisi, Khair al-Din, 10
Tunisia, 10, 152, 155
Turkey, 13, 34, 35

'Umar Pasha, 17
Umayyad Caliphate, 26, 31, 59, 175
Uncovering the Hidden in Europe's Civilization (al-Shidyaq, A.), 183
Université St. Joseph de Beyrouth, 18, 23
Unveiling and Veiling (al-Din, N.Z.), 40, 90
'Urabi Pasha, Ahmad, 14

Valéry, Paul, 178
Vie de Jésus (Renan, E.), 48
Voltaire, 24, 25, 30, 44, 74, 101
A Voyage to Paris (Marrash, F.), 129

Wendell, Charles, 177
Wilson, President Woodrow, 15
Wingate, Gen. Sir Reginald, 15
Our Women in the Shari'a and Society (H. Al-T.), 10
World War I, 15, 16, 19, 20, 131, 167, 168

Al-Yaziji, Ibrahim, 19
Al-Yaziji, Nasif, 19
Yemen, 155
Young Turks, 19, 130, 159, 168

Zaghlul, Fathi, 112
Zaghlul, Sa'd, 15–16
Al-Zahawi, Jamil Sidqi, 11
Al-Zahrawi, 'Abd al-Hamid, 11
Zaydan, Jurji
absolute rule; attack on, 130

anti-revolutionary attitude, 133
Arab nationalism of, 19
on Arabism, 162–3
capitalism, belief in, 121
on constitutional rule, 139–40
economic independence, belief in, 120–1
education, on power of, 133–4
education, views on, 98, 99
al-Hilal, founder of, 18
on individualism, 67, 68, 72, 74–6
on intolerance, 106
on language, 185–8
on laws (of God and man), 144–5
morality and knowledge, 105
on nationalism, 158, 159, 160–1
on patriotism, 161–2

reason, on limits of power of, 104
on religion, 47–9, 51–7, 60–1
scientific fundamentalism of, 113
spiritualism/temporalism, on separation of, 28, 31
traditional values, criticism of, 108
on women's status, 81–2, 84–5, 85–6, 87, 89, 91
Zaynab's Letters (Fawwaz, Z.), 82
Ziady, May, 12
Zionism, 164, 169, 219–20